Negotiating
the Siege of the
LAL MASJID

Negotiating The Siege of [the] Lal Masjid by Adam Dolnik and Khuram Iqbal is an insightful and scholarly examination of how the Pakistani government attempted to deal with one of the most significant and challenging confrontations ever experienced between secular authority and Islamist extremists. This book takes the reader on a fascinating journey of inquiry that sheds light on the specific thinking and decision making of both the government and the extremists they encountered during this tense and tragic standoff. Rarely do we get to see how the attitudes, decisions, actions, and behaviors of all involved parties can lead to such devastating consequences. This book should be read by everyone who wants to understand how effective negotiations can achieve better outcomes, if fully understood and supported by government decision makers. Sadly, and all too often, those charged with resolving conflict allow their preconceived notions, personal biases, and lack of knowledge lead to tragic decision making, with tragic results.

Gary Noesner, Chief (Ret.)
FBI Crisis Negotiation Unit, USA

This book is a must read in the quest to deeper understanding of the difficulties inherent to a hostage negotiator's worst nightmare: negotiating with radical extremists who have impossible demands and are willing to kill and die for their convictions. Dolnik and Khuram effectively elucidate with great candor the powerful lessons learned during the Siege of Lal Masjid and provide practical guiding principles for crisis negotiators, incident commanders, and political decision makers.

Lt. Jack J. Cambria, Commanding Officer
New York City Police Department's
Hostage Negotiation Team

Following on the success of his first book *Negotiating Hostage Crises with the New Terrorists*, Adam Dolnik teams with Khuram Iqbal to dissect yet another siege that challenged negotiators, commanders and a government to the breaking point. Insightful while being both critical and complimentary where warranted, they shed new light on the phenomena of extremist motivated behaviours that lie at the center of modern day sieges. The lessons so painstakingly researched by Dolnik and Iqbal highlight the need for Negotiators to develop new skill sets should they hope to contribute to the peaceful resolution to today's most challenging terrorist and extremist motivated events. Failing to learn from *Negotiating The Siege of [the] Lal Masjid* will leave Governments, Commanders and Negotiators struggling to find viable and peaceful solutions to these life threatening events that sadly continue to grow in number across the globe.

Gordon Black, Chief Superintendent (Ret.)
Founder and Team Leader, Domestic and
International Response Group
Royal Canadian Mounted Police

Through extensive fieldwork, Dolnik and his co-author Iqbal have captured the essence and intricacies of this complex incident. The masterful encapsulation of the true undercurrents, motives and previously discarded or unknown background data enhances this book. Dolnik sees the siege through the eyes of those closest to the incident 'whatever side they are from', which makes the explanations real, natural and enables the reader to make sense of the accounts from the diametrically opposed sides. This book is an engrossing and fascinating read from all levels, and will be especially useful to practitioners for whom learning from these complicated and multi-layered life changing incidents is vitally important.

Neil Stapley, Detective Chief Inspector
Head of New Scotland Yard's Hostage
& Crisis Negotiation Unit, UK

Through extensive research and numerous interviews with the parties involved on all sides of the standoff, Dolnik and Iqbal managed to analyze the siege of Lal Masjid in its historical, religious and cultural context. They focus on the successes and failures of the negotiation strategies and tactics. It becomes very clear that a solid and well-founded negotiation strategy (in combination with a tactical strategy and media strategy) is of lifesaving importance in incidents like this. I can only hope that not only negotiators, but also political decision makers and incident commanders will read the book.

'To negotiate or not to negotiate: that is NOT the question'.

Chief Inspector Heidi A. Nieboer-Martini
Trainer, Former Coordinator
Counter Terrorism Negotiation,
The Dutch National Police Agency

Professor Adam Dolnik and Khuram Iqbal, in this book, made a contribution to refining police crisis negotiation technology in describing the siege of Lal Masjid from different critical perspectives. The discussion and analysis can be utilised effectively when we as police crisis negotiators are confronted with a similar or more challenging incident in future. Their experience as "academics in hostage negotiation practice" brought the opportunity in sharing this landmark case with the police crisis negotiators cadre as a best practice for future reference.

Dr Ernst H Strydom, Lieutenant Colonel
National Commander, South African Police Service
Hostage Negotiation Team

Crisis Negotiation is an evolving art and science. Lessons learned from the 8-day Lal Masjid siege gave me tremendous insight on the importance of negotiation strategies, tactics, skills and trainings for law enforcement negotiators. This book has become one of my personal and professional reference guides and should be one of the textbooks for all crisis/hostage negotiation courses.

Dr WONG Kwong-hing, Gilbert, PhD
Commanding Officer of Police Negotiation Cadre
Hong Kong Police Force

Negotiating the Siege of [the] Lal Masjid by Adam Dolnik and Khuram Iqbal gives detailed insights into this prominent crisis and draws important lessons that are a must-read for both political and administrative decisions makers, as well as law enforcement tacticians and negotiators.

Stein Erik Mauseth, Detective Superintendent (Ret.)
Commander of the National Hostage Negotiations Team, Norway

Negotiating
the Siege of the
LAL MASJID

Adam Dolnik
and
Khuram Iqbal

OXFORD
UNIVERSITY PRESS

Oxford University Press is a department of the University of Oxford.
It furthers the University's objective of excellence in research, scholarship,
and education by publishing worldwide. Oxford is a registered trade mark of
Oxford University Press in the UK and in certain other countries

Published in Pakistan by
Ameena Saiyid, Oxford University Press
No.38, Sector 15, Korangi Industrial Area,
PO Box 8214, Karachi-74900, Pakistan

ISBN 978-0-19-940034-8

Typeset in Adobe Caslon Pro
Printed on 80gsm Imported Offset paper

Printed by Ilma Printers, Karachi

Contents

Acknowledgements

My deepest thanks go to all of my academic mentors past and present, in particular Michael Sample, Keith M. Fitzgerald, Jason Pate, Alex Schmid, Bruce Hoffman, William Monning, Amin Tarzi, Amy Sands, Stephen Garrett, Rohan Gunaratna, Clint Blandford, Kumar Ramakrishna, and William Potter.

A special thanks goes to Mia Fedele and Luanne Freeman for their superb assistance with my impossible travel schedule. For his contribution to this book I am grateful to my co-author Khuram Iqbal.

I owe my knowledge of hostage and crisis negotiation to my many mentors and colleagues in this unique field: Neil Stapley, Gary Noesner, Nigel Basham, Matt Todd, Kevin Taylor, Jack Cambria, Heidi Nieboer-Martini, Nicky Cross, Dave Bartley, Ian Williamson, Philip Williams, Paul Padman, Bryan Heard, Abdul Hye, Peter Doherty, Sean Cunningham, Timo der Weduwen, Phil Harper, Mark Thundercloud, Mike Yansick, Mark Flores, Vince Dalfonso, Tim Suttles, Christy Shaffer, Shawn VanSlyke, Mark Rossin, Scott Owens, Michael Helms, Steve, Kyle, Kevin Curerri, Wong Gilbert Kwong-Hing, Espen Scavenius, Matthias Herter, Eveline Van Werven, Marty Briggs, Greg Ringuet, Fi Bokulic, Pete Morgan, Lyndy Baker, David Plumpton, P. J. Hunter, Mark Jenkins,

Graeme Abel, Elias Petropoulos, Gordon Black, Jean-Marc Collin, Cal Chrustie, Jan de Graaf, Peter Kroon, Stephen McAllister, Jon Crawford, Sue Williams, Kirk Kinnell, Catriona Paton, Sharon Tait, Lance Burdette, Cathy MacDonald, Alan McCambridge, Ernst Strydom, Marc Perron, William Hogewood, Jan Dubina, Kevin Mitchell, William Kidd, Moty Crystal, Stein Erik Mauseth, Jenny Holden, Bill Cole, David Rausch and many others. Thank you for your trust and friendship; it has been an honour to learn from you.

Special thanks goes to my 'brothers in words' from the UK National Hostage and Crisis Negotiation Course: Marc, Paul, Guy, Rich Dave, Mark, Wes, Ahmed, Elang, Bryan, Rob, Simon H., Sara, Jim, James, John, Fiona, Justin, Wes, Pete, Denis, James, John, Mike, Ian, Simon F., Jay and Andy. I am equally grateful to my teammates from the FBI's National Crisis Negotiation Course: Walter, Angela, Marc, Patrick, Maurice, Alvaro, Bash, Payton, Jean, Ricardo, Victoria, Josh, Ron, Marni, Micah, Adam, Russell, Dan, Cliff, Charlie, Andy, Elliot, Laura S., Kathryn, Amanda, Henry, Sammy, Carrie, Laura M., Eric, Babs, Claudia and Brittani.

This book would not have been possible without the field research in Pakistan. My deepest gratitude goes to Sajjad Azhar, Muhammad Amir Rana, Masror Hausen, Jawed Rahman, Arslan Akbar, Mansur Mahsud, Hamid Ateeq Sarwar, Syed Adnan Bukhari, Zia Rehman, Zubair Shah, Faisal Hakim and Mairaj Ariff, and others for their assistance. I am grateful to the many policy makers, negotiators, investigators, Lal Masjid students, hostages, journalists, victims, family members, and witnesses, who were kind enough to share their insights. I will not name names, but you know who you are; thank you for your courage to speak.

Last but not least, I would like to thank my family, without whose encouragement and support this book would not have been possible. For their affection and for teaching me to rise above challenges and never give up, I thank my parents Vladislav and Jana, and my brother David. For their love and patience with my constant absences, I thank Zuzana and my children Tatiana and Max. You mean the world to me; this book is dedicated to you.

Adam Dolnik
Washington D.C., 2015.

I wish to thank my former colleagues at the International Centre for Political Violence and Terrorism Research (ICPVTR-Singapore), University Of Wollongong (Australia) and the Department for Policing, Intelligence and Counter-Terrorism at Macquarie University (PICT-Australia). My deepest gratitude to Professor Adam Dolnik (UoW-Australia) for inviting me to co-author this book, to Syed Adnan Ali Shah Bukhari and Dr Sadia Sulaiman (ICPVTR-Singapore) for their expert feedback on the manuscript, to Dr Dalbir Ahlawat and Dr Julian Droogan (PICT-Sydney) for their academic mentorship and to Dr Sara De Silva (KDU-Colombo) for her meticulous editing and archival support. Finally, my sincerest gratitude to my family and friends for their continuous encouragement and love. This book is dedicated to my parents for being a great pillar of support, and to my wife for piecing me back together.

Khuram Iqbal

Islamabad, 2015.

Introduction

Established in 1965, Lal Masjid is one of Islamabad's oldest mosques. It started to flourish in the late 1970s and early 1980s under the patronage of General Zia ul-Haq, the military general, who in July 1977 overthrew Prime Minister Zulfikar Ali Bhutto and launched a systematic campaign to 'Islamize'[1] Pakistani society. During the US-backed anti-Soviet jihad[2] in Afghanistan, the Lal Masjid rose to prominence as a centre for recruiting, radicalizing, and training mujahideen for the conflict. Following the Soviet withdrawal from Afghanistan in 1989, the Lal Masjid continued to serve the same purpose, only now supplying militant fighters for the jihad in Kashmir as well as for the sectarian anti-Shia campaign in Pakistan.

Following the dramatic events of 11 September 2001, Pakistan decided to join the international alliance against al-Qaeda, marking a key turning point in the relations between the Pakistani government and radical clerics[3] in the country. In order to mobilize popular resistance against the government and to provide religious legitimacy to local and foreign fighters in the Federally Administered Tribal Areas of Pakistan (FATA), the Lal Masjid clerics issued a fatwa[4] against Pakistani troops, advising Muslims not to give Islamic burial to the soldiers who lost their lives fighting against al-Qaeda and their local supporters in the tribal region. The mosque also declared that the true Shaheeds (martyrs) in this conflict were the militants, and not the soldiers of the Pakistan Army.

The Lal Masjid fatwas caused serious friction within the Pakistani security apparatus and a decision was reached that the clerics had to be contained, preferably in a way that would be both legal and easily justifiable to the masses. The fact that many other radical mosques and 'madaris' (singular: madrasa, Islamic seminary) were built illegally on encroached lands, provided an opportunity and a legal pretext for making this politically sensitive move. In January 2007, the Capital Development Authority (CDA) demolished the Amir Hamza Mosque in Islamabad, which was one of some eighty mosques and madaris in Islamabad that were to be demolished. The Lal Masjid madrasa for girls, the Jamia Hafsa, was also included on the list.

In order to pre-empt the government from continuing with the demolitions, hundreds of female students from Jamia Hafsa occupied the adjacent Children's Library in protest, stating their determination to be martyred for their cause. Eventually, the government caved in to the Lal Masjid demands and on 12 February 2007 the Minister for Religious Affairs, Ijaz ul-Haq, the son of the former dictator, General Zia ul-Haq, laid the foundation brick at the site where the Amir Hamza Mosque once stood, demonstrating the government's intent to rebuild it.

But this attempt at appeasement only fed the ambitions of the Lal Masjid students and other actions followed, including attacks on markets selling music CDs and DVDs, moral policing activities in the capital such as kidnappings of alleged prostitutes, as well as the kidnappings of policemen in order to trade them for the release of students arrested by the police. The clerics also established a Sharia court inside the mosque, which was seen as a challenge to the state, since it created a de facto parallel judicial system. As the Lal Masjid ambitions grew, the students also demanded the implementation of Sharia[5] throughout Pakistan, and threatened to use suicide bombings should the government choose to employ force against them. Although the rhetoric and actions of the Lal Masjid's clerics and students threatened the state, the government, fearing public fallout, avoided taking action, until the kidnapping of several Chinese citizens. The subsequent pressure by the Chinese government to do something served as the proverbial last drop that made the glass overflow.

A state of emergency was declared as troops and army trucks besieged the Lal Masjid. On 3 July 2007, violence suddenly erupted when several students from the mosque tried to storm the Estate Office in an apparent protest against the rumours of a plan to raid the mosque. During this incident, they engaged in a scuffle with the policemen, in which they snatched four of their rifles and walkie-talkies. In reply, the police fired teargas to disperse the protesters, which provoked a reaction from the armed students in the mosque who opened fire on both the police and the Rangers.

This confrontation marked the beginning of an eight-day siege, which was eventually ended by an armed assault that resulted in the deaths of at least 103 people and injuries to many more. Despite the government's initial determination to end the siege peacefully, the eventual tragic outcome of the standoff had a devastating spillover effect, as it turned into a rallying cry for Islamist militancy in the country. Further, it also became the main catalyst for the escalation of fighting in the tribal border areas, which led to the eventual breakdown of the truce that existed between Pakistan and the militants in the then North-West Frontier Province (NWFP). Since the Lal Masjid incident, the militant activities and suicide bombings in Pakistan have continued to escalate.

The importance of the Lal Masjid standoff in triggering a rapid destabilization of a key front in the 'War on Terror' cannot be overemphasized. It also serves as a vivid reminder of the crucial dilemmas any government will face in the event of a similar incident taking place on its soil. In essence, barricade/hostage crises constitute direct challenges to national governments by forcing them to choose among very unattractive options. With the rare exception of extremely successful rescue operations such as Entebbe, Mogadishu, or Lima, governments are almost always criticized for their response, either for 'giving in' to the terrorists, thus encouraging similar acts in the future, or for storming the location and thus being held responsible for civilian casualties. Barricade/hostage crises provide militants with an extremely effective tool to directly challenge the legitimacy of their enemies. Thus, governments need to use any available sources of knowledge to prepare for managing such incidents. In this context, the Lal Masjid case is an extremely suitable empirical source, as it provides a rare example of protracted negotiations with religious militants in the barricade setting.

ABOUT THIS BOOK

Despite the availability of numerous media accounts, the finer details and caveats of the Lal Masjid siege remain sketchy. It is the objective of this book to illuminate the issue by providing an in-depth analytical account of the events that unfolded, with specific emphasis on the successes and failures of the negotiation process. Further, the book attempts to translate the lessons learnt into practical guidelines for crisis negotiators, incident commanders, and political decision makers.

The Lal Masjid siege ended tragically. Thus, it is perhaps not surprising that our commentary in this book is sometimes highly critical of the steps taken by the authorities in charge. We should emphasize here, however, that our focus on pinpointing specific mistakes and failures is not motivated by the desire to ostracize the respective decision makers and responders for incompetence, but rather to facilitate an effective learning process from which we could all benefit in the future. We fully recognize the fact that the disastrous results were to some extent caused by imperfect decisions based on incomplete information, and that much of the useful detail that we have at our disposal today, was simply unavailable to the decision makers at the time of the crisis. That being said, in order to prevent unnecessary loss of life in the future, and the tremendous strategic fallout that followed, we have the obligation to critically evaluate past response strategies and to ask ourselves how things could have been done differently to achieve a better outcome.

Learning from past failures is not always easy, given the fact that official versions of barricade/hostage ordeals are frequently inspired less by actual events and more by the authorities' need to justify their actions in order to minimize the negative fallout from their own mishandling of the given crisis. Especially in the aftermath of high profile standoffs that result in a large number of casualties among civilians, there is a tendency to engage in a bipolar discourse about the legitimacy of the government's response to the incident. While this tendency to justify the respective course of action is understandable at the political level, the authorities' frequent manoeuvring of facts to fit this purpose does more than to protect individuals; it effectively inhibits the possibility of learning from mistakes, thus bringing about their likely repetition in the future.

Politically motivated manoeuvring of facts has been one of the reasons why, despite its global notoriety, the Lal Masjid incident still remains a poorly understood phenomenon. And understanding the finer points is, of course, essential to any analysis of barricade crises, as even small and seemingly insignificant details can provide a crucial piece of the puzzle that has the capacity to completely change our perspective with regard to the prospects of a negotiated outcome. For instance, a single conversation between the subject and the negotiator can have deep intrinsic meaning in relation to the negotiability of the incident. It happens frequently that incidents, which in a retrospective analysis of official versions would clearly be diagnosed as 'non-negotiable', actually start appearing in a very different light once more details begin to emerge.

Given the importance of specifics to the overall analysis of negotiability of hostage incidents, meticulous attention to detail constitutes a requirement for a meaningful analysis. Our research on the Lal Masjid siege took place between 2007 and 2011, and is based on exhaustive open source research of Pakistani and international sources in both Urdu and English, analysis of available video footage, and extensive field research in Pakistan, including the inspection of the target location and dozens of detailed interviews with the Lal Masjid students, government negotiators, members of the ulema delegation, members of tactical teams who responded at the scene, lawyers, journalists, government ministers, investigators, members of government security services, as well as ordinary bystanders and eye-witnesses. Among those we interviewed were Lal Masjid chief imam Maulana Abdul Aziz, Lal Masjid *Naib Khatib* Amir Siddiqi, defence attorney Hashmat Ali Habib, government negotiator and PML-Q President Chaudhry Shujaat Hussain, Ministers Tariq Azeem and Ijaz ul-Haq, National Crisis Management Cell director Brig (Retd) Javed Cheema, Maulana Sher Ali Shah, and dozens of

Lal Masjid students and members of Pakistan's Armed Forces who took part on different sides of the siege, and whose identities remain concealed owing to our pledge of confidentiality.

The sheer amount of data collected in this massive effort has made it impossible to include all of the fascinating details of the crisis in this book. Instead, only information that is relevant to our analysis of the negotiations will be featured here. Also, despite being one of this book's strengths, the importance of detail to the overall analysis of negotiability of hostage incidents also accounts for one of its greatest limitations, stemming from the fact that most available accounts of practically any barricade/hostage crisis differ significantly in their description of virtually every aspect of the given incident. This is frequently further complicated by government secrecy, vested interests, media censorship, as well as the fact that even eyewitness accounts are often contradictory, and tend to further mutate over time. Despite our efforts to ensure the reliability of witness testimonies by conducting second and third waves of interviews within two years after the first round, some details will inevitably remain disputed, inhibiting our ability to determine some aspects of the siege with absolute certainty.

It is important to highlight here what this book is not. It is not an investigative report looking to identify who is to blame for the tragic outcome of the standoff. Neither is it a journalistic account telling the dramatic and emotional stories of the people involved on the different sides of the crisis. Nor is it a travelogue, telling a gripping story of a western researcher's rendezvous with Maulana Abdul Aziz inside the Lal Masjid, the middle of the night discussions with armed militants in Karachi, the secretive meetings with former Lal Masjid students who participated in the standoff, and all the adrenalin rushes and human emotions encountered along the way. Rather, this book is a dispassionate, matter of fact analysis of the key aspects of the siege as they relate to the viability of crisis negotiation strategies and tactics as a possible means of achieving a less catastrophic outcome. Instead of focusing on the politically sensitive and highly contentious issue of 'responsibility', the book seeks to provide a critical evaluation of the successes and failures of the negotiation approach, with the aim of deriving lessons that would enhance our ability to manage similar standoffs more effectively.

This book is organized in the following manner. Chapter 1 provides a brief overview of the history of the Lal Masjid and its links to militant movements. Chapter 2 then describes the events that escalated the relationship of the Lal Masjid clerics with the government, starting with the Capital Development Authority's (CDA) decision to demolish mosques built illegally on government land, and the occupation of the Children's Library in protest of this decision. This is followed by a chronological description of the escalation of the crisis, through the emergence of the 'burqa brigade' and its engagement in self-appointed moral policing activities, the establishment of the Sharia court, and the kidnappings of alleged prostitutes and policemen that brought the Lal Masjid to the brink of open confrontation with the government. Chapter 3 then recounts the events of July 3 as well as chronology of the eight-day siege of Lal Masjid. Having provided backgrounds to the origins, evolution, and the outcome of the incident, Chapter 4 zooms in on the analysis of the failure to manage the situation effectively prior to its transformation into a barricade/hostage standoff, which is an important element in providing the negotiation context for the situation that followed later. Chapter 5 focuses on outlining the basic principles of crisis negotiation as a law enforcement tool for managing barricade/hostage incidents, followed by an analytical chronology of the negotiations that took place during the siege of Lal Masjid. The application of these principles to this case study then follows in Chapter 6, which offers an analytical negotiability assessment, along with highlighting the relevant indicators of volatility and de-escalation, as well as identifying successes, failures, missed opportunities, and the lessons learned during the Lal Masjid siege. And, finally, the epilogue analyzes the strategic fallout of 'Operation Sunrise', focusing especially on the mobilization of the various jihadi factions in the country, as well as the accompanying phenomenon of the radicalization of their tactics and targeting.

NOTES

1. In the context of Pakistani politics, the term denotes a set of laws and policies implemented in Pakistan over a period of several years, with particular reference to those legislated during General Zia ul-Haq's period (1978–88). Thus Islamization would mean the process of bringing the laws of Pakistan in accordance with a

specific interpretation of Islamic sources, an interpretation that did not necessarily have a particular methodology at its foundation.

2. From the Arabic root j.h.d, jihad means 'Striving'. Although originally encompassing a wide range of spiritual and religious activities, including armed struggle, it is now understood almost exclusively in the narrow, political context of militancy by extremist groups that identify themselves as representatives of Islam.

3. 'Cleric' and 'Clergy' denote formal positions and hierarchies inside the Catholic Church. However, no such institution exists in Sunni Islam—there is no formal center for the promulgation and implementation of Sunni doctrine, no ordained supreme leader, and no formal hierarchy of religious leadership. In the book we have, wherever possible, used the term 'imam' rather than 'cleric'. Where we have retained the latter, we mean someone whom the society may see as a trained religious scholar and who is associated with a mosque or a madrasa.

4. A fatwa is a non-binding, legal opinion of a Muslim scholar who is recognized as a mufti—an opinion that is informed by an interpretation of the religious sources.

5. The term 'Sharia' is defined in Islamic literature as 'the one true path'. In the early centuries it was taken as an assumption that any human endeavor to discover 'the one true path' will necessarily fall short of perfection. In the Sunni tradition, the attempt at deciphering 'the one true path', came to be called 'fiqh', literally 'understanding'. The body of these fiqh laws constitutes a *madhhab* (pl: *madhahib*). However, since Sharia is a term more familiar to people than the term 'madhhab'; we have retained it at some places within the book.

1

The Red Mosque: Cradle of Jihad

Established in 1965, Lal Masjid, or 'Red Mosque', is one of Islamabad's oldest mosques. How it acquired its name is unclear. While some believe it was mostly because of its red painted walls and interior, others believe it was called 'Lal' after Lal Shahbaz Qalandar, a revered Sufi saint buried in Pakistan's Sindh province.[1] Another account suggests that it was named by the Auqaf Department,[2] which had originally constructed and operated the mosque, because of its red coloured edifice.[3]

According to the records of the Capital Development Authority of Islamabad (CDA), the land for Lal Masjid was allotted some time in the 1960s and it was a 260' x 260' plot, or 8377.78 sq. yards. The mosque was constructed directly by the CDA itself with funding from the Finance Ministry. Legally, the mosque is the property of the Auqaf Department. In 1979, two small living rooms were added for the prayer leader (imam) and the muezzin (the person who calls for prayer at the mosque). The imam's quarters were built on 400 sq. yards and the muezzin's quarters were built on 111 sq. yards.[4]

From its inception, the Red Mosque had been a centre of fundamentalist religious ideologues hailing from Karachi's Jamia Binoria, which came to be known as the 'jihad factory of Pakistan'.[5] Once the mosque's construction was completed, an Islamabad-based religious organization named 'International Organization for the Administration of Mosques' wrote a letter to Maulana Yousaf Binori, founder of the Karachi seminary and the most powerful voice of Deobandi Islam in Pakistan, and requested him to designate a qualified person to lead prayers at the newly established mosque in the G6/4 area. Maulana Yousaf chose Maulana Abdullah, a young graduate of Jamia Binoria, and asked him to undertake this responsibility. Abdullah, who was struggling to make ends meet in Karachi, agreed and joined Jamia Masjid G6/4 that would later be renamed as the Red Mosque.

Having established a foothold in the newly built capital,[6] Maulana Abdullah started to work his way into the local religious scene with the intention of strengthening the Deobandi school of thought in the seat of power. He became a part of the 'International Organization for the Administration of Mosques' to influence the decisions to nominate prayer leaders for Islamabad's fast growing numbers of mosques. Maulana Abdullah also endeavoured to convert the Red Mosque into a stronghold of Deobandi religio-political groups. Although he was not an official member of any political party, the Maulana actively supported the Jamiatul Ulema-e-Islam, led by Mufti Mahmud, in the general elections of 1970, and took an active part in the anti-Ahmadiya movement[7] in 1974, during which he was arrested on four different occasions and imprisoned in Central Jail Rawalpindi, Jhelum, Faisalabad, and Haripur. He also participated in the religio-political movement to overthrow Zulfikar Ali Bhutto's government in 1977.[8]

Maulana Abdullah came to terms with the state when General Zia ul-Haq overthrew the elected government of Prime Minister Zulfikar Ali Bhutto in July 1977, and introduced various measures claiming to Islamize Pakistani society. Abdullah was a vocal opponent of Zia's predecessor Bhutto and declared his socialist policies to be against the fundamental tenets of Islam.[9] General Zia, who was desperately looking for the support of religious circles to sustain his unconstitutional rule, patronized the Red Mosque. In August 1981, on his directive No 833, PC-I, a grand rehabilitation of the Lal Masjid was done at a cost of Rs.7.255 million. General Zia was greatly interested in the expansion and renovation of the mosque so that larger congregations could be accommodated. Therefore, governmental funding was provided to the mosque in 1982 and again in 1984 for further renovation.[10]

THE IMPACT OF THE SOVIET INVASION OF AFGHANISTAN

In 1979, the Soviet Union invaded Afghanistan. With the intention of driving the 'Godless Communists' out of Afghanistan, an international jihad was launched under the patronage of the US, Saudi Arabia, Pakistan, and others.

Zia became the 'blue-eyed boy' of the US and the West. Pakistan's engagement in the war in Afghanistan against the Soviet occupation (1979–1989) created an opportunity for Zia and Maulana Abdullah to consolidate their appreciation of one another. The military dictator needed a regular supply of radicalized militants to fight shoulder to shoulder with the Afghan mujahideen in Afghanistan and Lal Masjid under Maulana Abdullah served this purpose by recruiting, radicalizing, and training such militant fighters.[11] The mosque also became a favourite place for high ranking military officials, politicians, and other elite of Islamabad to gather for prayers and socialization. This nexus between the army and the clergy laid the foundation of what became the well-known Military-Mullah Alliance.[12]

The ten-year long international military campaign in Afghanistan resulted in the withdrawal of Soviet forces. In February 1989, Lieut. Gen. Boris V. Gromov, the commander of the Soviet forces in Afghanistan, was the last Soviet soldier to leave the country. He crossed the Friendship Bridge to the border city of Termez, in Uzbekistan, and declared, 'There is not a single Soviet soldier or officer left behind me. Our nine-year stay ends with this.'[13]

The Soviet Union was defeated but the jihadi infrastructure built in Pakistan during the Afghan War remained intact and a number of jihadi outfits shifted their focus from Afghanistan to Indian-held Kashmir and other conflict zones around the world. A few thousand individuals referred to as mujahideen by the western media in the

1980s had proved their mettle in the fight against the world's largest land Army in Afghanistan. Pakistan saw this as an opportunity to confront her arch-rival India through jihadi proxies. Geostrategic interests aside, the state also lacked the resources to bring back thousands of mujahideen, who knew nothing except to wage war, and rehabilitate them into the mainstream of society. Under such circumstances, Pakistan's security establishment decided to continue supporting such assets as Maulana Abdullah, who could motivate the younger population to take up arms in Kashmir against India. Thus, state patronage of the Red Mosque persisted even after the Soviet troops departed from Afghanistan and the violent extremism that originated during the Afghan jihad crossed the Hindu Kush to engulf other regions of the world.

For more than a decade, the cause to drive the USSR out of Afghanistan had gelled together a fractious but powerful array of Muslim insurgents. With the Russian defeat, the ideological centre of gravity exploded and led to further diffusion of militant groups active in the region. Numerous jihadi factions got themselves involved in a prolonged and bloody civil war to capture power in Kabul. During this phase, a number of international fighters were relocated to other conflict zones, like Kashmir and Chechnya. Militancy in Kashmir intensified as thousands of Pakistani, Afghan and Arab fighters, trained and armed to fight in Afghanistan, were moved to fight Indian occupation. Meanwhile, sectarian conflict in Pakistan also escalated with the return of the 'Afghan-trained boys', who were instrumental in forming sectarian terrorist outfits, such as Sipah-e-Sahaba, which later gave birth to Lashkar-e-Jhangvi, Pakistan's deadliest sectarian terrorist outfit. Maulana Abdullah was one of the founders of Sipah-e-Sahaba. His firebrand speeches against the Shia community soon won him unprecedented support among the country's hard-line Deobandis and anti-Iran forces outside Pakistan.

General Zia died in 1988 in a plane crash and Pakistan, under Benazir Bhutto, Pakistan's first female Prime Minister, re-entered a decade of democratic rule. Maulana Abdullah and his jihadi allies regarded a female head of state as 'un-Islamic' and campaigned against her.[14] Abdullah's anti-Benazir rhetoric also echoed al-Qaeda's views regarding a woman ruling a Muslim majority state. The outfit was a strong opponent of Benazir and also attempted to assassinate her in 1993.

In the following years, the mosque continued to expand with the establishment of two madaris. Jamia Hafsa, a madrasa for female students, was established adjacent to the mosque, and a male student madrasa, named Jamia Faridia, was constructed not far away.

Maulana Abdullah's increasing role in promoting hatred and violence against the Shia branch of Islam made him the top target of Shia terrorist outfits operating in Pakistan with the logistical and financial support of Iran. In 1998, he was assassinated in a gun attack allegedly involving a Shia sectarian terrorist group. The assassin was caught but was not tried and was released owing to lack of evidence.

Abdullah's assassination catapulted his two sons, Maulana Abdul Aziz (the elder) and Abdul Rashid Ghazi, on to the scene. The two brothers took charge of the mosque and its complex.[15]

ABDUL AZIZ AND ABDUL RASHID GHAZI TAKE CHARGE

The tale of two brothers' journey to the religious life is an interesting story of contrasts. Abdul Aziz adopted the religious way of life from an early age, as an obedient son of his father. Rashid, however, was something of a rebel. He moved in liberal circles, preferred western-style clothes and refused his father's advice to grow a beard and receive religious education.[16] Instead, he studied for a Master's degree in International Relations at one of Pakistan's leading institutions, the Quaid-i-Azam University in Islamabad. Thereafter, he joined the Ministry of Education in Islamabad as an officer, and later served as an Assistant Director in the United Nations Educational, Scientific and Cultural Organization (UNESCO).[17] Ghazi's demeanour alienated him from his father, to the extent that the latter nominated only the elder son as sole heir of his property in his will.[18]

Nevertheless, the assassination of Maulana Abdullah and the absence of punishment for the killers had a life-changing impact on Ghazi. In a dramatic shift of character, he became very religious and joined Maulana Abdul Aziz in the mosque's administration. He began to offer regular prayers and grew a beard.[19] Although he hardly had any formal education to be an imam, his critical nature, analytical skills, rebellious temper, good English, and soft-spoken demeanour, turned him into the public face of the mosque, despite the fact that officially he was only second-in-command to his camera-shy brother Aziz.[20]

The Lal Masjid maintained the reputation of being a radical establishment, and the two sons of Maulana Abdullah preferred it that way. The mosque was frequented by several high profile radicals and militants from across the region, including some leaders of the Taliban and al-Qaeda, as well as figures from banned Islamist groups such as Jaish-e-Muhammad.[21] Ghazi himself seemed to have been inspired by Osama bin Laden, the ultimate name in modern Islamist terrorism and the head of al-Qaeda, whom he claimed to have met in Kandahar along with his father.[22] According to Ghazi, it was this meeting with bin Laden that also had a profound impact on his change of path. Recalling the events Ghazi stated: 'the meeting inspired me to work hard for the establishment of Islam.' He also told a story about how at the end of the meeting he picked up a glass from which bin Laden was drinking water, and drank from it. An amused bin Laden asked about why he did that, to which Ghazi allegedly replied: 'I drank from your glass so that Allah would make me a warrior like you.'[23] Only two weeks after the meeting his father was assassinated, solidifying Ghazi's complete transformation into a devout, radical Islamist.

The Lal Masjid imams' links with local, regional, and international jihadis survived the international campaign

against al-Qaeda and their local hosts in Afghanistan
and Pakistan. As soon as Pakistan decided to join the
international alliance against al-Qaeda and its support
structure, the religious hardliners emerged as strong
opponents. Their opposition to the government's anti-
terrorism policy was manifested in various ways. In order
to mobilize popular resistance against the government and
to provide religious legitimacy to al-Qaeda-linked local and
foreign fighters in the Federally Administered Tribal Areas
of Pakistan (FATA), the Lal Masjid in Islamabad issued
a fatwa in March 2004 against Pakistani troops, advising
Muslims to refuse Islamic burial to the soldiers losing their
lives fighting against al-Qaeda, other foreign fighters, and
their local supporters in the tribal region.[24] This fatwa had
profound implications for the Pakistan Army, which was
already struggling to motivate its soldiers to fight against
a newly identified enemy, previously known to them as
brothers and holy warriors. Following the religious decree, a
number of incidents were reported in which people refused
to offer Islamic burial to the soldiers killed by al-Qaeda
and its affiliates in tribal areas of Pakistan. Having sought
the endorsement of top Deobandi clerics, thousands of
anti-government individuals joined the Taliban against
the Pakistan Army. The mosque also declared that the
true martyrs in this conflict were the militants and not
the soldiers of the Pakistani Army.[25] This particular fatwa,
which condemned Pakistan's government and the Army,
and declared Pakistani Taliban as holy warriors, was
endorsed by more than 500 religious leaders from across
Pakistan.

The fatwa was further consolidated and elaborated by Maulana Noor-ul-Huda, a prominent Deobandi scholar with links to jihadi outfits, in his pamphlet entitled *Pakistan Mein Nifaz-e-Shari'at Kay Liye Jihad Ki Shar'i Haysiyyat* (The Islamic Justification of Waging Jihad in Pakistan for the Enforcement of Sharia).[26] In this document, he denounced, on Islamic basis, the military operation against the mujahideen in Swat and Waziristan, justified the killing of Pakistani soldiers and everyone siding with the government while also discussing the religious legitimacy of waging jihad to enforce Sharia in Pakistan. Noor-ul-Huda, who also authored a book to endorse suicide attacks in Pakistan, argued that the Pakistan Army is equally responsible 'for the killing of innocent Muslims of Afghanistan' by virtue of its cooperation with the US in logistical and intelligence sharing.[27]

The Lal Masjid's role in promoting militancy was not limited to providing ideological support to jihadi organizations but some evidence suggests that the mosque was involved more actively in actual militant activities. For instance, in July 2005, when the security forces sought to raid the premises on the allegation that those involved in the 7 July 2005 suicide bombings in London had connections to the Lal Masjid, a large number of burqa-clad, baton-wielding female students prevented them from entering the mosque complex.[28] Similarly, Pakistani intelligence agencies had reports of the Red Mosque being used as a 'transit' and a 'meeting point' by the militants en route to tribal areas to fight against Pakistani forces.[29]

Saleem Shahzad, the slain Pakistani journalist, mentioned one such meeting that reportedly occurred in the Red Mosque in 2003 between Maulana Abdul Aziz and Sheikh Esa, the Egyptian al-Qaeda leader who had declared war against Pakistan.[30]

The mosque's aggressive posture against the Army and alleged involvement in international terrorism irked General Pervez Musharraf and the security establishment. Musharraf also realized the dangers associated with attacking a mosque in a country where religious sentiment can easily be infuriated by such acts. Nevertheless, increasing desertions in the army, demeaning of the public reputation of the soldiers, and external pressure to eliminate al-Qaeda's support structure in Pakistan compelled him to contain the ideological centre of Pakistani Taliban located in the midst of Islamabad.

A showdown against the mosque had also become important for Musharraf's political survival, which was seriously threatened by the Lawyers' Movement ignited by the sacking of Iftikhar Muhammad Chaudhry, then Chief Justice of the Supreme Court of Pakistan, in March 2007. At home and abroad, this movement was gaining momentum. The secular outlook of the struggle against Musharraf impressed the international community, which until this point had seen Musharraf as the only available alternative to the rise of the religious Right in Pakistan. However, the participation of political workers, civil society activists, students, and journalists prompted democracies around the globe to revisit their options in Pakistan. As the country reverberated with revolutionary slogans demanding removal of the military dictator, western capitals realized the danger of growing anti-US, anti-western sentiment in the Pakistani populace, which could have further complicated the global fight against terrorism and extremism. General Musharraf had long relied on the support extended to him by western capitals to prolong his unconstitutional rule. The thought of losing this external support base was certainly discomforting and the most effective way to retain it went through the corridors of Lal Masjid, i.e. a powerful assault against the ideological centre of violent extremism in the country.

However, Pakistan's powerful security establishment was divided over the issue. Our extensive interactions with the serving and retired army officers in the country suggest that the Lal Masjid issue caused serious frictions. Whereas the Military Intelligence (MI) advocated full use of force against the rebellious clerics and their allies spread across mainland Pakistan, the Inter-Services Intelligence (ISI) opposed the proposal, fearing retribution and public dismay over attacking a mosque in the heart of the capital. It was the ISI that apparently succeeded initially. A decision was reached that the imams had to be contained, preferably in a way that would be both legal and easily justifiable to the masses.

As mentioned earlier, the government's Auqaf department is responsible for the administration of registered mosques located across Pakistan. Following the controversial fatwa in 2004, the Auqaf department sacked Maulana Abdul Aziz and appointed a new imam for the mosque. Abdul Rashid Ghazi, who was serving in the education department as an assistant secretary, was also dismissed from his job. In addition, Ghazi was also implicated in a terrorist plot to blow up the Presidency, the Parliament, and the Army Headquarters on Pakistan's Independence Day in 2004. Government sources accused Ghazi of fomenting the plot in collaboration with Egyptian al-Qaeda suspect Sheikh Esa, alias Qari Ismail.[31] A large cache of arms was also reportedly recovered from Ghazi's car. Critics argued that these were false charges aimed at muffling the criticism emerging from the mosque, of which Ghazi had become an unofficial spokesman. When the security forces came to round him up, Ghazi had already gone underground. In order to prove the case and convince the public, the government presented an explosives-laden truck to the media, which was allegedly owned by Ghazi.[32]

From his hideout in a small house in the heart of Islamabad, Ghazi contacted Ijaz ul-Haq, son of the former dictator, who was a family friend and at the time Minister of Religious Affairs. Haq mediated between the Military Intelligence (MI) and Ghazi. Terms of reconciliation remained unknown but, within a week, the government had changed its position, conceding that Ghazi was not directly involved in the plot but the militants who were, including the Egyptian national, had frequently visited the Red Mosque. This shift allowed Ghazi to return to the mosque. The government's attempt to implicate Ghazi in terrorism plots delivered a strong message that the state had reached its tolerance threshold over the Red Mosque's continuous support for anti-government militias and its provocative anti-government rhetoric. This rhetoric included speeches of Maulana Aziz calling for jihad to implement an Islamic Sharia system in Pakistan and even justifying 'suicide attacks' as a 'last resort' tactic to achieve this objective.[33] In many ways, this rhetoric was nothing new in the extremists' behaviour, but it was the target that had changed.

Notes

1. Hassan Abbas, 'The Road to Lal Masjid and its Aftermath', *Terrorism Monitor* (19 July 2007); <http://www.jamestown.org/single/?no_cache=1&tx_ttnews%5Btt_news%5D=4322> accessed 15 March 2010.
2. A government authority to look after mosques, shrines and other sacred places including Hindu and Sikh temples, and Christian churches.
3. Baqir Sajjad Syed, 'Changing colours of Lal Masjid', *Dawn* (Pakistan) (6 July 2007); <http://www.dawn.com/2007/07/06/nat13.htm> accessed 20 April 2010.
4. Noreen Haider, 'Stand-off grabbing attention', *The News On Sunday* (Pakistan) (8 April 2007); <http://jang.com.pk/thenews/apr2007-weekly/nos-08-04-2007/enc.htm#1> accessed 15 March 2010.
5. Besides providing ideological support to militant outfits, the madrasa has produced the top leadership of some of those outfits in Pakistan including Masood Azhar (founder of Jaish-e-Muhammad), Abdullah Mehsud (the deceased Pakistani Taliban commander) and many others. Jamia Binori Town maintained close links with Afghan Taliban and awarded an honorary degree to Mullah Muhammad Omar, the head of Afghan Taliban.
6. Prior to Islamabad, Karachi was the capital city of Pakistan until early 1960s.

7. The Ahmadiya community was founded by Mirza Ghulam Ahmad. Mainstream Muslims differ with the Ahmadiyya on the claims to prophethood of Mirza Ghulam Ahmad. The Ahmadiyas' religious status (as a sect within Islam or a separate religion) is disputed. Although they consider themselves Muslims, in a number of countries, including Pakistan, Ahmadiyas have been declared non-Muslims.

8. Maulana Mufti Riaz Mansoor Gilgati, *Hayat-e-Shaheed* (Lahore: Iqra Quran Company, 2010), 26.

9. Abbas, 'The Road'.

10. Haider, 'Stand-off'.

11. Abbas, 'The Road'.

12. Griff Witte, 'Mosque Siege Exposes Rift In 'Mullah-Military' Alliance', *Washington Post* (13 July 2007); <http://www.washingtonpost.com/wp-dyn/content/article/2007/07/12/AR2007071202083.html> accessed 12 April 2010.

13. Bill Keller, 'Last Soviet Soldiers Leave Afghanistan', *The New York Times* (16 February 1989); <http://partners.nytimes.com/library/world/africa/021689afghan-laden.html> accessed 23 November 2012.

14. Ibid.

15. Rageh Omar, 'Inside the Red Mosque (Video Documentary)', Witness on Al Jazeera Television Network (English) (2007); <http://www.youtube.com/watch?v=RrKEaOeZs2o> accessed 12 February 2010.

16. 'Obituary: Abdul Rashid Ghazi', *BBC News* (10 July 2007); <http://news.bbc.co.uk/2/hi/south_asia/6281228.stm> accessed 7 May 2010.

17. Abbas, 'The Road'.

18. 'Obituary'.

19. Ibid.

20. Isambard Wilkinson, 'Bloody Pakistan mosque siege ends', *Telegraph* (UK) (11 July 2007); <http://www.telegraph.co.uk/news/worldnews/1557151/Bloody-Pakistan-mosque-siege-ends.html> accessed 5 March 2010.

21. 'Banned terror group to help defend mosque', *Gulf Times* (23 April 2007); <http://www.gulf-times.com/site/topics/article.asp?cu_no=2&item_no=145195&version=1&template_id=41&parent_id=23> accessed 5 March 2010; Iqbal Khattak, 'Musharraf ready to raid mosque but...', *Daily Times* (Pakistan) (30 June 2007); <http://www.dailytimes.com.pk/default.asp?page=2007%5C06%5C30%5C story_30-6-2007_pg1_3> accessed 5 March 2010.

22. Declan Walsh, 'The Business is Jihad', *The Guardian* (UK) (20 March 2007); <http://www.guardian.co.uk/world/2007/mar/20/pakistan.declanwalsh> accessed 5 March 2010.

23. Zahid Hussain, *The Scorpion's Tail: The Relentless Rise of Islamic Militants in Pakistan and How It Threatens America* (New York: Free Press, 2012), 112.

24. Hussain, *The Scorpion's Tail*, 71.

25. Irfan Raza, 'fatwa against Nilofar issued', *Dawn* (Pakistan) (9 April 2007); <http://www.dawn.com/2007/04/09/top2.htm> accessed 5 March 2010.

26. A copy of this leaflet was collected from Swat by the authors.

27. *Pakistan Mein Nifaz-e-Shari'at Kay Liye Jihad Ki Shar'i Haysiyyat* (The Islamic Justification of Waging Jihad in Pakistan for the Enforcement of *Shariah*), 2002.

28. Walsh, 'The Business'.

29. Interview with a serving officer of the Pakistani Army, Islamabad, 5 November 2011.

30. Syed Saleem Shahzad, *Inside al-Qaeda and the Taliban: Beyond Bin Laden and 9/11*, 1st ed. (Pluto Press, 2011).

31. 'Pakistan foils plan for weeklong series of al-Qaeda attacks', *Taipei Times* (23 August 2004); <http://www.taipeitimes.com/News/world/archives/2004/08/23/2003199891> accessed 29 October 2011.

32. 'Obituary'.

33. Syed Irfan Raza, 'Lal Masjid threatens suicide attacks' *Dawn* (Pakistan) (7 April 2007); <http://www.dawn.com/news/241168/lal-masjid-threatens-suicide-attacks> accessed 19 November 2014.

2

The Dawn of the Crisis

As discussed in Chapter One, the Red Mosque's links with anti-state elements, including the most dangerous jihadi outfits, like Lashkar-e-Jhangvi and Jaish-e-Muhammad, predated the 9/11 attack and the subsequent 'War on Terror'. Following the international intervention in Afghanistan in October 2001, President Musharraf came under international pressure to dismantle the terrorist infrastructure and its ideological support bases within the country. To satisfy the international anxiety, it was imperative that the incubators of jihad—the chain of radical mosques established during Zia's era in the capital of Pakistan—be dismantled. This left Musharraf in a diffcult political position, forcing him to try to strike a delicate balance between satisfying international pressures and, at the same time, trying to sustain political and physical survival on the domestic front. The fact that most of the radical mosques were built illegally on encroached lands provided an opportunity and a legal pretext for making this politically sensitive move. The Capital Development Authority Ordinance, 1960, Clause 49C says: 'If any building, structure, work or land is erected or constructed in contravention of the provisions of this ordinance or any rules, regulation or order the DC or any person empowered on his behalf may by order in writing, require the owner, occupier or person in control to remove, alter or demolish the building'.[1]

LAL MASJID VS CAPITAL DEVELOPMENT AUTHORITY, ISLAMABAD

In 2001, the Capital Development Authority (CDA) prepared a list of eighty such mosques and madaris that had been built on encroached land. The Red Mosque was included in this list. From March 2001, the Jamia Hafsa madrasa had been expanding over a 3,389 sq. yard plot adjacent to the Lal Masjid, which had already been allotted and earmarked for a gymnasium. Several verbal notices were reportedly issued to the madrasa authorities and to the *khatib* of Lal Masjid, but to no avail. The first written notice was issued in 2002 but again failed to produce any result. Media reports suggest further land seizures were made in 2004, when a 450 sq. yards plot allotted to the Ministry of Education for the purpose of building a public library was also occupied by the madrasa. Following this development, another notice was forwarded by the CDA on 9 December 2004, according to the records, but to no avail.[2]

Eventually, an operation was planned by the CDA to demolish the illegally built part of the madrasa; but it was never carried out, allegedly because the Islamabad Capital Territory (ICT) did not provide the CDA with an adequate police force to guarantee the safety of workers and officials. Further notices were issued in December 2005, April

2006, and January 2007, as shown in the records, without producing any results.

Responding to a question as to why the CDA authorities failed to demolish the illegal construction site when it was not yet finished, CDA Member Estate Brigadier Asad reportedly said:

> At that time administration's anti-encroachment [wing] had only 25 people. There were no weapons, no equipment and no way to carry out an operation without the help of ICT chief commissioner and Inspector General (IG) Islamabad. They provide the necessary support through the magistrate and police for any demolition operation. Because of the fact that this particular seminary has female students the authorities were always apprehensive of taking any extreme action against them. The seminary authorities exploited this situation to the hilt. An operation was planned for 9 December 2004, for which the CDA authorities were ready, but the necessary backup was not there so it was called off.[3]

The encroachments subsequently turned into a major cause of rift between the government and the Red Mosque administration, and are discussed in more detail later.

The situation was further complicated by the fact that the mosque and its madaris contained thousands of students from all age groups, starting from as young as three years old. Most of the students in recent years had come from the earthquake-hit (2005) and war-torn northern and tribal areas of the country. The mosque and its madaris provided for their food and personal care, as well as giving them an education in religion, science, and languages such as Arabic and even English.[4]

The CDA provided the government with a legal justification for demolishing Jamia Hafsa and Jamia Faridia, the *madaris* adjacent to the mosque, which had become a source of ideological indoctrination for a number of militant organizations fighting the government forces. However, the Red Mosque administration was able to counter the state's moves, forging an alliance with other hardline clerics by presenting the government's move to demolish mosques as akin to 'inviting the wrath of God'.[5] In January 2007, an emergency meeting of over 300 leading religious scholars was held in Madni Mosque on Murree Road, Islamabad, where Maulana Abdur Rauf and Qari Saeed-ur-Rehman vowed to hold demonstrations against the action of the government. The ulema argued that demolishing mosques was un-Islamic, and that the government was acting on the behest of its European and American 'masters'.[6]

Protracted protests by the clerics could not force the government to reverse its decision to demolish more than 80 disputed mosques and madaris situated across Islamabad. In January 2007, the CDA razed the Amir Hamza Mosque located at Murree Road, Islamabad. This mosque was closely linked to the Lal Masjid clerics and reportedly caused Maulana Abdul Aziz a great degree of distress, as reported by his wife, Umme Hasaan, who claimed that during those days the Maulana could hardly sleep at night.[7]

The Emergence of the 'Burqa Brigade'

In order to pre-empt government action, hundreds of female students from Jamia Hafsa attacked the adjacent Children's Library and occupied it.[8] The madrasa administration, headed by the two brothers, claimed to have had no prior knowledge of this move by the students but, once the Children's Library was occupied, they approved the students' action in order to save the mosques.[9]

The government's intent having become apparent from the recent demolition of the Amir Hamza Mosque, the Jamia Hafsa girls broke into the public library the following day. They demanded that no further demolitions of mosques should take place and that all the six mosques demolished over the past two and a half years should be reconstructed by the government.[10] Umme Hasaan, the wife of Maulana Aziz and the madrasa's Principal declared, 'They will have to shoot me before they can touch this place.'[11]

In the meantime, Maulana Aziz gave public speeches and media statements in which he warned the government against challenging the 'writ of God' and urged the nation to support him in protecting the mosques against desecration. He warned that the 'weapons of his supporters were their lives', and they were willing to sacrifice their lives for this cause. He further claimed to be receiving death threats. But, he said, he would not give up until the demand to restore and rebuild the desecrated mosques was met.[12] Additionally, he issued a warning that, in case of an attack on the madaris, students would sacrifice their lives to protect them. He claimed that the students had already written their wills and that the government must abandon their 'anti-Islamic measures' immediately.[13]

Eventually, the government caved in to the pressure and, on 12 February 2007, the Minister for Religious Affairs, Ijaz ul-Haq, laid the foundation stone at the site where the Amir Hamza Mosque once stood, confirming the government's intention of rebuilding the mosque. An eleven-member committee was later formed to review the list of eighty-one mosques marked for demolition and the possibility of providing alternate land for their relocation.[14] However, according to reports in the media, the government avoided signing a written contract.[15]

Umme Hasaan said: 'This is a result of the bravery shown by the girls ... At most, we would have been killed and embraced martyrdom.'[16] Afterwards, the doors to the library were only opened conditionally as she declared: 'We will continue to have administrative control over the library until all the six desecrated mosques have been renovated and the notices to eighty-one other mosques are withdrawn by the government.' On 13 February, the activists rechristened the library as the Modern Islamic Children's Library.[17]

After the occupation of the Children's Library by the female students of Jamia Hafsa, the government officials started negotiations with the prominent ulema of Wafaq-ul-Madaris, the largest group of Deobandi madaris in Pakistan. The representatives of Wafaq-ul-Madaris demanded that Maulana Abdul Aziz should surrender to the government. Two meetings were held between Abdul Aziz and senior members of Wafaq-ul-Madaris to mediate the issue, but failed to yield an outcome. He refused to accept the standpoint of the government and said the protests would continue until the enforcement of Sharia in the country. Many ulema in Islamabad termed this demand 'a manifestation of extremism' and condemned it.[18]

The protracted negotiations yielded an agreement between Wafaq-ul-Madaris leaders and the government, whereby the latter again promised to reconstruct the demolished mosques. But Maulana Abdul Aziz said that this was only 'a part' of his demands and once again declared that the protests would continue until the enforcement of Sharia in the country. The ulema had condemned the occupation of the library by female students of Jamia Hafsa but Maulana Abdul Aziz attacked these critics in return for criticizing the occupation of a 'mere library' as not being in line with Sharia while no fatwa was issued against a regime that was 'destroying holy mosques.'[19]

THE ANTI-VICE CAMPAIGN GROWS

Having registered considerable success with its initial protest campaign, the Lal Masjid administration and its students' ambitions increased, as they expanded their agenda and list of demands, simultaneously escalating the radicalization process inside the mosque and its madaris. As a consequence, the students from both madaris began to assert themselves as a self-appointed 'moral police' in the capital, openly confronting the state and the top religious leadership.

At first, the female students had limited their demands to the reconstruction of the Amir Hamza Mosque and the receipt of a clear promise from the government not to raze any other mosque in Islamabad. But they later joined Maulana Abdul Aziz, when he vowed to continue the protest until the implementation of Islamic Sharia. The occupation of a government-owned building in the federal capital was a clear challenge to the authority of the state. However, the female students believed the government had actually challenged the 'Will of God' by bulldozing the mosques.

The Jamia Hafsa students wrote a detailed letter to President Musharraf with the following demands:

1. President Musharraf should extend an apology to the nation for demolishing and attacking mosques and seminaries.

2. The only solution to the problems of Pakistan lies in the complete enforcement of Islam, therefore immediate imposition of Islamic order is necessary.

3. Islamic law should be applied to the courts of the country so that people can obtain speedy and inexpensive justice.

4. Jihad is an Islamic obligation but the media is portraying it as terrorism. This sin should be stopped immediately.[20]

A note at the end of this letter read: 'We are followers of the Sharia, which does not teach us to give and take. Rather, it insists we firmly adhere to the path of Islam and be either martyrs or *ghazis*. Therefore, our demands are unbending and we are not willing to withdraw any one of the demands.'[21] Subsequently, the madrasa students engaged in a number of acts that were tantamount to direct confrontation with the government, as well as harassment of the general public. In January 2007, about 100 to 150 students of the Red Mosque armed with Kalashnikovs, pistols, and batons disrupted a marriage ceremony at Aabpara Community Centre in Islamabad, threatening to 'turn the celebration into a tragedy' if the fireworks display was not stopped.[22] In March 2007, a group of forty to fifty baton-wielding persons, some with covered faces, visited different markets and ordered owners of CD, audio, and video shops to cease this kind of business. Maulana Abdul Aziz endeavoured to link events in Islamabad with the larger Talibanization movement engulfing the Tribal Areas and North-West Frontier Province (now Khyber Pakhtunkhwa, KPK). In a telephonic address on the occasion of the inauguration of the basement of a mosque in Kohat, Maulana Abdul Aziz reportedly asked the Taliban to continue their militancy against obscenity, prostitution, video shops, and other social vices and expand it to every nook and corner of the NWFP.[23] 'Muttahida Majlis-i-Amal secured votes in the name of Islam and the Quran but failed to enforce Sharia and curb un-Islamic practises. Therefore, it is now the responsibility of all believers to support the activities of the Taliban in the province against CD shops and obscenity,' he said.[24]

Aziz advised the Taliban to also help the 'weak and helpless' segments of society in obtaining justice. He said the government would have to enforce Islam soon because they could not stop the movement of the Taliban which, he claimed, had the support of millions of people. 'People are fed up with the rulers and want immediate change for which time is ripe.'[25] In the following days, the Red Mosque's 'moral brigade' launched a series of attacks on the video and CD shops in Islamabad.

The 'anti-vice' campaign soon started targeting massage parlours located in the posh areas of Islamabad. On 27 March 2007, a group of students from the mosque's madaris—thirty women and ten men—broke into a massage parlour in the centre of Islamabad, alleging it was a brothel. The owner, known as Auntie Shamim, had allegedly ignored their warning to close it down.[26] The students took the owner, her daughter, and her daughter-in-law back to the madrasa, claiming the 'right to end immoral activity under Islamic law'. Initially, the police were reluctant to step in to rescue the women, but later registered the case and arrested two female teachers of the school. In an audacious response, the students reciprocated by kidnapping two policemen from a nearby patrol, and holding them captive inside the madrasa.[27] Aware of the importance of the battle for public opinion, the clerics paraded the policemen in front of the media, where one of them stated: 'They have not mistreated us, they have served us tea and allowed us to keep our mobile phones ...

We are told that negotiations are under way and we hope the matter will be over soon.'[28]

Commenting on the incident, Rashid Ghazi stated: 'The 'brothel' had been raided on the complaint of residents of the area who feared that Shamim Akhtar (a.k.a. 'Auntie Shamim'), who allegedly had links with senior police officials, would take revenge on them if they lodged any report against her.' He added that, despite complaints to the police by the residents, no action was taken and therefore, the students had to act.[29] He warned: 'We will not release the women unless a 'strong' FIR (First Information Report) is registered in a Police Station against them so that they can be taken to task through legal means for their immoral activities.'[30]

The alleged brothel owner was released on 29 March after making a 'confession' from inside the mosque at a press conference, wearing a full-face burqa and declaring that she had been involved in 'immoral activities'. The kidnapped women were then released, along with a demand for the release (within 15 days) of Khalid Khwaja, a former Inter-Services Intelligence (ISI) official, and five activists closely linked to the Red Mosque clerics.[31] Shamim Akhtar later retracted her 'confession' stating it was forced. Describing her ordeal, she said her daughter and daughter-in-law had been kept in separate rooms and alleged that, before being presented to the media for the press conference, she had been threatened that her family members could be killed if she said anything contrary to the written statement.[32]

PUBLIC REACTIONS

The involvement of female students in the above-mentioned incidents triggered a heated debate in Pakistani society, which generally discourages women's active participation in such activities, traditionally undertaken by men. Many parents interviewed by the media suggested that they had enrolled their daughters to study Islamic subjects, and not to carry sticks or guard their academy. Parents also filed complaints against the mosque's administration on the use of their daughters in violent activities both inside and outside the madrasa premises, while some also demanded assurances that their daughters would not be used for such purposes in the future. Some parents also complained that they were being taunted by their fellow villagers that their daughters were searching for prostitutes instead of concentrating on their studies. Further criticism was raised by parents who considered the use of the students for 'anti-vice' campaigns launched by the mosque as non-Pashtun, i.e. against their traditions. Therefore, some parents ordered their daughters to return and forbade them to stay in the mosque.[33]

Commenting on these issues, Rashid Ghazi stated that there was no restriction on students leaving the madrasa and that parents who wanted to remove their daughters from the madrasa should contact him. He said: 'We have not forcefully retained the students in the madrasa nor have we imposed any restriction on removing children.' He further added that Jamia Hafsa students would not be used for enforcement of Islamic law, but said they reserved the right to self-defence in case the government launched an operation against the students. He criticized the media for highlighting only the violent side of the Sharia movement.[34]

Pakistan's civil society was not a silent observer during these events, and a strong sense of anger and dismay prevailed across the country over the government's inaction. On 5 April, several hundred men and women protested against the religious militancy and ferocity of the students of the Lal Masjid madaris in launching their campaign 'to stop vices' in the city and for seeking the 'Talibanization' of Pakistan.[35] Although the demonstration took place a few hundred yards from the Lal Masjid, it drew no reaction from the 'moral squads' entrenched in the mosque. Law-enforcement personnel were present for a couple of hours as the slogan-chanting activists marched along the Aabpara Market. Towards the end of the protests, however, police intervened when some enthusiastic women activists wanted to march towards Lal Masjid and blocked their way, to prevent an escalation of the protests. Representatives of civil society and a number of political leaders made short speeches criticizing 'the self-proclaimed custodians of morality'.[36] They demanded that the government has to forcefully end the Jamia Hafsa students' occupation of the Children's Library and warned that if this was not achieved, 'the menace' would continue to be a threat for peaceful citizens.[37]

The Lal Masjid 'anti-vice' campaign also drew considerable criticism from the Pakistani political and religious elite. A number of prominent lawyers and politicians responding to a *Jang* (Urdu Daily) questionnaire stressed their view that Islam did not allow actions such as those taken by Jamia Hafsa and that this was not a legal way of eliminating vice from society. The government must act to demonstrate its authority, while at the same time acting 'responsibly'.[38] Several prominent Islamic scholars also condemned the Red Mosque clerics and students for taking the law in their hands. Maulana Rafi Usmani, the grand Mufti of Deobandism in Pakistan, also disagreed with Maulana Aziz. He declared that the people in the Lal Masjid were not serving Islam but were in fact defaming it with their actions. The grand Mufti also stated that Aziz's claim that he has an indication from God to launch jihad and impose Sharia in the country was meaningless.[39]

Representatives of various madaris of Lahore also later denounced the Ghazi brothers for damaging the image of Islam and Pakistan.[40] Commenting on the crackdown on the mosque and related madaris, the representatives of various other such institutions, including the Jamia Ashrafia (Deobandi), the Jamia Naeemia (Barelwi), the Jamiatul Muntazir (Shia), the Jamia Ahle Hadith (Ahl-e-Hadith), and the Jamia Manzoorul Islam (Deobandi), called for a military operation to end the crisis, and accused the government of indecisiveness.

On 9 February 2007, after gaining much-needed support from the mainstream clerics, the government decided to launch an operation to end the occupation of the Children's Library. Law enforcement agencies moved in, all the telephone lines of the madrasa and the mosque were cut, and water supply was also stopped. Police and administration unloaded a large number of barricades to block the roads. This step from the government was initiated after talks between the government and the students' mediator Javed Ibrahim Paracha had failed. The government's stance was that radical elements could plan a terrorist attack by exploiting the situation and therefore security forces were posted around the complex to prevent such an attack.

Talks between the two sides were in process, when security forces started to gather around the Jamia Hafsa. Maulana Abdul Aziz appealed to the neighbours through loud speakers to 'save the mosque, madrasa, and female students from the brutality of the security forces'. In the meantime, students and young men from nearby madaris and the university rushed to Lal Masjid and Jamia Hafsa, carrying batons to fight the government forces. Despite heavy rain and cold weather, the female students of Jamia Hafsa maintained their positions on the roof of the library. Representatives of international media were all present at the spot, as they expected a battle between the security forces and thousands of the madrasa's students, when Shah Abdul Aziz, a renowned politician with strong links among regional Jihadi forces, reached the spot. He appealed to both sides to remain peaceful. The security forces were called back and the government decided to look for 'alternative solutions'.

Intelligence sources claimed that Maulana Abdul Aziz sought a violent showdown to dramatize the mosque controversy. According to some reports, he had set up an anti-government force comprising 150 members of banned sectarian outfits. Several rounds of talks between the government and the Jamia Hafsa management had failed. The Vice Principal of Jamia Hafsa, Abdul Rashid Ghazi, had boycotted the dialogue with the government by saying that the 'government [was] not sincere about resolving the issue. They [wanted] to create justification for the use of force against us.' At the same time, Minister of Religious Affairs Ijaz ul-Haq asked the authorities to delay the operation in order to hold a 'final meeting' with the madrasa management.

THE SHARIA COURT

On 6 April 2007, there was another challenge to the Pakistani state. The mosque administration set up its own Sharia court inside its premises.[41] They also threatened a wave of suicide bombings if the government tried to shut it down. The so-called Sharia court, which represented a parallel judicial system to that of the state, was presided by ten clerics and its declared goal was to 'stamp out the vice in society'. At the inaugural session of the court, sermonizing, Maulana Aziz said to the attendees: 'Our youths will shake their palaces with suicide attacks.'[42] Defending the setting up of the so-called Sharia court, Ghazi refuted the claim that its establishment posed an unacceptable challenge to the state, arguing that 'if jirga and panchayat[43] are not considered parallel judicial systems, then why should a Sharia court be regarded as one?' [sic.][44] Maulana Aziz then.

issued a warning: 'The government has been saying that an operation against us is its last option. I want to tell the government that suicide attacks are our last option.' When he asked the worshippers whether they would be ready to sacrifice their lives the students responded with shouts: 'Yes, Yes, *Allah-u-Akbar*.'[45]

Ghazi claimed that the newly established Sharia court had begun to receive complaints but declined to say anything about the number of complaints received, the names of the complainants, or the nature of the disputes.[46] He also stated that anyone could bring their case to the Sharia court, and the only condition was that the parties involved in a dispute agreed to abide by the court's decision.

It is pertinent to mention here that the idea of Sharia courts has not been a new phenomenon among Islamic extremists in Pakistan. Even at the time when the Lal Masjid set up its court, fifty-four other similar private courts were already operational across the country. Of these twenty-four were run by Jamaat-ud-Dawa, five by the banned Sipah-e-Sahaba, and others by the local Taliban, not only in the tribal areas but also in towns like Tank and Bannu.[47]

As Muhammad Amir Rana has noted, the Jamiat-ul-Ulema-e-Islam (JUI) was the first organization to introduce the idea of private Sharia courts in 1975. At the JUI annual convention in Gujranwala, Mufti Mehmood and Maulana Abdullah Darkhwasti had presented the idea of the private courts. The participants approved the idea and a Sharia committee, comprising Mufti Mahmud,

Abdul Karim Qureshi, and Maulana Sarfaraz Khan, was formed to decide the mechanism for these courts. The plan for private courts was made part of the JUI's party platform and manifesto in 1976 but was not implemented at the time because of Zia ul-Haq's martial law.[48] Following the same plan, Sipah-e-Sahaba set up a Sharia court in Jhang district in 1998. Jamaat-ud-Dawa's head Hafiz Muhammad Saeed had announced the establishment of Sharia courts on 15 September 2005 in Lahore. The Jamaat-ud-Dawa had plans to set up similar courts at district level and, at this time, there were twenty-four courts operating in Punjab and Interior Sindh. These courts made it mandatory for rival parties to submit an affidavit that they would accept the court's decision.[49] The Pakistani Taliban, who started an armed struggle against the state in the Federally Administered Tribal Areas (FATA) region, were, in the course of the Shakai Agreement in 2004, allowed to enforce Sharia in their stronghold of South Waziristan. This did not only include the establishment of Sharia courts, but also the formation of a Sharia police. Following in Pakistani Taliban's footsteps, religious scholars in Dera Ismail Khan and Bannu districts adopted the same system. The Khyber Agency maintained two Sharia courts, established by the rival sectarian groups, Lashkar-e-Islam and Ansarul Islam. But the Lal Mosque's Sharia court plan was closest to the Sipah-e-Sahaba plan announced by Maulana Azam Tariq in 2000 in the 7th International Difa-e-Islam Conference at Karachi.[50]

The Lal Masjid Sharia court, named *Darul Ifta*, did not waste any time and only two days after its inception it issued its first fatwa (religious opinion), directed against the then Pakistani Tourism Minister Nilofar Bakhtiar after pictures of her embracing her parachuting instructor surfaced in the media. The fatwa demanded that the government 'punish and sack' her from the Cabinet for engaging with paragliders in Paris in an 'obscene manner'.[51] Nilofar reacted by encouraging the government to take action against the clerics. However, with the exception of a few public office holders and one minister, the government on the whole remained silent on the issue. Quoting the case of Zille Huma, a Punjab Provincial Minister, who was killed as a consequence of a similar fatwa, Nilofar told the Standing Committee of the Parliament that she feared for her life. Zille Huma was killed by an assassin after a fatwa was issued against her saying that a woman under Islam had no right to hold public office.[52] Another report suggested that she was killed because she was not wearing a veil.[53]

Nilofar Bakhtiar later resigned, feeling that the government was insufficiently supportive of her, and urged the Supreme Court to take *suo motu* notice of the fatwa, as well as against the setting up of an illegal and parallel system of justice in the form of the so-called Sharia court.[54] She was disappointed that her Cabinet colleagues had not stood by her and hurt by the way her sky diving had been sensationalized.[55] However, the fatwa did draw some limited reaction. For instance, the then Minister of State for Health Shahnaz Sheikh said that the *Darul Ifta* had no authority to issue a decree against anyone. 'These people are misinterpreting Islam and we strongly condemn this act.'[56] Pakistan Peoples Party Parliamentarians Information Secretary Sherry Rehman also said that no one should be allowed to take law into their own hands. Further, Human Rights Commission of Pakistan chairperson Asma Jahangir said the fatwa had no credibility and stated that no importance should be attached to it.[57] Nevertheless, an official governmental reaction to the fatwa was non-existent.

TENSIONS GROW

Encouraged by their earlier successes, which were constituted in the government's inaction against their 'anti-vice' campaign, the kidnapping of Aunty Shamim and two policemen, the establishment of a Sharia court and the resignation of Nilofar Bakhtiar, the feeling of strength inside the mosque and its madaris grew stronger. On 18 May 2007, events escalated further, as the female students of Jamia Hafsa (by now commonly known as the 'Lal Masjid Brigade') took hostage another four policemen, who were on duty in front of the mosque, accusing them of 'spying' for the government.[58] This audacious act raised general fears about the inevitability of a violent showdown at the mosque.

Later, a police report was lodged by the government authorities against both brothers and seventy-two of their followers, citing a number of different charges, including terrorism, and all security agencies were put on high alert as a precaution. The authorities then tried to negotiate the release of the kidnapped policemen. However, talks conducted by Magistrate Farasat Ali and Assistant Superintendent of Police Kamran Adil, broke down when Maulana Abdul Aziz and his brother Maulana Abdul Rashid Ghazi refused to release the policemen until eleven of their followers, who were detained by the security agencies, were also released.[59] Neither of the two brothers physically participated in the negotiations, communicating indirectly through Lal Masjid representatives instead.[60]

Ghazi, commenting on the breakdown of the talks, stated: 'We are releasing two policemen in exchange for five of our companions but will continue to hold the other two until all our men, arrested by the intelligence agency, are freed.' He added that the negotiations were now over and would be resumed when the administration was willing to release the six others in detention.[61]

Maulana Aziz, condemning the threats of an operation against the mosque, said that their supporters were ready to 'carry out suicide attacks if such an operation was launched'. Ghazi also argued that the policemen, who were in plain clothes, were outside the mosque on a 'spying mission'. 'We had already advised the local administration not to carry out such acts which could aggravate the situation, but it chose to ignore our warnings,' said Ghazi.[62]

Meanwhile, a Rawalpindi Anti-Terrorism Court ordered the release of four students and Mr Khawaja, a close associate of the brothers, but they could not be released because of non-submission of surety bonds of Rs 100,000 (approximately USD 1200). So, all but two policemen were released after sunset. Shaukat Aziz, Khalid Khawaja's lawyer, said Mr Khawaja could not be released on bail immediately because the court had issued another detention order against him under the Security of Pakistan Act.[63] Chaudhry Iftikhar Ahmed, the Islamabad Police Chief, denied the reports that the students had been released in reaction to the kidnappings of the policemen. He said that an Anti-Terrorism Court had ordered the students to be released on bail and their release was not related to the kidnapping of the policemen.[64] This move was seen as another effort to appease the brothers and pave the way for a prisoners' swap with the Red Mosque.

The same day, the military authorities, Interior Ministry, local administration, and police held separate meetings to find a 'permanent solution' to the Lal Masjid issue. The main meeting was held at the General Headquarters (GHQ) in Rawalpindi, which was attended by security and intelligence officials. However, there was a general impression in the media and the public that the government was still reluctant to launch any operation against the mosque's administration.[65] A high-ranking government official later revealed that in the Interior Ministry it was decided that 'force will not be used to free the police and the path of negotiations will be sought for the sake of public safety'.[66] In an interesting turn, following the government's declaration that it was not inclined to use force, the mosque's management finally released the remaining two policemen, after nearly a week of detention, on 24 May, on what it claimed to be 'humanitarian grounds'.[67]

On 25 May, the Lal Masjid administration once again announced that its students would attack audio and video shops, massage centres, and brothels in Islamabad if their owners did not wind up their businesses immediately. Warning the shopkeepers about the deadline issued on 29 March by the mosque's madrasa students, Maulana Aziz said in his Friday sermon: 'Our students can attack these outlets anytime because the deadline given to their owners had already passed.'[68]

The Lal Masjid and the government confrontation peaked when, on 2 June, a group of burqa-clad Jamia Hafsa students kidnapped nine people from a massage parlour and acupuncture clinic. These nine persons comprised six foreign women, of whom three were Chinese, together with one Chinese man and two Pakistani men. The Pakistani Interior Ministry called the abductions a 'shocking and unlawful act',[69] whereas Ghazi said the abductees were 'spreading obscenity' and 'running a brothel in [sic.] the cover of a massage parlour'.[70] He further added that the Lal Masjid administration had been receiving complaints about a prostitution racket at the parlour.[71]

Given the involvement of foreign nationals, this crisis was handled at a much higher level than before. Reportedly, Luo Zhaohui, the Chinese Ambassador to Pakistan, sought the help of the ruling party Pakistan Muslim

League–Quaid-i-Azam Group (PML-Q) and the army. In a meeting with President Musharraf, he presented the Chinese government's displeasure at the incident and put pressure on the President to tame the extremists in the heart of the country.

After fifteen hours of negotiations, nine people were released.[72] Ghazi later claimed that the detainees were released because they had regard for Pakistani-Chinese friendship and because the government gave an undertaking that it would shut down all 'illegal' massage parlours.[73] He, however, did not disclose the nationalities of the three other women, nor were the details of the negotiations and terms of the deal ever made public.

PONDERING THE STORMING OF THE MOSQUE

All the events, which took place between January and June 2007,[74] posed a serious challenge to the government. A first attempt to end the occupation of the Children's Library was made on the night of 9 February, when the authorities were about to launch an operation that included the use of force. But, keeping in mind the perceived threat from the religious hardliners, the government recalled the forces and started to think about alternate solutions. On 29 June, President Musharraf claimed that suicide bombers were holed up in Lal Masjid. He said that an operation could be launched against the Lal Masjid and Jamia Hafsa brigade, but a raid was expected to lead to heavy casualties on both sides because a large number of suicide bombers were allegedly inside the mosque and the madaris. Elaborating further, he claimed that militants with links to Jaish-e-Muhammad and al-Qaeda were hiding in the mosque and the madaris and were in possession of explosives.[75]

Aware that an operation may cause havoc and a hostile reaction, but simultaneously worried about a lack of action being perceived as governmental weakness, Musharraf declared, 'Let it be clear that the action against the Lal Masjid and Jamia Hafsa brigade was not withheld because of government's weakness or cowardice in the face of an enemy.' He further added, 'Critics should understand that the seminary (Jamia Hafsa) houses 2,500 women students, and suicide bombers inside are equipped with sophisticated arms. While police are not capable of launching such a complex operation, the army cannot be involved, for it can give a wrong message to the world.' He continued, 'We have involved senior clerics of the country, the Council of Islamic Ideology and the Imam-e-Kaaba, the highest religious authority in the Muslim world, to end the standoff. Shall we now call Allah to help these elements shun their wrongdoings?'[76]

Another reliable news source covering the same speech by Musharraf, however, quoted him also saying, 'Action is ready but will be taken at the right time.' The television channel *Aaj* quoted him saying, 'Government will take action against the mosque if the media guarantee that it will not show any dead bodies in electronic or print media.'[77]

On 2 July, at around 4:00 p.m., there was a large meeting held inside the mosque, in which Ghazi revealed that 'certain elements' in the government had been successful in their objectives and that the mosque was going to be cordoned off starting that evening. He reportedly lamented to the crowd, 'How can we stop the fight? Who should we talk to? All our supporters in the government are helpless. The major clerics have already deserted us so there is no point in talking to them. If these clerics had backed us from day one, the situation would not have deteriorated to this point. Perhaps, partially, our demands would have been met. There is nothing in my hands except following the orders of the Amir [i.e. Maulana Aziz].'[78]

Responding to the query of the anxious crowd, Maulana Aziz reportedly stated, 'I am sure that the government cannot be so ruthless. There may be cordoning off of the mosque but there will be no violence. You gentlemen should not worry. We are in our own country and want the religion of God to prevail. We may be harsh in our tone so there will be some reaction but I am not expecting an operation by the security forces.'[79]

Around 8:00 p.m., Ghazi reportedly received a phone call and then rang Maulana Aziz to inform him that the government had called in the security forces and the army had decided to blockade the mosque from all sides. According to those present, Maulana Aziz's face turned red and he asked all senior members of the mosque to gather at one place to devise a strategy to deal with the unfolding crisis. It was allegedly decided that 'no action will be taken unless provoked. No shot should be fired and no stones will be thrown. However, if anyone tried to make a forced entry into the mosque or the seminary, then he would be stopped.' A committee was also constituted under the leadership of Abdul Rashid Ghazi to open dialogue with senior officials in the government and resolve the issue, quickly and amicably, and at the same time inform the media and press of the unfolding situation. After this, the senior members of the mosque also devised a defense strategy in case of an operation or attack.[80]

After the meeting ended, Maulana Aziz reportedly spoke with the students at the madrasa and the mosque about the situation and sought their opinion, which allegedly overwhelmingly opposed the idea of withdrawal of demands 'under any circumstances'. As they spoke, the noise of army trucks let those inside know that a siege had begun. Maulana Aziz then went into the mosque's hall where around three thousand men were present and addressed them for a few minutes, followed by early morning prayers (*fajr*), after which several people left the mosque's premises, all without being stopped.[81]

NOTES

1. Noreen Haider, 'Stand-off grabbing attention', *The News On Sunday (Pakistan)* (8 April 2007); <http://jang.com.pk/thenews/apr2007-weekly/nos-08-04-2007/enc.htm#1> accessed 15 March 2010.
2. Ibid.
3. Ibid.
4. Rageh Omar, 'Inside the Red Mosque' (Video Documentary), *Witness on Al Jazeera Television Network (English)* (2007); <http://www.youtube.com/watch?v=RrKEaOeZs2o> accessed 12 February 2010.
5. Umme Hasaan, *Saniha Lal Masjid: Ham par kya guzri* (The tragedy of the Red Mosque: What befell us) (Islamabad: Lal Masjid Publications, 2007), 7.
6. Khuram Iqbal, 'Children Library to Enforce Sharia?', *South Asia Net* (2011); <http://san-pips.com/print.php?id=25> accessed 5 March 2011.
7. Umme Hasaan, *Saniha*, 10–11.
8. Iqbal, 'Children Library'.
9. Umme Hasaan, *Saniha*, 10–21.
10. Mariana Baabar, 'Who wears the pants?', *Outlook India* (26 February 2007); <http://www.outlookindia.com/article.aspx?233987> accessed 5 March 2010.
11. Thaksina Khaikaew, 'Female Pakistani students protest Gov't', *Fox News (US)* (10 February 2007); <http://www.foxnews.com/printer_friendly_wires/2007Feb10/0,4675,PakistanMadrassaProtest,00.html> accessed 10 March 2010.
12. '*Masajid-o-madaris ke tahaffuz ke liye kashtian jala di hain, qaum saath de—Molana Abdul Aziz* (We have burnt our boats for the sake of the mosques and the seminaries: the nation should support us—Molana Abdul Aziz)', *Daily Islam* (*Urdu*) (27 January 2007).
13. '*Madrasa Jamia Faridia par hamla hua to talibat apni jaanein de dain ge—Molana Abdul Aziz*', *Nawae Waqt* (*Urdu*) (27 January 2007).
14. Baabar, 'Who wears the pants'.

15. Wajiha Ahmed Siddiqui, '*Tahriri mu'ahida karne se sarkari idaron ka gureiz*' (Reluctance of the government departments to sign a written agreement)', *Ummat* (Urdu) (10 February 2007).
16. Baabar, 'Who wears the pants'.
17. Ibid.
18. Iqbal, 'Children's Library'.
19. Ibid.
20. The letter was published in the February 2007 edition of Monthly 'Aab-e-Hayat' magazine linked to the Red Mosque.
21. Ibid.
22. 'Lal Masjid clerics had contacts with terrorists, commission told' *Pakistan Today* (26 March 2013); <www.pakistantoday.com.pk/2013/03/26/news/national/lal-masjid-clerics-had-contacts-with-terrorists-commission-told/> accessed 26 November 2014.
23. 'Lal Masjid gears up for attack on CD, video shops: Taliban jihad in NWFP backed', *Dawn (Pakistan)* (26 May 2007); <http://archives.dawn.com/2007/05/26/top7.htm> accessed 31 October 2011.
24. Ibid.
25. Ibid.
26. Matthew Pennington, 'Pakistani Students Abduct Brothel Owner', *Washington Post (USA)* (28 March 2007); <http://www.washingtonpost.com/wp-dyn/content/article/2007/03/28/AR2007032800290.html> accessed 2 March 2010.
27. 'Students raid Islamabad 'brothel', *BBC* (28 March 2007); <http://news.bbc.co.uk/2/hi/south_asia/6502305.stm> accessed 12 March 2010.
28. Ibid.
29. Wajiha Ahmed Siddiqui, '*Shikayat ke bawajood police ne karawai nahin ki; makinon ki shikayat par hamein ikdam karna para—Jamia Hafsa ke Naib Maulana Abdul Rashid Ghazi se guftugu*' (Despite complaints Police did not take action: We had to take action on the request of the residents—Talking to Maulana Rashid Ghazi, the deputy of Jamia Hafsa), *Ummat (Urdu)* (31 March 2007).
30. Syed Irfan Raza, '*Madressah* force on the offensive in Islamabad: Move to impose Talibanisation; three women kidnapped', *Dawn*

(Pakistan) (29 March 2007); <http://www.dawn.com/2007/03/29/top4.htm> accessed 5 March 2010; Syed Irfan Raza, *'Badkari ka ilzam: Jamia Hafsa ki talibat ne teen khawateen ko aghwa kar liya* (Allegations of Corruption: Students of Jamia Hafsa kidnap 3 women)', *Jang* (*Urdu*) (29 March 2007).

31. Syed Irfan Raza, 'Women freed after forced confession', *Dawn (Pakistan)* (30 March 2007); <http://www.dawn.com/2007/03/30/top2.htm> accessed 3 March 2010.

32. Ibid.

33. Irfan Raza, 'Fatwa against Nilofar issued', *Dawn (Pakistan)* (9 April 2007); <http://www.dawn.com/2007/04/09/top2.htm> accessed 5 March 2010.

34. Ibid.

35. Khawar Ghumman, 'Protests in Islamabad against 'moral police'', *Dawn (Pakistan)* (6 April 2007); <http://www.dawn.com/2007/04/06/top7.htm> accessed 5 March 2010.

36. Ibid.

37. Ibid.

38. *'Jamia hafsa aur Tank jaese waaqe'at ki Islam mein ijazat nahin hai—hukumat apni writ qaim kare'* (There is no permission for acts such as Jamia Hafsa and Tank in Islam—Government must establish its writ), *Jang* (*Urdu*) (30 March 2007).

39. 'Ulema reject claim of Lal Masjid mullah', *Daily Times* (5 July 2007).

40. Ali Waqar, 'Lahori clerics distance themselves from Ghazi brothers', *Daily Times* (7 July 2007).

41. 'Lal Masjid set up *Shariat* Court today', *The News (Pakistan)* (6 April 2007); <http://www.thenews.com.pk/top_story_detail.asp?Id=6945> accessed 5 March 2010; Wajiha Ahmed Siddiqui, *'Lal Masjid mein qazi ki adalat—hukumat ka ikdam kya hoga?'* (Establishment of Court in Lal Masjid—What will the government do?), *Ummat* (*Urdu*) (7 April 2007).

42. Isambard Wilkinson, 'Radical cleric sets up vigilante *Sharia* law court in Pakistan's capital', *Telegraph (UK)* (7 April 2007); <http://www.telegraph.co.uk/news/worldnews/1547930/Radical-cleric-

sets-up-vigilante-sharia-law-court-in-Pakistans-capital.html>
accessed 2 March 2010.

43. Jirga and Panchayat are traditional assemblies of elders in Pakhtun
and Punjabi cultures, respectively, intended to resolve disputes
through consensus.

44. Muhammad Amir Rana, 'Conflict: Lal Mosque's Terror Link',
Pakistan Institute for Peace Studies Network <http://san-pips.com/
print.php?id=28> accessed 15 March 2010.

45. Wilkinson, 'Radical cleric'.

46. Raza, 'Fatwa'.

47. Rana, 'Conflict'.

48. Ibid.

49. Ibid.

50. Ibid.

51. Raza, 'Fatwa'.

52. 'Fatwa makes minister fear for her life', *Indian Express* (India)
(16 April 2007); <http://www.indianexpress.com/news/Fatwa-
makes-minister-fear-for-her-life/28473/> accessed 10 March 2010;
Akram Malik, 'Woman minister killed by fanatic', *Dawn* (Pakistan)
(21 February 2007); <http://www.dawn.com/2007/02/21/top2.
htm> accessed 4 March 2010.

53. Zahid Hussain, 'The leap of faith that cost tourism minister her
job', *Times Online (UK)* (21 May 2007); <http://www.timesonline.
co.uk/tol/news/world/asia/article1820247.ece> accessed 4 March
2010.

54. Masood Haider, 'Nilofar Urges SC action against Lal Masjid',
Dawn (4 July 2007); <http://www.dawn.com/2007/07/04/nat1.
htm> accessed 26 November 2014.

55. Hussain, 'The leap'.

56. Raza, 'Fatwa'.

57. Raza, 'Fatwa'.

58. 'Lal Masjid 'brigade' kidnaps 4 policemen', *Dawn (Pakistan)*
(19 May 2007); <http://www.dawn.com/2007/05/19/top1.htm>
accessed 3 March 2010.

59. Ibid.

60. Shakeel Anjum, 'Govt gives in to Lal Masjid clerics', *The News (Pakistan)* (20 May 2007); <http://thenews.jang.com.pk/top_story_detail.asp?Id=7963> accessed 4 March 2010.
61. Ibid.
62. 'Lal Masjid "brigade"'.
63. Irfan Raza, 'Two policemen freed in Lal Masjid swap: GHQ meeting looks for final solution', *Dawn (Pakistan)* (20 May 2007); <http://www.dawn.com/2007/05/20/top1.htm> accessed 2 March 2010.
64. 'Lal Masjid operation called off', *Ibnlive.com (India)* (22 May 2007); <http://ibnlive.in.com/news/lal-masjid-operation-called-off/41078-2.html> accessed 1 March 2010.
65. Raza, 'Two policemen'.
66. Anjum, 'Govt gives in'.
67. Nirupama Subramanian, 'Pakistan policemen released', *The Hindu (India)* (25 May 2007); <http://www.hindu.com/2007/05/25/stories/2007052506751500.htm> accessed 3 March 2010.
68. 'Lal Masjid gears up'.
69. 'Islamists Free 3 Chinese Women, 6 Others After Massage Parlour Kidnapping in Pakistan', *Fox News (US)* (23 June 2007); <http://www.foxnews.com/story/0,2933,286390,00.html> accessed 21 March 2010.
70. Ibid.
71. '*Madrassa* students in Pak release Chinese nationals', *The Hindu (India)* (23 June 2007); <http://www.hinduonnet.com/thehindu/holnus/001200706232169.htm> accessed 24 March 2010.
72. 'Islamists Free 3 Chinese Women'.
73. '*Madrassa* students in Pak'.
74. 'A Chronology of the Lal Masjid Standoff', *Dawn* (Pakistan) (4 July 2007); <http://www.dawn.com/2007/07/04/nat6.htm> accessed 26 March 2010.
75. Ahmed Hassan, 'Suicide bombers holed up in Lal Masjid: President', *Dawn (Pakistan)* (30 June 2007); <http://www.dawn.com/2007/06/30/top1.htm> accessed 26 March 2010.
76. Ibid.

77. Iqbal Khattak, 'Musharraf ready to raid mosque but', *Daily Times (Pakistan)* (30 June 2007); <http://www.dailytimes.com.pk/default.asp?page=2007%5C06%5C30%5Cstory_30-6-2007_pg1_3> accessed 5 March 2010.

78. Akram Bukhari, '*Lal Masjid ke andar ki kahani—lamha ba lamha*' (The inside story of Lal Masjid—moment by moment)', *Islam (Urdu)* (8 July 2007).

79. Ibid.

80. Bukhari, '*Lal Masjid ke andar ki kahani*'.

81. Ibid.

3

The Barricade Siege

DAY 1: 3 JULY 2007

The critical situation in which army trucks besieged the Lal Masjid would soon escalate even further. On 3 July 2007 violence suddenly erupted when several students from the mosque tried to storm the Estate Office in an apparent protest against the rumours of a plan to raid the mosque. During this incident they were drawn into a scuffle with the policemen, in which they snatched four of their rifles and walkie-talkies. The police in reply fired teargas to disperse the protesters, which provoked a response by armed students holed up in the mosque, who opened fire on both the police and the Rangers. Unsurprisingly, it is still disputed who fired the first shot. Media reports overwhelmingly suggest that the first provocation came from inside the mosque in the form of rocks and bricks targeting the patrolling Rangers, to which the riot police responded with heavy tear-gassing. Armed attack then allegedly came from inside the madrasa in the form of dozens of rounds from automatic weapons.[1] One of these bullets hit a Ranger Lance Naik, Mubarik Hussain, who died in the hospital. Within no time, the Rangers started firing back.[2] The Lal Masjid militants claim a converse sequence of events, claiming that it was the Rangers who started firing first.[3] The accuracy of either claim is at this point impossible to verify with certainty; what is certain, however, is that this exchange of fire marked the beginning of the eight-day standoff.

Reports suggest that a number of people were injured in this initial exchange of fire, including several female students. The mutual realization of this fact led to a brief period of calm in which the security forces retreated to their original positions. However, this calm proved to be short-lived and probably counter-productive, as it provided a window of opportunity for hundreds of the mosque's supporters from two neighbouring mosques to gather inside and outside of the Lal Masjid, armed with Kalashnikovs, grenades, and petrol bombs. Wearing masks, they began to gain ground by spreading into the directions of the main road and the front of the mosque. The madrasa students also set fire to a Ministry of Environment building near the Lal Masjid.[4] As the situation deteriorated, the security forces retaliated with full force. Militants, who had taken positions on the mosque's roof and behind several trees, returned fire at will. This second round of clashes was so abrupt that a number of journalists, locals and other innocent bystanders were caught off guard. Nine persons died and about 150 were severely injured as a result. Those who died included four students of the mosque, a TV news channel cameraman, a businessman, and a pedestrian.[5] As the clashes erupted, threats were issued from inside the mosque through loudspeakers demanding that the security forces stop the attack or suicide bombings would be launched. Security forces closed off the area, a state of emergency was declared in the capital's hospitals, and the siege of the Lal Masjid began.

When the fire-fights broke out, the Pakistani government reportedly put all key services on high alert and the Interior Minister announced that a joint operation of the Pakistan Army, police, the Rangers, and the Special Services Group (SSG) was under way, adding that the media were advised to stay away from the area.[6] Hours after this announcement, Pakistan's President General Pervez Musharraf held a high-level meeting to assess the Lal Masjid situation after day-long clashes between students of Lal Masjid and the security forces. All roads to the Red Mosque were already blocked off and a complete blackout was enforced in the area. During the meeting, senior military commanders expressed concern over the possible fallout from attacking a mosque in a religiously sensitive society like Pakistan. President Musharraf, who also held the position of the Army Chief, asserted that the Ghazi brothers had shunned negotiations and a military operation was inevitable. According to reports, this meeting gave the go-ahead to the plan of action against the Lal Masjid occupants.[7]

In a clear sign that the Pakistani authorities were preparing to storm the mosque, the government asked all doctors to report to hospitals and put the Islamabad Airport on high alert. The government also dropped many hints that it was going to deal with the situation 'with an iron hand'. For instance, a government spokesman told the press after the crisis meeting that what the government was doing was 'for the common good of Pakistan and Islam', adding that all the religious seminaries preaching extremism would be 'dealt with severely'.[8] Further, the government spokesperson also specified that a curfew had been imposed in the Lal Masjid area and announced that the plan was to first ask the militants to surrender via loudspeakers and those that would heed the call would be spared. Those who did not surrender and tried to fight back would 'face what people who break the law face'.[9]

Apprehensive of a decisive action by the government forces, the Red Mosque administration skillfully played the suicide bomber card. Umme Hasaan, wife of Abdul Aziz, repeatedly warned about the use of suicide bombings in case the government resorted to force.[10] Red Mosque's allies in the tribal areas of Pakistan also intensified their activities and rhetoric. The public mood was rapidly turning against the state. Religious political parties and madaris across Pakistan opposed a military approach to resolving the matter. A number of public protests were organized by religious bodies from tribal areas, which sent their supporters to the heart of Pakistan.

DAY 2: 4 JULY 2007

With the intention of minimizing casualties, the security forces announced the government's promise that all those who surrendered and came out of the mosque without a weapon would be provided amnesty and would be given Rs 5000 and a 'better institution' to study in.[11] This offer was linked with a deadline to surrender by 11:30 a.m. Several students began surrendering at around 11:15 a.m. The deadline was regularly extended with the help of loudspeakers in the hope that more may surrender. By dusk, 1,100 students had left the mosque and the adjacent madaris.[12] Among those who surrendered were two hundred burqa-clad girls. However, the number of remaining militants in the mosque and the women's madrasa was not known. To maintain pressure, armoured personnel carriers and helicopter gunships provided a strong show of force.[13]

A curfew was imposed in the area surrounding the mosque and electricity for the complex was cut during the night. Despite these measures, the authorities made repeated pleas through every possible means, including megaphones, telephone, and the media, to those inside the complex to surrender. Having made preparations for government actions, the mosque's administration restored the electricity through the use of power generators. The Pakistani forces resorted to tear gas shelling to drive out those holed up in the mosque, which apparently resulted in firing from inside the mosque, leading to a heavy exchange of fire between the two sides.

Meanwhile, negotiations were going on between a delegation of the country's top clerics and Abdul Rashid Ghazi. The former insisted on unconditional surrender of the brothers and the other militants holed up in the mosque and madaris. Ghazi accused the clergy of compromising their Islamic obligations in favour of a heretic, authoritarian ruler. The trust deficit between the two parties was not very likely to be resolved soon, given the emotionally charged atmosphere within the mosque. Intelligence agencies cautioned regarding the presence of terrorists linked to Jaish-e-Muhammad and Lashkar-e-Jhangvi inside the mosque. Government estimates of the remaining militants varied from 2,000 to 5,000. However, this figure was most likely exaggerated and the number of armed personnel inside the mosque and the madaris probably did not exceed 1,000. The alleged presence of Mufti Abdul Jabbar, a senior commander of Jaish-e-Muhammad, was another source of concern for the authorities. Mufti Abdul Jabbar was very influential among regional militants and could have mobilized thousands of militants in one call.

As some of the students surrendered, they were thoroughly screened, in the light of the clerics' repeated threats of using suicide bombers. While the male students who surrendered were sent to Adiyala prison for interrogation, the women of Jamia Hafsa were kept for debriefing at the Haj Terminal in Rawalpindi. Those found innocent would be given Rs 5,000 to enable them to return home, as most of them hailed from the Khyber Pakhtunkhwa province. Umme Hasaan, however, disputed this before a judicial commission formed in December 2012 to investigate the issue, arguing that the mistreatment of those who surrendered at the hands of the security forces discouraged more students and clerics from leaving the mosque. 'Students were humiliated, they were asked to strip off their clothes and number of students were shot dead by the security forces at the surrender point,' she claimed.[14]

As evening fell, the Ghazi brothers showed some signs of flexibility and reconciliation. Rashid Ghazi offered a negotiated settlement that included their surrender, not to the military, but to a delegation of religious clerics. He also demanded safe passage for his family and companions to their hometown in Rajanpur district. However, senior officials at the scene said they were not prepared to discuss any such condition. The government insisted that the Ghazi brothers would have to face legal action for challenging the authority of the state in its own capital. Furthermore, it declared that the brothers would not get amnesty and would face trial for terrorism, murder of Rangers personnel, as well as for the abduction of Chinese nationals in Islamabad on 27 June.[15]

DAY 3: 5 JULY 2007

As the battle of nerves between the heavily-armed security forces and the besieged militants continued for the third day, desertions by the madrasa students continued amid the exchanges of fire and continued hovering of Cobra helicopters. The surprise of the day came at dawn when, just after the fourth deadline, Maulana Abdul Aziz was caught escaping the mosque disguised as a veiled woman. Reports suggest that he was arrested when a female constable, who was watching the women who had surrendered, noticed something unusual about one of the women. This woman was stopped and, when she was asked her name, there was no reply. Other girls accompanying the burqa-clad Aziz told the constable 'Do not search her, she is our aunt.' The supposed 'aunt' was later told to remove her burqa and 'she' turned out to be Maulana Aziz, the mosque's leader. The officer later told the reporters that his height and a pot-belly gave him away.[16] He was later searched and arrested on the spot by the intelligence agencies.[17]

Maulana Aziz's plan to escape in a burqa was not without precedent. His father Maulana Abdullah had already set an example in the 1970s, when he was banned from delivering a sermon in the mosque. According to details available in the biography of Maulana Abdullah:

> During Bhutto's era, Maulana Abdullah was banned from leading prayers and delivering Friday sermons at the Red Mosque. But the Maulana was determined to lead Friday prayer at any cost. On that particular Friday, police had surrounded the mosque in order to deny him access. Maulana went to meet his friend Haji Shoaib at his house, where he wore a shuttlecock burqa,[18] carried a shopping basket in his hands and asked Haji Shoaib to accompany him to the bazaar adjacent to Red Mosque. Haji Shoaib pretending to be the disguised Maulana's 'husband', they shopped in the bazaar and, after a while, sneaked into the mosque through a small door. The policeman guarding the door was informed that 'the lady' is thirsty and wants to drink water from the mosque. The Maulana went inside the mosque, took off his burqa and led the prayer.[19]

However, the son had failed to outsmart the police in the manner of his father. For a radical religious militant who encouraged violent militancy until the last moment of one's life and who propagated 'martyrdom' in the war to achieve an Islamic state, little could be more humiliating than being caught running away from the scene of battle in a burqa. Deputy Information Minister Tariq Azeem, expressing the government's views on the arrest, said: 'After all the things he (Maulana Aziz) has said and all the oaths he took from his students that they should embrace martyrdom with him, look at this man.'[20] He was spirited away by the intelligence agencies to an undisclosed location. Later, the government also confirmed the news that he was arrested together with his wife who, the government believed, was instrumental in preventing most of the female students from surrendering.[21]

The arrest of Maulana Abdul Aziz provided a huge opportunity to use the cleric's authority in an effort to persuade more of his students to surrender peacefully. Unfortunately, this opportunity became a double-edged sword, when Maulana Aziz was openly ridiculed in a television interview aired on the following day. Maulana Aziz was taken to the head office of Pakistan Television (PTV), where he encountered Ijaz ul-Haq, the Minister for Religious Affairs. An exchange of smiles was allegedly followed by a plea by the Maulana to get him released. Ijaz ul-Haq reportedly ensured him of the possibility of this happening, if Maulana agreed to order the surrender of his brother and the remaining students. In the TV interview, which was broadcasted live, Aziz was made to appear in the burqa and was ordered to remove it in front of the TV audience. When asked why he chose this shameful method of escaping the mosque, Maulana Aziz said that this was allowed under Islam and there was no shame in it. He added that he would recommend all the students to either escape or surrender, because, given the large deployment of the security forces outside the mosque, they could not hold out for long.

While Aziz's statement convinced a huge wave of students (almost 800 male, and 400 female students of Jamia Hafsa) to surrender,[22] and also significantly reduced popular support for the Lal Masjid movement and its demands,[23] the manner in which the Maulana was ridiculed on television only made those who decided to stay inside more defiant and averse to a peaceful end, since they feared being ridiculed in a similar manner. This was especially true in the case of Rashid Ghazi, whose rhetoric and stance hardened and became less amenable to a negotiated outcome.

While bouts of intense tear-gassing continued in phases throughout the day, the security forces took further measures to end the siege. They carried out controlled explosions to create a number of breaches in the outer wall of the mosque-madrasa complex, including one 14-foot breach, which was the first clear indication that the option of storming the building was being seriously contemplated. Senior officials of Pakistan Rangers and the Interior Ministry said that, even though they had flatly rejected Rashid Ghazi's terms for surrender, they were still delaying the storming of the complex in order to allow parents of some of the trapped students to use their influence and get their loved ones out. Some of them did succeed and several men and women came out voluntarily. There was another round of intense firing around midnight outside the besieged mosque, as the security forces captured five more militants trying to escape by scaling the mosque's wall.

The curfew was relaxed for two hours from 1:30 to 3:30 p.m. to allow the residents of the G6 sector to buy essentials. A fire fight between the armed students of the Red Mosque and security forces escalated during those two hours. First, a rocket-propelled grenade was fired from inside the mosque, followed by firing at a military helicopter.[24] Throughout the day, tensions also arose between security forces personnel and parents of those madrasa students who had been taken away for questioning after they had voluntarily surrendered. Some of the parents accused security forces of deceiving them, saying that their children had left the mosque on their persuasion and under the promise of amnesty, but when they came out they were arrested and treated like 'terrorists'. The security personnel covered the students' faces with their shirts, tied their hands behind their backs, and sent them to the Central Adiyala Jail in Rawalpindi. The parents were not allowed to meet the arrested students and were told to visit the jail.[25] Some of them also complained that they did not receive the Rs 5,000 promised by President General Pervez Musharraf for those students who would leave the madrasa. However, around 5:00 p.m., eyewitnesses confirmed that a female assistant commissioner was distributing Rs 5,000 each to some of the departing female students. Most of the young women hailed from Peshawar, Attock, Mardan, Murree, and Rawalpindi (all in northern Pakistan) and had been at Jamia Hafsa from six months to over two years.[26]

Meanwhile, Abdul Rashid Ghazi contacted Maulana Taqi Usmani, the grand Mufti of Deobandi Islam and a former judge of the Federal Shariat Court, and requested him to mediate his safe passage. The Interior Ministry, however, refused this offer of conditional surrender and maintained that the time for negotiations had passed.[27]

DAY 4: 6 JULY 2007

As the standoff continued, the Red Mosque's allies throughout the country explored various ways of dissuading the government from an all-out operation. But the unexpected unfolding of the events complicated such efforts. On the fourth day of the siege, an assassination attempt on President Musharraf, involving elements linked to the mosque, took place around 10:15 a.m., when the President's aircraft came under attack soon after it took off from the Chaklala airbase.[28] Thirty-six rounds were allegedly fired by a sub-machine gun installed on the roof of a two-storey house in Asghar Mall, not far from Islamabad Airport.[29] Police, army, and intelligence agencies rushed to the location immediately and seized a sub-machine gun, two anti-aircraft guns with tripods, and two satellite antennas. The law enforcement personnel also arrested the house owner, Muhammad Sharif, and sealed the premises.[30] The Red Mosque's leadership later reportedly admitted that it were 'their people' who carried out the attack.[31] Neighbours testified that three bearded men, a woman, and two children had lived in this house and that two of the men were seen fleeing the area on a motorbike shouting slogans of '*Allah-u-Akbar*' after the attack. They did not know when the third man, woman, and the children escaped.[32]

With the siege continuing into the next day, the Lal Masjid militants stood defiant. Abdul Rashid Ghazi repeated that he would prefer death to arrest after the government called again for an unconditional surrender. Security forces kept announcing safe passage for surrendering students throughout the day and the number of students who abandoned the mosque premises reached 1,221: 795 male and 426 female students on Friday night.[33]

The authorities simultaneously continued to increase pressure on the militants, suspending gas supply to the area. The troops also reportedly conducted the longest spell of firing and shelling on the mosque, lasting two hours from 10 a.m. to noon, and another attack was carried out at 6 p.m. when two additional blasts took place, one of which allegedly destroyed the outer wall of the Lal Masjid complex. The curfew was relaxed for three hours—from 12:30 p.m. to 3:30 p.m.—for Friday prayers.[34] In the Lal Masjid, the prayer was led by Qari Inamullah and not by Maulana Abdul Aziz, who had been taken into custody.[35]

Earlier that day, Begum Bilqees Edhi appealed over the megaphone to Rashid Ghazi to hand over the children, who were allegedly being used as human shields, to the Edhi Foundation. Mrs Edhi was permitted by law enforcement agencies to make the appeals on behalf of her husband and

Edhi Foundation chief Abdul Sattar Edhi. The authorities, however, did not allow her to enter Lal Masjid or the Jamia Hafsa madrasa, despite her repeated requests. She later stated that she had made the announcements six times from locations close to the Lal Masjid, and that she was certain that her voice had reached the people holed up inside. She also said that the Edhi Foundation would look after the children and try to locate their parents.[36] Nevertheless, no one from inside the mosque responded to her appeals.

DAY 5: 7 JULY 2007

Rations and ammunition inside the mosque started to run short, but the individuals inside the compound were still not willing to accept unconditional surrender. At 1:18 a.m. three powerful explosions were carried out by the security forces which blew up parts of the wall of the compound. Subsequent cross-firing injured Hasaan, the son of Maulana Abdul Aziz, as well as Colonel Haroon, a senior commander of the SSG, who had been leading the operation, who succumbed to injuries in a local hospital later that day. The killing of a senior army officer and a personal friend by Lal Masjid militants infuriated President Musharraf, and is frequently credited as the final tipping point in the President's decision to storm the mosque.

Religious leaders and some senior politicians, on the other hand, were bent on continuing to seek a peaceful resolution to the crisis. A meeting of leading Deobandi scholars was held in a local madrasa called Jamia Muhammadia, and the delegation later headed to the Prime Minister's House to request him to allow the religious scholars to enter the mosque and hold talks with Rashid Ghazi. However, citing security concerns, Prime Minister Shaukat Aziz turned down their requests. A similar request for a meeting with Ghazi by prominent leaders of Muttahida Majlis-e-Amal (MMA), an alliance of religious political parties, was also denied. On the night of 7 July, Ghazi announced that he was 'ready to leave and settle in my village in Rohjan, if safe passage is given to [him] and [his] colleagues'.[37] The authorities continued to demand unconditional surrender.

DAY 6: 8 JULY 2007

On the sixth day of the siege, government negotiator Chaudhry Shujaat Hussain was formally joined by a group of ulema from Wafaq-ul-Madaris, who were seen as useful intermediaries because they seemed equally acceptable to Rashid Ghazi and to the government, in the effort to convince the former to surrender. The ulema team was led by Maulana Salimullah Khan.[38] While the mediation through Chaudhry Shujaat alone was perceived as heading for a failure over the conditions of surrender, the chances of a solution to the crisis brightened with mutually respected clerics and religious scholars on board. However, as explained in Chapter 5, some of the most dramatic events of the crisis unfolded as the ulema and Chaudhry Shujaat sought to negotiate a deal with Ghazi.

While the negotiations were under way, allegations surfaced that 'fifty hardcore militants' among the several hundred confined in the Lal Masjid had put on suicide jackets and were ready to resist any raid on the complex, following reports that Musharraf had given a go-ahead for his troops to finally storm the facility in order to end the six-day long standoff.[39] Abdul Rashid Ghazi also accused the security forces of allegedly killing more than 300 students in overnight shelling and bombing, making any possibility of a peaceful resolution seem even more distant.

DAY 7: 9 JULY 2007

On the seventh day, the Prime Minister extended the mandate of the ulema and Chaudhry Shujaat to continue their efforts at negotiating a peaceful resolution of the crisis,[40] as the Supreme Court in a *suo motu* action ordered a negotiated solution of the siege and the surrounding tensions, and also ordered the government to release all the students who were arrested upon surrender from the mosque.[41]

Earlier in the day, the guns had fallen silent, as a government-ulema team allegedly tried, but failed, to conduct face-to-face talks with Ghazi. A twelve-member delegation, which included PML-Q President Chaudhry Shujaat Hussain, Ministers Ijaz ul-Haq and Muhammad Ali Durrani, social workers Abdus Sattar Edhi and Bilqees Edhi, and religious leaders Mufti Rafi Usmani and Dr Abdur Razzaq, reached the 'Red Zone' at 6:30 p.m. and conveyed to Rashid Ghazi an invitation for talks through a megaphone.[42] However, he refused to come outside for the talks, claiming that he would be immediately arrested or killed, but invited the delegation to come inside instead. This suggestion was turned down by the authorities, who in turn feared that the delegation might be taken hostage. In the end, the meeting never took place, but they managed to talk for ten to eleven hours from outside the premises through mobile phones and walkie-talkies. These negotiations will be further examined in Chapter 5.

DAY 8: 10 JULY 2007

On 10 July at 1:30 a.m. the government allegedly agreed to Ghazi's request to engage Maulana Fazlur Rehman Khalil (head of Harkat-ul-Mujahideen, a Pakistan-based, Kashmir-focussed militant group) as a new negotiator. Recounting the events, Maulana Fazlur Rehman Khalil stated in March 2013:

Ghazi Abdul Rashid had accepted all the conditions of Musharraf and talks had been hundred per cent successful. While in the vehicle, Chaudhry Shujaat had informed Pervez Musharraf of the success of talks, but he had refused to rely on Ghazi Abdul Rashid. In the first place, Musharraf demanded handing over of five persons. When this demand was accepted by Ghazi Abdul Rashid, the number was raised to 30. Ghazi Abdul Rashid had accepted even the new demand. After acceptance of one demand, there was an unending series of fresh demands. Even in spite of these things, we had prevailed upon Ghazi Abdul Rashid. The talks continued for three to four hours and were successful and we had congratulated each other. We had also informed Ghazi Abdul Rashid of the success of talks and he too was very happy. After the talks, the government delegation said that they were going to Musharraf to inform him of the successful talks. But the president overturned success to failure and ordered that operation be carried out.[43]

Just before the storming, the government claimed that there were still 100 militants and around 300 to 400 children inside the mosque.[44] At 4 a.m. upon receiving final approval from the President, the commandos, primarily comprising the Special Services Group (SSG),[45] attacked from three directions and quickly cleared the ground floor of the mosque.[46]

Pakistan Army spokesman General Waheed Arshad said that the troops began by attacking and breaching the mosque from the south and assaulted it from three different directions.[47] The forces immediately came under fire from heavily armed militants firing from behind sandbagged positions on the roof and through holes in the building walls. The SSG quickly cleared the mosque's ground floor, amid explosions coming from the mosque. While the SSG secured the ground floor of the mosque, they were continually under fire from the mosque's minarets, which slowed down their progress. The militants had allegedly piled sandbags at the base of the minarets, which they used as steps to shoot at the troops below.[48] After the minarets were taken, the SSG progressed deeper into the complex, and the militants reportedly threw gasoline bombs in a suspected unsuccessful attempt to set fire to the mosque and stop the assault. According to General Arshad, once the ground floor was secured, the SSG attempted to enter the Jamia Hafsa madrasa but were delayed by booby traps, which had to be disabled before they could continue into the complex.[49]

After the booby traps were disarmed, the SSG entered the Jamia Hafsa complex and engaged in a firefight in the main courtyard, where the militants reportedly fired on them from makeshift bunkers beneath the stairwell. General Arshad later stated that the militants must have been fortifying the bunkers for several months.[50] Once the courtyard was cleared, the SSG entered the labyrinth of the Jamia Hafsa building, which was complicated since the building had been built illegally and there were no blueprints available. Militants inside were equipped with guns and bullets, and explosion-proof vests, while some areas were still booby-trapped.

General Arshad said that after the troops had secured eighty per cent of the complex, they started moving slowly, as the resistance in the remaining areas was intense. He also claimed that the heavily armed militants had retreated into the basement, allegedly using women and children as human shields.[51] In the basement, the militants resisted with machine guns, shoulder-fired rockets, and Molotov cocktails.

In the last interview with Geo TV on 9 July 2007 during the operation, Abdul Rashid Ghazi, who was hunkered down in the basement, claimed that his mother had been wounded by gunfire and was quoted as saying, 'The government is using full force. This is naked aggression . . . my murder is certain now.' Consistent with claims he had made earlier, he also asserted that thirty rebels were still battling Pakistani troops, but they only had fourteen AK-47 assault rifles.

At about 7 p.m. Ghazi was finally killed in the clashes. Yet the exact circumstances of his death continue to remain a matter of dispute. Some government sources claim that he was killed when he was trying to surrender and was shot by his fellow militants who wanted to prevent this from happening.[52] However, in another version, the Interior Ministry's spokesman Javed Iqbal Cheema said that he was killed as troops were flushing out militants still inside the girls' madrasa. According to this version, he was spotted in the basement and asked to come out, which he did, but with four or five militants who kept on firing at the security forces. The security forces responded and Rashid Ghazi was allegedly killed in the cross-fire.[53]

The operation lasted for more than fifteen hours.[54] Reporting on the final hours of the siege as well as post-operation events, *The Washington Post* informed its readers that more than 80 people died in the combat. 'The number of casualties was much lower than it could have been,' Prime Minister Shaukat Aziz was quoted as saying. The operation still had a high cost for the responders: of the 164 elite army commandos who laid siege to the mosque, 10 had died and 33 were wounded. Officials indicated that most, if not all, of the 73 bodies allegedly recovered from the mosque on 11 July were those of militants and not civilians. The government, however, would not provide a fact sheet of who was killed, saying an investigation was ongoing.[55]

AFTERMATH

Later, Prime Minister Shaukat Aziz said in a statement that there were only a few women and children left inside as the operation began, and that he did not know of any women or children who had been killed. He also credited the commandos with ensuring the safety of civilians by moving methodically through the compound. At the same time, he conceded, 'The resistance that the law enforcement agencies faced was much more than what anyone expected. These people were trained, hard-core fighters who knew very clearly what they were doing.'[56] In addition, it must be objectively acknowledged that fighting in a large and illegally built structure such as the Jamia Hafsa is incredibly challenging, given the fact that no blueprints of the layout were available and thus it was very difficult to plan and prepare in advance the assault team movements inside the stronghold.

After 48 hours since the completion of the operation, the media were shown a huge cache of arms and ammunition during an officially arranged visit to Lal Masjid and Jamia Hafsa by the Pakistan Army. The weapons, the Inter-Services Public Relations claimed, were recovered from bullet-riddled Lal Masjid and Jamia Hafsa and included rockets, landmines, suicide belts, light machine guns, Kalashnikovs, rocket-propelled grenades, automatic guns, pistols, revolvers, night vision goggles, and over 50,000 live bullets of different calibres.[57] Three crates of petrol bombs made out of green soft drink bottles, gas masks, recoilless rifles, two-way radios, large plastic buckets filled with tennis ball-sized homemade bombs, and knives were also displayed.[58]

Inside the mosque the scene looked like a battlefield. Flies were swarming over the blood in a corner full of debris, where militants had created a defence position under a stairwell. It was not clear if any human remains were underneath. Cartridge cases were reportedly littered on the mosque's roof, while the interior of Lal Masjid had turned coal black, blamed on the militants by the authorities, who claimed the former had set the mosque on fire with petrol bombs.[59] Although its entrance hall was totally burned out, the ceiling scorched and its red walls above the oval doorway blackened, the mosque sustained less damage than the madrasa.[60]

General Waheed Arshad, despite the journalists' inquiries regarding the death toll of civilians, averred that 75 militants and 11 personnel of security forces were killed. He also added that 19 bodies remained unidentified, and these were handed over to the civil administration for further investigation. He said: 'Out of these 75 bodies, 19 are beyond recognition while autopsies of others have been carried out'. General Arshad said that a suicide bomber had detonated himself in the mosque located at the opposite side of the complex to the madrasa and that the security forces had 'recovered the head of the suicide bomber and his body parts ... and also found five bodies that were burned beyond recognition.'[61]

Arshad also noted that militants had used the mosque's two white minarets as vantage points; the dome, however, appeared undamaged. The Director General of Inter-Service Public Relations said investigations were being carried out as some of the photographs showed that the bodies seemed to be of foreigners. However, he stated that any confirmation of this fact could only be made after the tests and investigations were completed. He further declared that 85 people were rescued from the complex (56 male and 29 female), of which 39 were allegedly under 18 years of age.[62]

Many questions have remained. Subsequent analysis of these events in the print and other media criticized the government's blocking them from showing footage in the hospitals where the wounded were taken. Journalists were allowed to only show ambulances rushing to the scene. Apparently, there were very few survivors and it is unclear how many were killed inside the mosque complex. The government's official figure also allegedly left 'a few hundred people' unaccounted for. Hastily dug graves around Islamabad, and burials at night only encouraged rumours of a massacre and a cover up.[63] In a news report in the Urdu daily *Jinnah*, the figure of 102 was quoted as those who were killed and 198 as injured. Cases were allegedly filed against 608 persons, whereas 503 students and 152 children were released. The newspaper further reported that 73 of those killed could not be identified and were buried as such, and that 90 women were among those injured.[64]

While the overall number of the fatalities resulting from the assault cannot be independently verified, it is clear that at least a hundred people had died in 'Operation Sunrise', making it one of the most lethal peacetime sieges in modern history. Was such an outcome inevitable? Did other options exist? Did the negotiations have a chance? These are some of the critical questions that will be explored in the following chapters.

NOTES

1. 'Fierce gun battles rock capital: •Army troops deployed around Lal Masjid •Curfew imposed in area •Rangers man, journalist among 10 killed •Govt buildings torched', *Dawn* (Pakistan) (4 July 2007); <http://www.dawn.com/2007/07/04/top1.htm> accessed 18 April 2010.
2. Ibid.
3. Interviews with Lal Masjid students and leaders in January 2010 in Islamabad.
4. Sohail Khan, 'Environment Ministry building, vehicles set on fire', *The News International* (4 July 2007), accessed 24 May 2008.
5. 'Fierce gun battles rock capital'.
6. 'Pak forces set to storm Lal Masjid; state on alert', *IBN Live* (4 July 2007); <http://ibnlive.in.com/news/pak-forces-set-to-storm-lal-masjid-state-on-alert/44008-2.html> accessed 12 April 2010.
7. Ibid.
8. Ibid.
9. Ibid.
10. 'Suicide bombers are present in Red Mosque: Umme Hasaan', *Urdu Daily Express* (Lahore) (4 July 2007).

11. 'Chief cleric held in burqa escape bid: 1,100 students surrender, G-6 residents brave siege', *Dawn* (Pakistan) (5 July 2007) accessed 2 April 2010.

12. Syed Irfan Raza, '1,100 students surrender', *Dawn* (Pakistan) (5 July 2007).

13. K. Varma, 'Lal Masjid: 800 Students Surrender', *Rediff* (4 July 2007); <http://www.rediff.com/news/2007/jul/04pak3.htm> accessed 4 April 2010.

14. Abdul Quddus Mirza, '*Pervez Musharraf ki hatdharmi ki wajh se* surrender *nahi kiya th*a [We did not surrender because of Pervez Musharraf's arrogance]', *Ummat* (Urdu) (4 January 2013).

15. Varma, 'Lal Masjid'.

16. 'Chief cleric held'.

17. Ibid.

18. This is also known as *chadri* in Afghanistan, which covers the wearer's entire face, except for a small region about the eyes covered by a concealing net. This type of covering is also common in North Western Pakistan close to the Afghan border. It is frequently referred to as 'Shuttlecock Burqa' in Pakistan to differentiate it from other burqa styles and due to its resemblance with a badminton shuttlecock.

19. Gilgati, '*Hayat-e-Shaheed*', 215.

20. 'Chief cleric held'.

21. Ibid.

22. 'An Interview with Molana Abdul Aziz after his arrest [Urdu]', *Pakistan Television* (2007); <http://www.youtube.com/watch?v=3Z4Ss7OdgdM> accessed 15 March 2010.

23. '*Sadr Musharraf ke tayyare ko nishana banane ki koshish aur khudkush hamla Lal Masjid Operation ka radd-e amal?*' [Attack on President Musharraf's plane and suicide attack reaction to Lal Masjid Operation? *Ausaf* (Urdu) (Pakistan) (7 July 2007).

24. Urdu *Daily Express* (Lahore) (6 July 2007).

25. Syed Irfan Raza, 'Besieged cleric seeks safe passage: •Nerves as standoff continues •Govt sticks to its guns', *Dawn* (Pakistan) (6 July 2007); <http://www.dawn.com/2007/07/06/top1.htm> accessed 4 March 2010.

26. 'Veiled women leave Jamia Hafsa, dazed and confused', *Dawn* (5 July 2007); <http://www.dawn.com/2007/07/05/nat2.htm> accessed 3 March 2010.

27. Ibid.

28. 'Musharraf escapes yet another assassination bid', *Daily Times* (Lahore) (7 July 2007).

29. Ajai Sahni, 'Pakistan: A Progression of Crises', *South Asia Terrorism Portal;* <http://www.satp.org/satporgtp/sair/Archives/5_52.htm> accessed 27 November 2014.

30. Ibid.

31. Urdu *Daily Express* (Lahore) (6 July 2007).

32. Ibid.

33. Zulfiqar Ghuman, Irfan Ghauri, and Azaz Syed, 'Lal Masjid militants stand defiant', *Daily Times* (Lahore) (7 July 2007).

34. Syed Irfan Raza, 'Ghazi, militants vow to fight till bitter end', *Dawn* (Pakistan) (7 July 2007); <http://www.dawn.com/2007/07/07/top1. htm> accessed 3 March 2010.

35. Ibid.

36. 'Lal Masjid ignore Bilqees Edhi's offer', *Daily Times* (Lahore) (7 July 2007).

37. Zahid Hussain, *The Scorpion's Tail: The Relentless Rise of Islamic Militants in Pakistan and How it Threatens America* (New York: Free Press, 2012), 110.

38. Abid Ullah Jan, 'Lal Masjid Massacre: What really happened?' *Haqeeqat.Org* (15 July 2007); <www.haqeeqat.org/.../lal-masjid-massacre-what-really-happened-abid-ullah-jan/> accessed 3 May 2010.

39. 'The chronology of Lal Masjid clashes', *Times of India,* (10 July 2007); <http://timesofindia.indiatimes.com/world/pakistan/Chronology-of-Lal-Masjid-clashes/articleshow/2190609.cms> accessed 13 May 2010.

40. Maulana Zahid Al-Rashdi, '*Lal Masjid tanaza'e par muzakarat kaise sabotazh kiye gaye*' [How the Lal Masjid talks were sabotaged], *Islam* (Urdu) (12 July 2007).

41. Nirupama Subramanian, 'Bid to hold talks with Lal Masjid cleric', *The Hindu* (India) (10 July 2007); <http://www.hindu.

com/2007/07/10/stories/2007071057990100.htm> accessed 21 March 2010.

42. Shakil Anjum, 'Solution to Lal Masjid crisis in sight', *The News* (Pakistan) (10 July 2007); <http://server.kbri-islamabad.go.id/index.php?option=com_content&task=view&id=1101&Itemid=53> accessed 14 March 2010.

43. 'Musharraf changed success into failure, ordered Lal Masjid operation: Shujaat', *The News* (Pakistan) (21 March 2013).

44. Isambard Wilkinson, 'Chief siege cleric killed as rebel mosque falls', *Telegraph* (UK) (10 July 2007); <http://www.telegraph.co.uk/news/worldnews/1557036/Chief-siege-cleric-killed-as-rebel-mosque-falls.html> accessed 11 March 2010.

45. Shakeel Anjum, 'Army shows huge cache of "recovered" arms", *The News* (Pakistan) (13 July 2007); <http://www.thenews.com.pk/top_story_detail.asp?Id=8988> accessed 10 March 2010.

46. Wilkinson, 'Chief siege cleric killed'.

47. Griff Witte, 'Pakistani Forces Kill Last Holdouts in Red Mosque', *Washington Post* (12 July 2007); <http://www.washingtonpost.com/wp-dyn/content/article/2007/07/11/AR2007071100367.html> accessed 2 November 2014.

48. Ibid.

49. Ibid.

50. Ibid.

51. 'Pakistani soldiers storm mosque', *BBC News* (10 July 2007); <http://news.bbc.co.uk/1/hi/world/south_asia/6286500.stm> accessed 10 May 2008.

52. 'Pakistan's Red Mosque leader killed', *Al Jazeera* (English) (10 July 2007); <http://english.aljazeera.net/news/asia/2007/07/2008525124430212996.html> accessed 4 March 2010; '*Sadr Musharraf ke tayyare ko*'.

53. 'Pakistan militant cleric killed', *BBC News* (10 July 2010); <http://news.bbc.co.uk/2/hi/south_asia/6288704.stm> accessed 12 March 2010.

54. Wilkinson, 'Chief siege cleric killed'.

55. Witte, 'Pakistani Forces Kill'.

56. Ibid.

57. Anjum, 'Army shows huge cache of "recovered" arms'.

58. Ibid.; Khalid Qayum, 'Pakistan Red Mosque Was "Fort Ready for Battle", Musharraf Says', *Bloomberg* (US) (13 July 2007); <http:// www.bloomberg.com/apps/news?pid=20601091&sid=aWFb. nCpxO.o&refer=india> accessed 3 May 2010.

59. Anjum, 'Army shows huge cache of "recovered" arms'.

60. Ibid.

61. Ibid.

62. Ibid.

63. Hassan Abbas, 'The Road to Lal Masjid and its Aftermath', *Terrorism Monitor* (19 July 2007); <http://www.jamestown.org/ single/?no_cache=1&tx_ttnews%5Btt_news%5D=4322> accessed 15 March 2010.

64. '*Operation Khamosh: 102 jan bahaq, 198 zakhmi, 608 ke khilaf muqaddimat, 403 talibat, 152 bache riha*' [Operation Silence: 102 killed, 198 injured, Cases filed against 608, 403 students, and 152 children released], *Jinnah* (Urdu) (17 July 2007).

4

Pre-Barricade Crisis Negotiations

As dust and smoke from the siege of the Lal Masjid began to settle, questions about the appropriateness of the government response gained increasing momentum. Proponents of government action argued that a rescue operation was the only available option after negotiations had failed, also stressing the symbolic value of taking a tough stance on militants who ignore the rule of law and directly challenge the legitimacy of the state. Critics, on the other hand, pointed to the large number of casualties, and the strategic fallout of the incident, which only contributed to a greater polarization of Pakistani society, as well as the unification of various militant groups against the Pakistani state. As with most such debates, the discourse had been ideologically and politically charged, and the focus misplaced and framed as an argument over 'giving in' and 'legitimizing extremism' by talking with militants versus being 'tough' by refusing to talk. Such a discourse is understandable, but ultimately focused in the wrong direction, because it completely ignores the issue of the *quality* of the negotiation effort—in other words, whether negotiation is judged as a positive or negative strategy very much depends on how skilfully it is applied and whether it succeeds in meeting its objectives. The ultimate question should therefore not be about *whether* to negotiate or not, but rather *how* to use negotiation strategies effectively to achieve the best possible result. This chapter will focus in detail on the negotiations that preceded the actual barricade standoff, in order to identify the trends and patterns that set the stage for the expectations and conduct of all parties involved in the final showdown.

TO NEGOTIATE OR NOT TO NEGOTIATE: THAT IS NOT THE QUESTION

Sieges such as the Lal Masjid serve as a vivid reminder of the crucial dilemmas any government will face in the event of a similar incident taking place on its soil. In essence, barricade crises constitute a direct challenge to national governments by forcing them to choose from some very unattractive options. With the rare exception of extremely successful tactical rescue operations such as Entebbe, Mogadishu, or Lima, governments are practically *always* criticized for their response, either for 'giving in' to the terrorists, thus encouraging similar acts in the future, or for storming the location, and thus being held responsible for any civilian casualties, as well as the damage to the site of the attack, which in some cases has extremely high religious or symbolic value (the sieges at the Grand Mosque in Mecca (1979), the Golden Temple in Amritsar (1984), and the Lal Masjid are good examples of this). In short, barricade/hostage crises provide militants with an extremely effective tool directly to challenge the very legitimacy of their enemies.

But as Keith M. Fitzgerald and I have argued elsewhere,[1] the question of whether or not to negotiate with militants ultimately hinges, not so much on our opinions about their cause or methods, but rather on our definition of negotiation. Politicians who 'refuse to negotiate with terrorists' are taking a tough stance that is intuitively understandable, and invariably politically popular. But, in essence, these leaders do not actually mean that they will not negotiate. What they are really saying is that they will not make deals with terrorists, make concessions to terrorists, compromise with terrorists, or reward terrorists' behaviour. One of the key reasons why leaders often make the mistake of declaring that they will not 'negotiate' is simply their limited view of negotiation as merely bargaining, compromise, and deal making.

To be sure, bargaining—the practice of offers and counter-offers—is by far the most common process used when negotiating and some negotiations are indeed expected to end with compromises, in which each side gets less than what they want. But while these procedures frequently constitute parts of the negotiation process, they are certainly not synonymous with the term itself. If one assumes that negotiation is only about bargaining, making deals, or concessions, then of course we should not negotiate with militants, as this action is likely to ultimately lead to some rewards for their undesirable behaviour. However, if one understands that *negotiation, ultimately, is the use of communication to exercise influence in order to change someone's thinking, behaviour, and decision making,* then negotiating with militants does not necessarily require making foolish concessions, nor is it rewarding and further incentivizing condemnable behaviour. Unfortunately, this fine point is frequently missed, often resulting in the a priori dismissal of 'negotiations' as an option.[2]

One question we always ask political leaders who 'refuse to negotiate with terrorists' is: How does *not talking* to them (rebels, terrorists, hostage takers, hijackers) in the midst of a barricade/hostage crisis help the situation? They never seem to have an answer. *Who* should do the negotiating is another question, and—in most cases—we would not recommend that heads-of-state talk directly with terrorists in the midst of a terrorist incident.[3] But, in order to effectively influence the outcome of a crisis, it is absolutely essential to overcome this debilitating assumption that negotiation means 'giving in', making concessions, compromise, or making deals, and that negotiation is a 'weaker' approach to terrorism than tactical operations, such as assaults, raids, and rescue operations. Tactical tools and influence tools are two parts of the same toolkit; we cannot afford to throw half of that toolkit away by being too quick to discard negotiations during crises.[4]

In the case of the Lal Masjid, a blanket rejection of negotiations as an option was not the problem—quite on the contrary. Unlike in many similar incidents in other parts of the world, where governments declare that they will 'not negotiate with terrorists', the Pakistani authorities did invest considerable effort into negotiating a peaceful resolution to the crisis. Ever since the beginning of the standoff, following the takeover of the Children's Library in January 2007, various government officials and religious leaders communicated with the Lal Masjid administration in an effort to reach some sort of peaceful resolution. Government Ministers such as Ijaz ul-Haq, influential political figures such as Chaudhry Shujaat Hussain, a Wafaq-ul-Madaris delegation, and even the Imam-e-Kaaba were enlisted in an effort to influence the religious leaders' hard-line position. Aware of the potential consequences of a violent resolution for Pakistan, the government also showed an incredible amount of patience in relation to handling issues such as the occupation of the library, the concession to the demand to start rebuilding the Amir Hamza Mosque, even demonstrating a willingness to release people from custody in exchange for the release of policemen kidnapped by the Lal Masjid students. But while such efforts can be commended for seeing past the common 'no negotiations' policy trap, they ended up representing the opposite, yet just as detrimental, problem in relation to the general understanding of negotiations as a tool. In this sense, the outcome of the Lal Masjid case does not by any means 'prove' that negotiations with militants in barricade or hostage situation do not work—it simply shows that the particular negotiation approach selected to deal with the issue was not the right one. The following sections will chronologically revisit the key aspects of the negotiations in more detail.

THE NEGOTIATION CONTEXT

Although not the primary focus of this book, the failure to manage the situation effectively prior to its escalation into a barricade/hostage standoff is an unavoidable topic, as it sets the scene for the management of the tactical barricade situation that followed later. From the very start, the government approached the negotiations from a position of weakness, demonstrating a willingness to change its own legal verdicts just to appease some religious leaders and push the problem under the rug. And, while the willingness to hold a dialogue with the religious leaders was in principle the right decision, the whole process by which the negotiations were conducted, was fundamentally flawed.

This of course has a historical context, which cannot be overlooked. Support for radical religious leaders like Abdul Aziz had for many years been a state-sanctioned policy and, as a result, many precedents for simply fulfilling their demands had been set. This is true, not only of the times in which radical religious leaders and militants were essentially state employees, but more crucially even during more recent years, in which different factions had already started turning against the Pakistani state. Consider for instance the Shakai Agreement (2004) with Nek Muhammad, in which the Pakistani government agreed to release Taliban prisoners, pay compensation to tribesmen for property damage resulting from military operations, and provide money to the militants so that they could 'repay their debt to al-Qaeda'. All the government achieved in return was a vague agreement to register foreign militants and stop cross-border attacks into Afghanistan, an agreement that the militants simply failed to uphold.[5] Similarly, in the Srarogha Peace Agreement (2005) with Baitullah Mehsud, the government also agreed to compensate militants for homes razed or damaged during military operations and not to target Baitullah or his supporters, in exchange for an empty promise by the militants to cease attacks on Pakistani targets and deny shelter to foreign militants. According to Daud Khattak, both of these agreements not only failed to achieve the desired outcome, they also ended up sidelining tribal elders and providing both Nek Muhammad and Baitullah Mehsud with a new level of stature. In both cases, the government never enforced its demands of disarmament or the surrendering of foreign fighters, while itself providing significant financial resources to the militants on the pretext of compensation for property damage.[6] This pattern of negotiating from a position of weakness, bending over backwards to unconditionally fulfil the stated demands of the militants, while at the same time failing to get anything substantive in return, set the backdrop for the Lal Masjid negotiations.

It is not easy to step away from previously established patterns of negotiating behaviour, which is especially true in cases where former partners become adversaries. While, on the one hand, the previous partnership provides personal contacts and open communication links between specific people that can be very useful in the negotiations, the former partnership often also introduces perception of historical betrayal, which can result in great difficulties in building enough initial trust to hold negotiations in the first place. In addition, when past partners turn enemies, this is frequently accompanied by perceptions of humiliation, as nothing humiliates more than crushed expectations and unfulfilled promises.[7] Given the importance of humiliation as a driver of conflict, such situations have a tremendous potential to escalate the clash between the two parties to much higher levels than in cases where the opposing parties have no prior history of close relationships. As a result, the high level of tensions and aggressiveness of the conflict between the government and the religious leaders was hardly surprising.

Moreover, a similar dynamic can be observed at the interpersonal level as well. For instance, the first government negotiator, Ijaz ul-Haq, had deep personal connections to the brothers, since his father, General Zia ul-Haq, had been the main patron of the Red Mosque from the very beginning. It was also Ijaz ul-Haq who, back in 2004, had used his personal influence to free Maulana Rashid Ghazi of terrorism charges. Given this historical background, in dealing with Ijaz, the religious leaders had naturally approached the situation with a perception that meeting any of their demands would be easily achievable. This perception was not helped by the fact that Ijaz ul-Haq began the first meeting by touching Maulana Abdul Aziz's feet as a sign of respect, which only reinforced his perceived position of power. As the talks dragged out and as the clerics lost confidence in Ijaz, their formerly amicable relationship reached a new level of hostility, and Ijaz was frequently pinpointed by Rashid Ghazi as the main reason for the failure of the talks. Unsurprisingly, in the aftermath of the crisis, the labelling of Ijaz ul-Haq as the 'fall guy' led to multiple assassination attempts against him by suicide bombers allegedly linked to the Lal Masjid.[8]

In short, given this perception of humiliation and betrayal by past partners, it is not surprising that the negotiations about the main impasse issue were related to the CDA verdict to raze mosques built illegally on government land. They were not conceived as a dialogue of two sides trying to explore the possibilities for an amicable resolution within the legal framework, but instead became a game in which one side made extreme demands and the other looked for ways to keep things from escalating at virtually any cost.

AGREEMENTS, THREATS, AND 'MOVING GOAL POSTS'

In the beginning, an opportunity clearly presented itself to resolve the crisis around the occupation of the Children's Library, quickly and yet without 'giving in' to the Lal Masjid tactics, as the Wafaq-ul-Madaris who had campaigned around the same issues but had condemned the occupation of the library, sat down with the government. On 3 February 2007, an agreement was signed between a Wafaq-ul-Madaris official Qari Hanif Jalandhry and Interior Minister Aftab Sherpao to reconstruct the Amir Hamza Masjid, fulfilling some of the Lal Masjid's core demands, while not involving the mosque's administration directly. The agreement allegedly stated that a tripartite committee, including religious leaders, the CDA, and the capital city administration officials, would be formed to resolve the issue of demolition of illegally built mosques. Following the signing of the agreement, Sherpao also stated that if the students did not vacate the Children's Library, the government would 'take action'.[9]

The agreement was however rejected by the students of the Jamia Hafsa the next day, despite the fact that it addressed their earlier demands to rebuild the Amir Hamza Masjid, and to form a committee to oversee the issue of withdrawal of demolition notices. Justifying the rejection of the agreement, Amna Adeel, a member of the self-proclaimed student action committee of the Jamia Hafsa, stated: 'The ulema of Wafaq-ul-Madaris have termed the occupation of the library illegal and un-Islamic, which is deplorable because we took over the building to put pressure on the government for the acceptance of *their* [emphasis added] demands'. She also said that the committee being formed on the issue did not include religious scholars. Other Jamia Hafsa students argued that the assurance by the government to rebuild the Amir Hamza Masjid was just an 'empty promise that would not be met'.[10] Part of the problem here was the fact that while the Lal Masjid campaign was largely successful in the beginning in pressuring the government into concessions on all the core issues, the fact that the religious leaders were personally sidelined from reaching the agreement with the government contributed to their lack of commitment to the deal, and to the expansion of demands and prolongation of the conflict in order to achieve alternative success for which they themselves could take credit.

This rejection of the government's 'olive branch' triggered an immediate reaction, at least at the public diplomacy level. As early as 6 February, 2007, news reports suggested that a major operation was being planned by the law enforcement agencies to evict the students from the Children's Library by force. Citing inside sources, the reports suggested that massive arrests would be made in a pre-dawn raid within a week. Acknowledging the risks of taking action, Iftikhar Ahmad, the Inspector General of Police stated, 'Yes! The retaliation from religious groups could be severe, but the operation would be conducted at all costs to keep the supremacy of the law.'[11] The next day, the President's Secretariat confirmed that the Interior Ministry had been instructed to use force if necessary to vacate the library. 'There will be no compromise on principles and the writ of the law for vacating the Children's Library', the orders said. According to the plans, the operation was to be conducted by female police officers only, and no male police personnel would be involved. In addition, the policewomen would not be wearing shoes, but only leather socks.[12] (Despite the fact that this sensitivity to the sanctity of the religious sites was thought of as early as February, five months later cameras would capture images of SSG troops walking around the mosque in boots—these images were later heavily featured in militant propaganda videos.) Unfortunately, this show of strength was just that—a show. Instead of upholding its strong public stance about the importance of maintaining the writ of law, and using this principle as an immovable baseline for future negotiations from the position of authority, the government backed down. In what would become the first of many publicly futile attempts to intimidate the militants with the threat of force, the government set the precedent of weakness and created a situation in which any future show of force could easily be dismissed as mere sabre rattling. As a result, not only did future threats to use force become futile, the Lal Masjid students also became desensitized to the threats, leading them to the erroneous belief that nothing could possibly happen to them. Abdul Rashid Ghazi had also been heard personally dismissing the possibility of an operation against the mosque. He presumed that the government would avoid launching an operation against a sacred place in the heart of the capital.[13]

The following day, former MNA (Member National Assembly) Javed Ibrahim Paracha, who played a role of mediator between the government and the students, announced that the students would vacate the library after the government had approved the rebuilding of the Amir Hamza Masjid at its original site, and that an ulema board, the Interior Ministry, and CDA would have to decide on the demolition of any mosque jointly. In addition, Paracha said that the government had also nodded to the implementation of Islamic system in the country.[14] Despite his earlier strong words about upholding the writ of law at all costs, Iftikhar Ahmad, the Inspector General of Police, acknowledged that the police were trying to 'avoid confrontation by being lenient'.[15] Two days later, despite implicit promises made earlier, Paracha and Ijaz ul-Haq still failed to persuade the students to vacate the library. In response, the government once again deployed police and Rangers around the mosque and surrounding streets, and also cut the mosque's telephone lines.[16] And yet, several days later, the library still remained occupied. Facing media pressure over the question of why the library was still being occupied despite the government's consent to the key demands, Rashid Ghazi responded: 'Only one of seven demands has been met. We are not satisfied at all with the negotiations.'

Expanding on the original list, he now claimed that the Lal Masjid demanded '*all* the mosques that have been razed [to] be built again, *all* notices issued to the mosques [to] be withdrawn, and the decision to raze mosques [to] be cancelled permanently.'[17] He also added, 'The girls are also demanding the announcement for the initiation of Islamic Sharia in Pakistan, and there are other items on the list.'[18] This approach of 'moving goal posts during the match' would become a signature characteristic of the crisis. In essence, the government rushed to appease the religious leaders who, however, always found a reason not to commit to a deal and to sabotage the process by continually increasing their demands (and leaving the door open for yet more demands in the future by incorporating vague phrases such as 'there are other items on the list'). In addition, the fact that the government played this game only solidified the perception of the religious leaders that they were by all means equal partners to the government, and that their position was strong enough to warrant their uncompromising stance. By failing to refuse to deal with them as with an equal partner from the start, based on the principle of the state monopoly on law enforcement, the government unnecessarily lost considerable leverage and control in further negotiations.

Nevertheless, on 9 February 2007, in yet another attempt to show strength, the government declared its intent to launch an operation to end the occupation of the Children's Library, as troops surrounded the mosque. Representatives of international media were present at the scene, expecting the mosque to become a battleground between the security forces and thousands of madrasa students. Eventually, MNA Shah Abdul Aziz, a renowned jihadi figure and close aide of the Afghan Taliban, arrived at the scene and appealed to both sides to 'remain peaceful'. After some time, the security forces were called back and the government again decided to look for 'alternative solutions'. The show of force once again appears to have been merely a symbolic gesture designed to help the government save face, as only three days later it practically gave up. After several weeks of tough positional bargaining, which involved various mediators and government representatives, the government simply heeded the pressure and, on 12 February 2007, Ijaz ul-Haq laid the foundation brick at the site where the Amir Hamza Mosque once stood, as a sign of the government's intent to rebuild it. In another step designed to satisfy the Lal Masjid administration's demand to form a committee to discuss the issue of 81 illegal mosques marked for demolition, an 11-member committee was formed to review the list and the possibility of providing alternative land for their relocation.[19] In an attempt to defuse criticism of giving in to extortion, the government refused to enter any sort of a written contract.[20] This however proved to be a fatal flaw, as the terms of the agreement were never fully articulated, and there was no declaration of commitment to any deal by the Lal Masjid administration. Since the government agreed to satisfy some of their core demands, what was it getting in return? If the government was interested in fostering a public perception of not being easily bullied, then this failure to achieve any sort of commitment from the clerics certainly backfired. Not only did the government look weak, the perception of unconditional success also increased the appetite of the Lal Masjid students for more.

Declaring victory, the wife of Abdul Aziz, Umme Hasaan stated, 'This is a result of the bravery shown by the girls ... At most we would have been killed and embraced martyrdom.'[21] This statement clearly marks growing confidence, as well as the perception that it was the uncompromising nature of the students' demands and the boldness of their actions that were to be credited for their success in the negotiations. Accordingly, Maulana Abdul Aziz reacted to the government's actions by saying that the reconstruction of Amir Hamza Mosque and the forming of the committee, constituted only *a part* of his demands and declared that the occupation of the Children's Library would continue until the enforcement of Sharia in the country. Such an open-ended demand then cast doubt on the sincerity of the negotiation effort from the side of the Lal Masjid administration, as it provided yet another 'moving goal post' that made the negotiations progress in the wrong direction—from the more concrete and manageable issues to more abstract and open-ended demands.

In the beginning, the female students limited their demands to the reconstruction of Amir Hamza Mosque and a clear promise from the government not to raze any other mosques in Islamabad. Now they insisted on the implementation of the Sharia, which is such an open-ended demand that it could never be fully fulfilled without being susceptible to perpetual accusations of 'only' partial compliance. In a note to the President, the students also articulated their approach to negotiations: 'We are followers of Sharia, which does not teach us give and take. Rather, it says that we firmly stick to the path of Islam and either be a martyr or a *ghazi*. Therefore, our demands are definitely unbending and we are not willing to withdraw any one of the demands.'[22]

This rigid negotiating stance was reinforced by Rashid Ghazi's shrewd if populist dismissal of the CDA rules and regulations in relation to building of mosques, regardless of whether these were built legally or illegally, and on whose land. 'When a mosque is built on state land, it is sacred and should stay forever. We don't care what the law says. Even the library is not an important issue at all,' he claimed. 'If other buildings and property of the highups could be legalized, so can a mosque,' he added.[23] Justifying the encroachment of government land for the expansion of the mosque and the Jamia Hafsa, Rashid Ghazi said, 'According to the Islamic law of *Haq Shufa* (law of pre-emption), we had the first right to buy the land next to the mosque. When we wanted to buy it, the CDA did not allow us, so we had no choice but to grab it. It is our right.'[24] In essence, Ghazi dismissed the legal norm as an objective criterion to be used in the negotiations, relying instead on public sentiment for leverage, in full awareness that it was the reaction of the public rather than the legal norm that held the key to his success (more on this later). In playing the religious card and in criticizing the rich and powerful for their 'un-Islamic and corrupt' ways, Ghazi was playing to the sentiments of a large percentage of the Pakistani population. In return, the government completely failed to undermine this bizarre argument by publicly questioning the applicability of the Islamic law of *Haq Shufa* in relation to a mosque already built on government land and owned by the Auqaf department, by two former state employees that had long been fired from their jobs, and who possessed no building permits for Jamia Hafsa.[25]

That being said, the Lal Masjid campaign did have its critics, not just from the more liberal circles in society, but also from its own ideological allies. For instance, the alliance of religious parties in Pakistan, Muttahida Majlis-e-Amal (MMA), declared the actions of Lal Masjid students as un-Islamic, because they were led by girls, and 'Islam does not allow leadership by women'.[26] Maulana Rafi Usmani, a leading Deobandi scholar of in Pakistan, also disagreed with Maulana Aziz. He declared that Lal Masjid clerics were not serving Islam but were defaming it with their actions instead. The Grand Mufti also stated that Aziz's claim that he has an indication from God to launch jihad and impose Sharia in the country had 'no importance'.[27] In an effort to appeal to the public opinion in religious terms, Minister Ijaz ul-Haq also stated: 'We have an edict of 53 leading ulema in the country against the activities in which the two brothers were involved.'[28] The Council on Islamic Ideology had ruled that such mosques were un-Islamic and should be demolished.[29] Despite all these rulings supporting the government position, the Lal Masjid religious leaders remained defiant.

LAL MASJID AMBITIONS INTENSIFY

Almost a month after the agreement, the Children's Library had still not been vacated. And, as the madrasa students' audacity grew, they issued a list of seven mosques that had been demolished by the CDA in the last three years, and gave the government a 'one month deadline' to rebuild all seven mosques and to withdraw the demolition notice against Safa Mosque: otherwise they vowed to rebuild the mosques themselves.[30] Just one day before the expiry of the deadline, the Lal Masjid committee accused the government of not fulfilling its promises. The next day, girl students, wearing burqas and armed with sticks, purged several markets around the city and raided the alleged 'brothel'. While this was portrayed as a separate moral policing issue, it appears that the timing of the raid was not accidental, and was designed to increase the pressure on the government right before the stipulated deadline for the rebuilding of the razed mosques. In yet another failure of the state to assert its authority, the Aabpara police station, under whose jurisdiction the affected area belonged, did not take any action, stating that no complaint had been filed against the madrasa students, and that the police would only take action after a formal complaint.[31] This complacency and reluctance to take action reinforced the fact that the previous raids on the markets and the kidnapping of policemen and 'prostitutes' had gone unpunished, allowing the students' audacity to grow even further. During the last Friday prayers of March at the Lal Masjid, Maulana Abdul Aziz issued a 'one week deadline' to the government for the implementation of Sharia in the country, stating 'if the government does not impose Sharia within a week, we will do it!'[32]

Aware of the importance of public perceptions and of the fact that simple criticism is not enough, the Lal Masjid administration needed to also provide some constructive alternatives. In April, they announced the formation of *Taibaat Adibaat* Centre for repentant prostitutes, which would provide shelter to women who gave up their 'immoral activities', by providing 'security and protection' through 'marriages'. Maulana Abdul Aziz himself offered to marry a woman between 35–40 years of age.[33] On 6 April, Lal Masjid also opened a Qazi court, which was supposed to provide ordinary people with 'quick and just' trials, an issue that appealed to many who were frustrated with the bureaucratic and corruption-infested judicial system in the country. This step, however, also increased the pressure on the government to take action against the mosque, as the Qazi court, which constituted a parallel judicial system, was perceived to be yet another challenge to state authority.

As mentioned in preceding chapters, one of the first actions of the Lal Masjid Sharia court was to issue a fatwa against the then Pakistani Tourism Minister Nilofar Bakhtiar, demanding that the government 'punish and sack' her from the cabinet for engaging with paragliders in Paris in an 'obscene manner'.[34] In yet another perceived Lal Masjid victory, Bakhtiar later resigned because she felt that the government was not supportive enough.[35] Strengthened by this result and sensing an opportunity to intensify the campaign, Abdul Aziz's fiery speeches during Friday sermons called for action with an increasing sense of urgency. 'There were only six Taliban who enforced Islamic law in Afghanistan, and we are 10,000. Then, how can we not enforce Sharia, at least in Islamabad?' he shouted.[36] Later that month, the Lal Masjid demands were specified again, as follows:

1. Immediate reconstruction of demolished mosques
2. Immediate promulgation of Quran and Sunnah in the courts of law
3. Removal of un-Islamic clauses of the Women's Protection Bill
4. Immediate discontinuation of declaring jihad as terrorism by the government, as it is a great sacred duty of Muslims.[37]

As of 9 April, more than two and a half months since the occupation of the Children's Library, the government still refrained from any use of force. In another effort to negotiate the crisis, the chief of the ruling party Pakistan Muslim League (PML-Q) Chaudhry Shujaat Hussain played the role of mediator between the brothers and the authorities. By this time, the demands set by the Ghazi brothers also included 'compensation for the damage caused to mosques and seminaries'. According to some sources, the engagement of Chaudhry Shujaat was intended to appease the anger of the brothers, who were upset with the administration for refusing to give support to institutions run by them. They allegedly stated that the administration had agreed to financially support the Lal Masjid and the Jamia Hafsa as part of an earlier deal.[38] In other words, the imams of a state-owned mosque, who had been sacked from their respective positions as government employees and thus had no right to even function in their respective capacities in the first place, were now demanding the state to finance their aggressive campaign against itself! The situation was bordering on the absurd.

To increase pressure, militants started appearing with assault rifles on the mosque's walls, and Rashid Ghazi made threats to 'defend the mosque and embrace martyrdom' in case the government took action against the Lal Masjid. In addition, Maulana Abdul Aziz repeated his threats to launch 'thousands of suicide attacks' if the government took forceful action. Alongside these threats, however, the clerics kept their door open for talks with the government, even as they ruled out the possibility of any flexibility on the issue of enforcement of Sharia. 'We will not budge an inch from our principled stand on the enforcement of the Islamic system,' Rashid Ghazi stated in an interview. Simultaneously, they also specified that the mosque's campaign for Sharia would be 'peaceful'. 'But this policy of keeping the door open for talks and launching a peaceful campaign must not be misconstrued as a sign of our weakness!' Rashid Ghazi warned. An indication of the Lal Masjid interpretation of what Sharia meant can be found in the 'guidelines for enforcement of Sharia in all spheres of life' issued on 12 May 2007, which featured 50 specific guidelines on the issue. Among them were 'general amnesty for all exiled political leaders', reforms in taxation system under which 'all unjustified taxes were [to be] withdrawn', abolishment of interest-based banking, employment of Sharia as the only way to protect women from sexual harassment and gender discrimination, declaration of Urdu as the sole official language of Pakistan, formulation of a 'code of conduct for media' to deal with obscenity in print and electronic media, and special training of government officials so that they would 'fully understand their Islamic duties'. The list of demands kept increasing.

Following the commencement of talks with Chaudhry Shujaat Hussain, reports emerged that the Lal Masjid administration had suspended functioning of the Qazi court, as a confidence-building measure for the talks, but this was later denied by Rashid Ghazi.[39] Despite this fact, there were indications that the brothers were treating the talks seriously, as they expressed public confidence in the efforts of Chaudhry Shujaat, stating that he was 'doing what he can'. However, the negotiation process was fragile, and was threatened by outside events, such as a Lal Masjid style raid on CD shops in Bhara Kahu (a suburb of Islamabad), which was immediately and unconditionally condemned by Rashid Ghazi, who claimed that it had 'nothing to do with Lal Masjid, and that someone [was] trying to sabotage [the] talks'.[40] Similarly, the talks were suspended on 16 April, after the clerics claimed that a military helicopter that passed overhead sprayed 'suffocating gas' on the mosque. 'Spraying of gas and taking snaps of girl students with very low flight of chopper on civil population is violation of the dialogue process as well as international laws!' claimed the outraged Ghazi. No one from the local population confirmed the incident, and no hospitals reported treating any victims, despite the fact that Ghazi claimed that many of the female students in the madrasa fell unconscious because of the use of gas. In response, the Lal Masjid administration suspended talks with Shujaat, and students from the seminaries staged a demonstration outside the mosque and blocked several surrounding streets.[41]

Despite this suspension of talks, the government announced the next day that it would provide land for the reconstruction of the second of the seven demolished mosques, and that land for the remaining five would be provided within the next 'few days'.[42] In addition, the area around Lal Masjid was declared a 'no-go zone' for law enforcement personnel, in order to 'avoid an unpleasant situation'.[43] In a familiar pattern, the government relented to appease the brothers, rewarding them by yielding to their threats. The scenario in which the law enforcement agencies were forbidden from entering an area in the middle of a capital city just to avoid a potential confrontation with a group of militants was truly very unusual, and heavily undermined the perception that the government was in control of the situation.

Unsurprisingly, this further demonstration of government's weakness was not lost on the Lal Masjid brothers, who rejected the concessions as insufficient, and demanded that the mosques be rebuilt at their *original* locations. Talks with Shujaat continued and, on 24 April, he announced a major breakthrough, stating the government had agreed to 'all of the Lal Masjid demands, including the enforcement of Sharia.' 'No Muslim rejects the enforcement of the Islamic system in the country,' he claimed.[44] However, Ghazi strictly denied Shujaat's claim that that the crisis had been 'amicably resolved', claiming that 'there's been an understanding from the beginning that [the government] would rebuild [the] mosques and enforce Islamic laws and in return the students [would] vacate the library. He also stated that the students would hand over the library only 'into the hands of an Islamic government'.

On 8 May, Shujaat once again claimed the successful conclusion of the talks, announcing, 'I have completed all my tasks and hope that all the agreed points will be implemented immediately and no one would be allowed to sabotage the whole process.'[45] A few days later, he specified that the government had agreed to rebuild the razed mosques at their original locations, and accepted the implementation of the Islamic system. In turn, the brothers agreed to allow access to the Children's Library and to vacate it as soon as a female librarian was appointed, after which no male or female student would be allowed to carry batons. The clerics also reportedly agreed that only 'genuine madrasa students' would stay inside the compound; moral policing activities, such as raids in massage parlours or markets, would stop; the self-proclaimed Sharia court would be abolished; all 'observation posts' would be removed from the mosque and seminary walls; weapons 'if there were any inside the compound' would be removed; provocative speeches would be stopped; and all banners suspended around the two institutions would also be taken down.[46] However, this optimism about an imminent end to the crisis disappeared only days later, after the clerics accused the government of violating the agreement by the CDA issuing a public notification to rebuild the razed mosques at alternative locations (as opposed to the original locations), and by the arrest of several Lal Masjid students, as well as the government's alleged complicity in the 12 May MQM killings of more than 30 people in violence in Karachi.[47]

The situation escalated even further a week later, with the 18 May abduction of four policemen near the mosque, whom the militants held under allegations that they were on a 'spying mission'. This, however, seemed to be little more than a pretext for the otherwise instrumentally designed abduction, the goal of which was transparent in the Lal Masjid demand for the release of 11 of their activists who had been detained by the security services in the days prior. Indeed, the negotiations about the release of the policemen, which were conducted by Magistrate Farasat Ali and Assistant Superintendent of Police Kamran Adil, broke down when Maulana Abdul Aziz and his brother Maulana Abdul Rashid Ghazi refused to release the policemen until 11 of their followers were also released.[48] Neither of the two brothers was physically participating in the negotiations, communicating indirectly through other Lal Masjid representatives instead.[49] Whether the primary motivation for this move was to introduce another layer of negotiators to create a buffer as part of the negotiation strategy, or whether the brothers simply wanted to keep their distance from involvement in this clearly criminal act, remains unclear. What is clear, however, is that this situation made negotiations even more complicated, as the inability of the authorities to speak directly to the decision makers introduced the 'deferment of authority' dynamic (more on this later). In another show of weakness, the Anti-Terrorism Court released five of the eleven detainees on bail, which was reciprocated by the release of two of the four policemen, accompanied by a statement from Rashid Ghazi stating: 'We are releasing two policemen in exchange for five of our companions but will continue to hold the other two until all our men, arrested by the intelligence agency, are freed.' He added that the negotiations were now over and would be resumed only when the administration was willing to release the six others in detention.[50] In a move to pre-empt criticism for showing weakness, Islamabad Police Chief Chaudhry Iftikhar Ahmed denied a possible link between the release of prisoners and the release of the policemen, stating that an Anti-Terrorism Court had ordered the students to be released on bail and their release was not related to the kidnapping.[51] Hardly anyone could be fooled anymore.

TO THE BRINK

Interestingly, the government decided to accept this quid pro quo game, and on 20 May there was a massive deployment of troops and armoured personnel carriers around the mosque. All of the roads leading to the mosque were barricaded, a state of emergency was declared and doctors from Islamabad hospitals were even called in for duty during the Sunday holiday. In the course of the operation, an additional 40 madrasa students were detained, and then, after a day of tensions, the troops were called off once again. The next day, another showdown took place at the boys' madrasa Jamia Faridia, located at the foot of the Margalla Hills in the E-7 sector, where the students abducted three more policemen. Confronted by 2,500 Punjab Constabulary personnel, backed up by armoured personnel carriers, the militants released the policemen. In essence, a clear quid pro quo pattern had been established, in which both sides were trying to improve their chances of getting their own 'prisoners' released by arresting/abducting additional persons to be used in a trade. Needless to say, such an approach is completely counterproductive, as it has a tendency to motivate each side to engage in more and more radical steps, inevitably escalating the entire scenario in the long run.

Despite the increasingly serious situation, negotiations clearly continued in the background, as on 23 May the security services released 26 of the 40 students arrested three days earlier.[52] In addition, the government declared that it was not 'inclined to use force'. The next day, the mosque's management finally released the remaining two policemen, after nearly a week of detention, on what it claimed to be 'humanitarian grounds'.[53]

Despite the public proclamations about a reluctance to use force, media reports leaked that the security forces already had an assault plan finalized, with 7,000 personnel of the Punjab police having reached the capital and over 1,500 Rangers ready to assist about 7,000 local police. 'We can take over the Lal Masjid and its allied seminaries and the government library occupied by the Jamia Hafsa students in a few minutes if an operation is launched,' a senior official was quoted as saying. The plan envisaged suspension of water and electricity and full containment.[54] In response to this development, the Lal Masjid students started to erect sandbag bunkers around their fortress-like complex in apparent preparation for a violent showdown.

The crisis rose to its final stage on 2 June, when a group of burqa-clad Jamia Hafsa students kidnapped nine persons from a massage parlour that also included an acupuncture clinic and accused them of prostitution. The abductees included four Chinese citizens. But, while the students had gotten away with similar action during the Aunty Shamim incident several months earlier, this time the involvement of foreign nationals resulted in handling of the case at a much higher level. Luo Zhaohui, the Chinese ambassador to Pakistan became involved, and President Musharraf also received a personal phone call from the Chinese President regarding the unacceptability of the incident. To some extent, the Chinese pressure can be credited with being the proverbial last drop that made the glass overflow. The Chinese ambassador called Chaudhry Shujaat for help, who in turn called Rashid Ghazi and was told that the foreign nationals would be released in 'a couple of days'. In his own words, Shujaat 'insisted that given [Pakistan's] close and special relations with China, [the hostages] must be released [that day].'[55] Ghazi allegedly reluctantly agreed and also allowed a Chinese representative to visit the captives inside the mosque and to facilitate a phone call between them and the Chinese ambassador. After fifteen hours of negotiation, the nine people were released.[56] Ghazi later claimed that the detainees were released because the Lal Masjid had a high regard for the Pakistani-Chinese friendship and because the government gave an undertaking that it would shut down all 'illegal massage parlours'.[57] But despite this relatively quick resolution of the last of the Lal Masjid excesses, the saga was heading for a bloody climax, which culminated on 3 July.

ANALYSIS

There are numerous ways by which the pre-barricade crisis negotiations with Lal Masjid militants influenced the process and outcome of future negotiations. First, the negotiation approach employed in the Lal Masjid case did not rely on negotiations as a tool of influence, where communication is used to de-escalate the situation and to *decrease* the expectations of the militants in an effort to alter their behaviour in a positive way; it achieved exactly the opposite. The Lal Masjid students took radical and illegal action, only to be allowed to do so time and time again. This, in combination with intense media coverage, only *increased* their sense of righteousness and importance and strengthened their belief that by engaging in more radical and illegal actions, they could achieve even more. Moreover, the concessions granted throughout the initial stages of the crisis also clearly signalled to them that they could get away with acts that clearly violated the laws of the state, which only complicated the use of the legal norm as an objective standard in future negotiations. In other words, since the government showed the willingness to bend laws in early negotiations, it set a precedent for more and more unreasonable and illegal demands, growing from the premise that if the provisions of law could be overlooked in the past, this could also be done in the future. In such a situation, negotiators have a much harder time explaining effectively why certain demands could not be met, and using standard strategies for talking through deadlines. In this sense, the 'negotiation' approach used in the Lal Masjid case was exactly the type of approach that gives the concept of negotiation in similar situations a bad name. Once again, we need to stress that negotiation is not necessarily about compromises and rewarding the other side, nor is it primarily about the substantive issues and demands presented by both sides. It is, above all, about expressive dimensions, communication, and influence.

Secondly, the pre-crisis negotiation behaviour of both parties established a consistent pattern of predictable action and reaction. The seminary students engaged in radical actions, which followed a constant escalatory trajectory, following each perceived success. The government's actions shifted between appeasement, through fulfilling the students' demands, and intimidation techniques, based on a display of force to signal the possibility of an armed strike on the mosque and its madaris. In order to nullify the government threat level, the Lal Masjid administration relied on proclaiming their commitment to martyrdom, and using threats of using suicide bombers in retaliation. Fearing public reaction to an assault, the government routinely backed off its threats, creating the perception that the mobilization of troops around the mosque was nothing but a bluff. This situation was damaging in more ways than one. Not only did the perception that the government was just 'sabre rattling' decrease the effectiveness of any future pressure tactics, it also desensitized the students to the threat of a possible use of force, which is a key factor that assists barricade/hostage negotiation strategies. Every time the troops were called off, the students felt more and more powerful and invincible. In addition, the process of repeatedly standing for prolonged periods face to face with armed police officers and special forces, reduced the fear of guns, tactical gear and armored personnel carriers that in other situations might have a rather intimidating effect. One can 'cry wolf' only so many times before the call completely loses its effect.

Thirdly, there are important lessons in relation to the use of intermediaries. In an effort to persuade the clerics, the government enlisted the help of the Wafaq-ul-Madaris ulema, who had condemned the occupation of the library by the female students of Jamia Hafsa, but whose overall worldview was quite similar to that of the brothers. To some extent, this was a potentially fruitful strategy, as the similarity in worldview had the potential of establishing trust and rapport between the parties (more on this in Chapter 6). In addition, the Wafaq-ul-Madaris campaigning for the same goals as the Lal Masjid, yet refraining from using the same extreme methods, provided an opportunity to discuss and resolve the key issues without creating a public perception that this openness to dialogue meant simply 'giving in' to the pressure tactics of Lal Masjid. In theory, at least, having resolved the core issues used as justification for the illegal occupation of the Children's Library with an alternative and more acceptable partner, would have allowed the government to save face while leaving the Lal Masjid extremists with very little in the way of justification for continuing the occupation. However, theory does not always translate well into practice. In negotiations, relationships and personal emotions are at least as important as the substantive issues that are the subject of discussions. In this case, Maulana Abdul Aziz felt betrayed by the ulema and condemned them for considering the occupation of 'a mere library as not in line with Sharia while at the same time failing to issue a fatwa against the regime which was destroying holy mosques'.[58] In essence, the Lal Masjid administration felt that, while it was taking great risks to campaign for the same goals and ideals articulated by Wafaq-ul-Madaris, the ulema were 'too cowardly' to openly support them in their struggle. Not only that, it was Wafaq-ul-Madaris that had signed a deal with the government, effectively depriving the Lal Masjid activists of the credit they thought they deserved for forcing the government into compliance. This soured relations between Wafaq-ul-Madaris and the Lal Masjid administration and led to the Lal Masjid expanding and augmenting its demands in search of an outcome where they alone could take credit for eventual success.

There is another important fallout from the souring of relations between Wafaq-ul-Madaris and the Lal Masjid staff. With the government having turned from active supporters to enemies, and even the Wafaq-ul-Madaris as their natural ideological allies now publicly siding with the government, there was a growing sense of betrayal and isolation felt by the Lal Masjid militants. This isolation, accompanied by a growing external threat of existential proportions, along with a perceived divine sanction for their actions, led to increased radicalism and a siege mentality among the students, which contributed significantly to their assuming extreme and aggressive positions throughout the negotiations. The brothers' growing isolation also meant that, in their quest for allies, they relied increasingly on militant elements in the country, such as Maulana Faqir Mohammad, the most wanted commander of militants in Bajaur agency, Maulana Fazlullah of Swat, who openly announced his support for the Lal Masjid cause on his notorious illegal FM radio station, and Maulana Masood Azhar, the leader of Jaish-e-Muhammad. Since these militant outfits, as well as the Lashkar-e-Taiba (LeT), Sipah-e-Sahaba (SSP), Harkat-ul-Jihad-e-Islami (HuJI) and the Taliban, had openly supported the cause of the Lal Masjid, while radical but non-violent groups and organizations had abandoned them, this had only pushed the mosque's administration closer to militancy and violence. The end result was not only increased radicalization of the clerics to please militant allies, but also the diminished influence of non-violent clerics on the outcome of the negotiations.

Finally, it is important to analyse the background to the goals and the stated demands of the Lal Masjid militants, in order to identify the core interests underlying their negotiation positions. As discussed in this chapter, the Lal Masjid students had throughout their campaign stated all sorts of demands, mostly relating to the demolition of the Amir Hamza Masjid, but also to a wide array of other issues. However, the real issue stayed in the background and received only peripheral attention. That was the issue of the Lal Masjid itself, and the threat of the Jamia Hafsa, the largest female madrasa in the country, being taken down as well, as it was also built illegally on encroached land. In this case, the total 'land grab' was 7,439 sq. yards, which according to a conservative estimate at the time was worth at least Rs 400 million.[59] As a result, the CDA had issued 19 notices to Jamia Hafsa and Jamia Faridia to end the illegal occupation of the land, but the brothers always threatened to launch an all-out war if the government tried to vacate the land.[60] So, in this case, the razing of the Amir Hamza Mosque was highly symbolic, as it represented the CDA's move from formal notifications and warnings to the actual action of tearing down illegal mosques around Islamabad. If the clerics remained silent, the Jamia Hafsa and Jamia Faridia would be next. In the words of the then Interior Minister Aftab Sherpao, 'The real issue is not Masjid-e-Hamza. It never was. The real issue is that they were issued notices about the illegal construction of their own madrasa and masjid and they have staged this "protest" in order to avert that.'[61] Indeed, despite all the other demands the brothers had made, it was the fate of the Lal Masjid madaris that was the key to ending the crisis.

NOTES

1. Adam Dolnik and Keith M. Fitzgerald, *Negotiating Hostage Crises with the New Terrorists* (Westport, CT: Praeger Security International, 2008), 1.
2. Ibid. 2.
3. Although we would not necessarily rule it out, *prima facie*, either.
4. Dolnik et al., *Negotiating*, 2–3.

5. Daud Khattak, 'Reviewing Pakistan's Peace Deals with the Taliban', *CTC Sentinel* (26 September 2012); <http://www.ctc.usma.edu/posts/reviewing-pakistans-peace-deals-with-the-taliban> accessed 2 November 2012.

6. Ibid.

7. Evelin Lindner, *Making Enemies: Humiliation and International Conflict* (Westport, CT, London: Greenwood/Praeger Security International), 183.

8. In December 2007, two suicide bombers namely Kaleem Ullah and Sana Ullah blew themselves up prematurely before reaching electoral public gathering of Ijaz ul-Haq in Haroonabad, South Punjab—'No one injured in Pak suicide attack', *One India News* (30 December 2007); <http://news.oneindia.in/2007/12/30/no-one-injured-in-pak-suicide-attack.html> accessed 1 November 2012.

9. Mohammad Imran, 'Government will rebuild Hamza mosque', *Daily Times* (Lahore) (4 February 2007).

10. Mohammad Imran, 'Seminar students reject govt-clerics agreement', *Daily Times* (Lahore) (5 February 2007).

11. Shakeel Anjum, 'Big plan to evict seminary students', *The News* (Lahore) (6 February 2007).

12. Naveed Siddiqui, 'President allows use of force', *Daily Times* (Lahore) (7 February 2007).

13. Tariq Asad, *Lal Masjid ka muqaddimah qanoon ki nazar mein* (Azmat-e-Quran Foundation, 2008), 11–12.

14. 'Jamia Hafsa to end library's occupation conditionally', *The News* (8 February 2007).

15. Anjum, 'Big plan'.

16. 'Security personnel deployed around Lal Masjid', *Daily Times* (Lahore) (10 February 2007).

17. Noreen Haider, 'Time for a showdown?', *The News* (Lahore) (18 February 2007).

18. Ibid.

19. Mariana Baabar, 'Who wears the pants?' *Outlook India* (26 February 2007); <http://www.outlookindia.com/article.aspx?233987> accessed 19 March 2010.

20. Wajiha Ahmed Siddiqui, '*Tahriri mu'ahida karne se sarkari idaron ka gureiz*' (Reluctance of the government departments to sign a written agreement), *Ummat* (Urdu) (10 February 2007).
21. Baabar, 'Who wears the pants?'
22. Ibid.
23. Haider, 'Time'.
24. <http://jang.com.pk.thenews/apr2007-weekly/nos-08-04-2007/enc.htm#1>
25. Ibid.
26. 'MMA raps capital clerics', *Daily Times* (Lahore) (5 April 2007).
27. 'Ulema reject claim of Lal Masjid mullah', *Daily Times* (Lahore) (5 July 2007).
28. Ahmed Hassan, 'Ijaz hits hard at Islamabad clerics', *Dawn* (Karachi) (4 April 2007).
29. Mohammad Imran, 'Seminar students reject govt-clerics agreement', *Daily Times* (Lahore) (5 February 2007).
30. 'Seminary students warn of protests', *Daily Times* (Lahore) (28 February 2007).
31. 'Jamia Hafsa students start drive against video centres', *Daily Times* (Lahore) (27 March 2007).
32. 'Cleric gives govt a week to impose Sharia', *Daily Times* (Lahore) (31 March 2007).
33. Syed Irfan Raza, 'Lal Masjid threatens suicide attacks', *Dawn* (Karachi) (7 April 2007).
34. Irfan Raza, 'fatwa against Nilofar issued', *Dawn* (Online Edition) (9 April 2007); <http://www.dawn.com/2007/04/09/top2.htm> accessed 5 March 2010.
35. Masood Haider, 'Nilofar Urges SC action against Lal Masjid', *Dawn* (Online Edition) (4 July 2007); <http://www.dawn.com/2007/07/04/nat1.htm> accessed 2 November 2012.
36. Inamullah Khattak, 'Seminaries plan 'Islamic Revolution', *Dawn* (Karachi) (4 April 2007).
37. 'Grabbing Attention', *The News* (Lahore) (8 April 2007).
38. Ahmed Hassan, 'Government decides to negotiate more with clerics', *Dawn* (Karachi) (4 April 2007).

39. Iftikhar A. Khan, 'Lal Masjid cleric urges ulema to enforce Sharia', *Dawn* (Karachi) (4 April 2007).

40. Asim Yasin, 'Lal Masjid not involved Ghazi tells Shujaat', *The News* (Lahore) (4 April 2007).

41. 'Clerics suspend talks after 'surveillance'', *Dawn* (Karachi) (17 April 2007).

42. Syed Irfan Raza, 'Major demand of Lal Masjid clerics accepted', *Dawn* (Karachi) (18 April 2007).

43. Shakeel Anjum, 'Lal Masjid declared a no-go area for cops', *The News* (18 April 2007).

44. Syed Irfan Raza, 'Government accepts Lal Masjid demands', *Dawn* (Karachi) (25 April 2007).

45. Asim Yasin, 'Government, Lal Masjid talks end on positive note', *The News* (8 May 2007)

46. 'Shujaat fears failure of Lal Masjid deal', *Dawn*, Karachi, 12 May 2007.

47. Syed Irfan Raza, 'Lal Masjid clerics break off talks with government', *Dawn* (Karachi) (17 May 2007).

48. 'Lal Masjid 'brigade' kidnaps 4 policemen', *Dawn* (Online Edition) (19 May 2007); <http://www.dawn.com/2007/05/19/top1.htm> accessed 3 March 2010.

49. Shakeel Anjum, 'Govt gives in to Lal Masjid clerics', *The News* (Online Edition) (20 May 2007); <http://thenews.jang.com.pk/top_story_detail.asp?Id=7963> accessed 4 March 2010.

50. Ibid.

51. 'Lal Masjid operation called off', *Ibnlive.com* (India) (22 May 2007); <http://ibnlive.in.com/news/lal-masjid-operation-called-off/41078-2.html> accessed 1 March 2010.

52. Shakeel Anjum and Mobarik A. Virk, 'Lal Masjid standoff continues', *The News* (Lahore) (24 May 2007).

53. Nirupama Subramanian, 'Pakistan policemen released', *The Hindu* (Online Edition) (India) (25 May, 2007); <http://www.hindu.com/2007/05/25/stories/2007052506751500.htm> accessed 3 March 2010.

54. 'Operation plan ready, but government hesitant', *Dawn* (Karachi) (24 May 2007).

55. Interview with Chaudhry Shujaat Hussain, Islamabad, 16 January 2009.
56. 'Islamists Free 3 Chinese Women, 6 Others After Massage Parlor Kidnapping in Pakistan', *Fox News* (US) (23 June 2007); <http://www.foxnews.com/story/0,2933,286390,00.html> accessed 21 March 2010.
57. '*Madrassa* students in Pak release Chinese nationals', *The Hindu* (Online Edition) (23 June 2007); <http://www.hinduonnet.com/thehindu/holnus/001200706232169.htm> accessed 24 March 2010.
58. Ibid.
59. Haider, 'Time'.
60. 'Students being trained for suicide attacks: report', *The News* (Lahore) (23 April 2007).
61. Haider, 'Time'.

5

Negotiating the Barricade Crisis

Following the breakout of violence on 3 July, the crisis progressed to the actual barricade/hostage crisis stage, in which hundreds of militants and madrasa students were holed up in the stronghold, while security forces cordoned off the area and negotiations began. This chapter will first focus on outlining the basic principles of crisis negotiations as a law enforcement tool for managing barricade/hostage incidents, followed by an analytical chronology of the negotiations that took place during the siege stage of the Lal Masjid standoff. The application of these principles to this case study will then follow in Chapter 6.

THE CRISIS NEGOTIATION APPROACH

Crisis negotiations differ from other negotiations in that the stakes are extremely high; the life of at least one person is in immediate danger leading to increased tension and stress to all parties. Such an environment impairs the rational decision-making ability of the actors and introduces perhaps more extreme positions than any other type of negotiation. As a result, the negotiation approach on the part of the barricade subjects is positional bargaining at its worst. It is the negotiator's task to break through these extreme positions and to facilitate de-escalation and, ideally, achieve a peaceful resolution of the incident, while working within the legal and political boundaries.

ORIGINS

Development of specialized hostage response teams dates back to an incident known as the 'Munich Massacre', in which members of the Black September Organization killed 11 Israeli athletes at the 1972 Munich Olympics. While two of the athletes were killed during the initial takeover in the Olympic village, nine others died at the Munich airport in a hostage rescue operation that went terribly wrong. In the aftermath of this high-profile incident, a debate took place within the law enforcement community about alternative means of resolving barricade/hostage incidents.

Prior to Munich, the vast majority of barricade/hostage sieges were handled by confrontational strategies, such as containing the location and issuing a demand for the subject(s) to surrender, along with a deadline for compliance. Such strategies, however, tended to push the standoff toward altercation and were associated with a high probability of violence. In response to the Munich Olympics attack, a new approach was founded within the New York City Police Department (NYPD), which emphasized the need for containment, in combination with understanding the hostage taker's motivation, and the importance of slowing the incident down so that time can work for the negotiator.[1] While the detailed history, evolution, and specific dynamics and tools used in this approach are beyond the scope of this book, other excellent sources can be consulted on the issue.[2] This chapter will focus only on the basic principles of the crisis negotiation approach, and on those aspects that are relevant to the Lal Masjid case study. It is also important to emphasize that the principles addressed here apply to 'barricade/hostage' incidents, defined as incidents in which the location of the victim(s) as well as that of the perpetrator(s) is known, and is located in an area in which the security forces are able to achieve full containment.[3] This is quite different from the kidnapping scenario, in which the location of the perpetrator(s) and the victim(s) is unknown, and thus containment cannot be achieved, resulting in rather different negotiation dynamics.

PROGRESSION OVER TIME

In the barricade scenario, the location of the barricaded subject is contained and it is only a matter of time before the individual(s) inside is worn out. In this scenario, time is typically on the side of the negotiator,[4] as with the passage of time the subjects tend to regress from their original demands to more primary needs, such as food, water, sleep, and safety. The hostage takers are under extreme stress, and their ability to think rationally is often initially severely impaired or completely disabled. The high level of adrenalin in the suspects' blood often results in rapid transition between a wide range of human emotions. According to research conducted by the German elite counterterrorism unit *Grenzschutzgruppe-9* (GSG-9), most barricade situations begin with the hostage taker experiencing rage and making the decision to take hostages or to barricade himself in a stronghold. This stage is later substituted by excitement, as the hostage taker is getting accustomed to the perceived position of absolute power. When the suspect discovers that not everything is going according to his or her initial plan, he or she becomes increasingly frustrated. Frustration then increases the already high level of stress, resulting in a more rational approach to the situation. At this point, the level of the captor's adrenalin drops and he or she begins to feel signs of fatigue, which later turn into complete exhaustion.[5] It is vitally important to note, however, that this emotional decline is a cyclical, rather than a linear process. As a result, the gradual de-escalation usually appears in a seemingly confusing pattern, which has many peaks and valleys, especially at the end, when the hostage taker is about to surrender (see Figure 1).[6] The negotiator's primary job is to essentially facilitate this decline, by 'buying time' in order to defuse tense situations, to return the subject to his/her normal functioning level, to build rapport and communicate empathy, and to gather intelligence.

Figure 1: Psychological progression in barricade situations

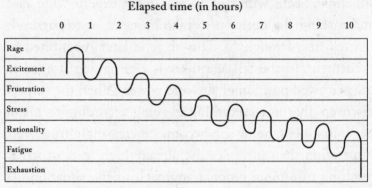

Source: Strentz, Thomas, *The Cyclic Crisis Negotiations Time Line*, Law and Order, March 1995

ACTIVE LISTENING

The principle method used by negotiators relies on the use of active listening, a loose system of style, manner, and technique that demonstrates the listener's caring, concern, and attentiveness.[7] Useful communication techniques to achieve this aim include paraphrasing, reflection, asking clarifying questions, open-ended probing, interpretation, and self-disclosure.[8] The purpose is to make the subject feel 'heard', satisfying one of the core needs we all have as people.[9] Not only does the negotiator's attentive style encourage a greater sharing of information, it can also have a positive rapport-building effect, especially with people who see themselves as self-defending victims who frame their involvement in barricades/hostage taking as the 'only way to be *heard*'. An essential part of this effort is to maintain a non-judgmental mindset in which the negotiator is not talking to a 'terrorist' or a 'criminal' but rather to a rational human being who, for some set of reasons, has chosen—or felt forced into—an extreme, violent course of action.[10] Militants rarely dispute the observation that their actions are extreme; they do, however, see them as justified. This acknowledged extreme nature of hostage taking is one of the possible reasons why militants have a tendency to passionately explain and rationalize their actions, especially when speaking to a person whom they perceive, (at least initially) as someone who does not understand the true drivers and 'root causes' of their actions. This is where empathetically listening to their grievances and validating some of their frustrations helps contradict many of the subjects' demonized perceptions of their counterpart, and makes it harder for them to label the negotiator as unreasonable. Active listening and expressed empathy (not sympathy) also create chances to build rapport, in order to gain influence on the decision-making and behaviour of the subject. This continuum, first described by Gary Noesner of the FBI's Crisis Negotiation Unit, is sometimes called the 'behavioural change stairway' (see Figure 2).

Figure 2: Behavioural Change Stairway

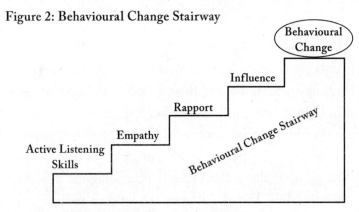

Source: Gary Noesner, Chief, FBI Crisis Negotiation Unit (retired)

DEFERMENT OF AUTHORITY

The next basic principle of crisis negotiation is that 'the boss does not negotiate', under the logic that such an action would disrupt one of the key 'tricks' in the crisis negotiation toolbox—the deferment of authority or a version of the 'good cop, bad cop' routine. One of the keys to gaining strategic advantage in a hostage crisis is achieving the perceived position of intermediary between the authorities and the hostage takers, which allows the negotiators to stall for time by pointing to the difficulty of locating a key decision-maker, or some other obstacle to meeting the terrorists' deadline. Further, the negotiators' lack of decision-making authority also allows them, in theory, to disassociate themselves from any official refusal to comply while empathetically validating the reasonable component of the demand and promising to keep trying to convince the authorities in favour of its fulfilment. This tactic is useful in stalling for time, decreasing the hostage takers' expectations, and creating a bond between the negotiators and the suspects.

DEMANDS

Demands are an indispensable part of any crisis negotiation. In barricade situations, the hostage taker is likely to issue a set of extreme demands at the beginning of the incident. These should become more realistic through the course of negotiation, as the perpetrator's approach becomes more rational as a result of the cyclical psychological processes described earlier. The negotiator can help in reducing the quantity of demands by focusing on a particular demand and by asking clarifying questions. If, for example, the hostage taker asks for a getaway vehicle, the negotiator can focus the discussion onto the characteristics of the vehicle, such as type, model, make, colour, etc. Such conversation has the potential of occupying the perpetrator's mind to the point that he or she simply forgets about the other demands made earlier.[11] In dealing with politically or religiously motivated barricade subjects, who have deliberately put themselves into the situation and who have engaged in prior strategic planning, such tactics have only limited use since the subjects usually have articulated their political demands in advance, and are unlikely to easily forget about them. That being said, the basic principle of asking good questions in order to understand the motivations and thought processes behind the subjects' demands and positions is still a cornerstone of a successful negotiation approach.

In essence, any demand formulated by a hostage taker or a barricaded subject is essentially a *conclusion of a thought process*. The job of the negotiator is to facilitate a dialogue throughout which this thought process can be traced back from the conclusion (the demand) toward the beginning (initial grievances, frustrations, etc.) The more negotiators listen, the more likely they are to learn about interests, alternatives, and persuasive criteria. This process alone has the capacity of de-escalating the situation emotionally by making the barricaded subject feel heard and understood, and also presents opportunities for the negotiator to learn more about the thought process and its key elements. Having learned about the key underlying emotions and interests behind the demands, the opportunity now exists to steer the thought process in a slightly different direction. This in turn can lead to generating different options in which some of the subject's core interests are addressed in alternative ways that do not require unwise concessions. Through this process, negotiators can give the subjects, who frequently feel like they have nothing to lose anymore, a stake in the outcome, one that can be perceived as a partial success that the subject will become worried about losing. This frequently happens at the emotional rather than the substantive level. For instance, in hostage situations, a negotiated deal that results in safe release of a hostage can be used to build momentum, in which the negotiator praises the subjects' decision to release hostages as a 'kind', 'generous' and 'humanitarian' step, one that clearly 'proves' that the hostage taker really is 'not a bad person'. For frustrated hostage takers, who feel misunderstood and at the end of their tether to the point of thinking they have nothing to lose, this can quickly build a perception of a suddenly positive reputation that the subject is motivated to uphold and maintain. In such a situation, chances of future harm to hostages rapidly decrease.

Giving the subject something to lose, also frequently has a moderating effect on future demands and behaviour, often without a single *substantive* concession related to the hostage taker's original demands. It is particularly important to keep in mind here that demands have both *instrumental* and *expressive* values.[12] In other words, each substantive demand also constitutes an expression of a certain type of emotion or a psychological need. It is especially the expressive value of the demand that the negotiator should concentrate on and seek to understand as this provides insight into the captor's underlying interests. The negotiator then should engage the hostage takers in dialogue whenever possible, and work with them to find alternative ways to satisfy the legitimate interests that can be identified, sometimes by acknowledging the validity of the hostage taker's grievances. And, in some cases, such interests can be satisfied, at least to some degree, simply by listening empathetically.

DEADLINES

Closely related to the issue of demands is the issue of deadlines. Especially in barricade hostage cases, a strict deadline will usually be attached to the fulfilment of demands, accompanied by a threat to start killing hostages. It is the negotiator's job to make these deadlines pass while keeping the hostages out of harm's way. This is usually achieved by introducing some of the 'objective' obstacles to meeting the deadline that were described earlier, and by reminding abductors that if anyone is hurt a violent resolution of the incident may become inevitable. The key is to provide a credible justification for not being able to meet the time limit, helping the hostage taker save face. In non-ideological cases, hostage and barricade situations are typically associated with criminal activity or domestic violence, where the hostage taker is essentially not determined to kill in the first place, and where his or her main objective in the standoff is to minimize the consequences of past behaviour, thus providing strong incentives not to harm the hostages. This lack of readiness to carry out threats, as well as the hostage taker's dependency on cooperation with the authorities in order to fulfil the core objective, works in the negotiator's favour, by creating an environment in which the risk to hostages is low. The hostage taker often willingly engages in bargaining to get the best possible terms, and the negotiator operates from a position of strength, backed up by the threat of force and the warning that any violent acts by the hostage takers will only get them into more trouble.

The nature of the demand that is attached to the deadline plays an important role in assessing its credibility and urgency. Some demands are simply too unrealistic to be credibly backed by the threat of killing hostages. Murdering someone in cold blood is an extreme measure that most hostage takers are not eager to resort to, unless they truly feel that no other option exists. Based on the theory of cognitive dissonance, which states that we seek consistency in our beliefs and attitudes in any situation where two cognitions are inconsistent, the reluctance to kill enables negotiators to talk through deadlines as long as they provide a believable explanation for not being able to fulfil them.

'NON-NEGOTIABLE' DEMANDS

Some demands in crisis negotiations are referred to as non-negotiable, either because of running contrary to legal norms or because of the potential of making the situation more volatile. In barricade situations, for instance, additional weapons will not be given to the hostage taker under any circumstances, as the suspect might be using a fake or a non-functional weapon; satisfying his or her demand would only provide the tools necessary for a violent exchange. Another example of a non-negotiable demand is the exchange of hostages, as the desire to bring a specific person to the scene may indicate the hostage taker's intent to hurt this person.[13] Other non-negotiable demands in a barricade situation also include supplying the hostage taker with alcohol or drugs, as these substances have the potential of escalating the suspect's violent behaviour.[14]

It is the negotiator's responsibility to handle non-negotiable demands. This is usually done by the deflection of the focus toward a different demand or by introducing issues pertaining to primary needs, such as hunger or thirst.[15] If these attempts fail and the hostage taker is insistent, the negotiator should carefully explain why the demand is not going to be fulfilled. It will be crucial to convey in a non-threatening manner that the non-negotiability of the entire package does not mean that individual demands cannot be discussed.[16]

That being said, it is important to emphasize that an a priori ruling out of certain demands is often not helpful. The general idea should be to be flexible in the area of demands, as there is nothing to be gained by dismissing a demand immediately as 'non-negotiable'. Rather than seeing the choice as 'negotiate or not' or as 'agree or deny' any particular request, negotiators should use anything the hostage takers say as a basis for good questions in an attempt to understand motives and to gain information. While providing hostage takers with a nuclear weapon in exchange for a hostage is certainly not a good idea, any demand that is put forward by the hostage taker carries tacit messages and provides clues to the hostage taker's interests. For instance, a subject's demand that the security forces leave the scene will not be fulfilled, yet it serves as an indication of the subject's concern about personal safety, which is not only an important analytical indicator in itself, but can also serve as a starting point for a whole new discussion. For this reason, any demand put forward by the hostage takers should be discussed, and the negotiator must always be looking for ways to exercise influence.

DELIBERATE DECEPTION

A frequent question that comes up in discussions about managing barricade/hostage sieges, relates to the use of deception, and the granting of concessions that the authorities never intend to fulfill. The proponents of this issue highlight the fact that deception provides a viable tactical alternative for resolving high stakes incidents where many lives may be at stake, also pointing to the fact that in some countries legal precedents exist which state that promises made to hostage takers during hostage negotiations are not legally binding contracts.[17] In addition, Hays' analysis has shown that bluffing, even if detected, does not reduce the likelihood of a negotiated solution,[18] suggesting that the benefits of deception may very well outweigh the risks. However, there are a number of additional factors that should be taken into consideration. First of all, the effort invested into building rapport with the barricaded subject could be jeopardized and the difficulties of reestablishing credibility are usually not worth the risk. Secondly, the wide media coverage barricade situations receive can make bluffing costly in the long run, as public familiarity with deceptive police tactics will make establishing credibility in future crisis negotiations even more challenging. Consequently, negotiators are taught in their training never to lie.

NEGOTIATION WITH IDEOLOGICAL/RELIGIOUS MILITANTS

Although the practice of crisis negotiation was inspired by the aforementioned Munich Olympics attack and was thus originally designed to fit hostage situations involving political extremists, over the years its focus has gradually shifted in favour of non-terrorist incidents. In fact, only about one fifth of situations to which crisis negotiation teams are called today involve any hostages at all, with the vast majority of those cases consisting of interrupted criminals, domestic violence cases, 'suicides-by-cop', and mentally disturbed individuals—who all share the fact that their decision to become involved in a barricade siege is typically a product of a spontaneous decision, without any detailed prior planning. Since most of the crisis negotiation guidelines have been built incrementally over time, through evaluation of past experiences, many of the paradigms and presumptions on which contemporary practice is based simply do not reflect the reality of incidents perpetrated by ideologically or religiously driven militants, who have deliberately placed themselves in the situation with a predetermined plan of action. Negotiating such sieges presents some additional challenges.

One successful way to deal with politically motivated incidents in the past has been for the negotiator to stress the widespread attention the perpetrators' cause had already received. Since publicity has usually been one of the main goals the terrorists strove to achieve in barricade hostage incidents, the captors could often be persuaded that they have succeeded in their mission, and that killing hostages would only hurt their cause in the eyes of the public. Since most militant movements use the rhetoric of liberation from oppression and inhumane treatment, the same language could be used to reiterate the innocence and suffering of the hostages, in order to appeal to the moral beliefs of the captors. And, while these standards were typically automatically deflected, their pronouncement still played an important role in the effort to humanize the victims to their captors as much as possible, in order to make cold-blooded execution of hostages psychologically more difficult.

The stressing of the attention the terrorists' cause had already achieved, in combination with a guarantee of a free passage for the terrorists, has historically been the most frequent formula for the negotiated resolution of politically inspired barricade incidents. Such an outcome is sometimes called the 'Bangkok Solution', referring to the 1972 incident in which members of the Black September group took over the Israeli embassy in Thailand but, after nineteen hours of negotiation, agreed to release their hostages and drop all other demands in return for safe passage out of the country. Such a solution of course is not without its problems, and ultimately would have to involve a political decision taken at the very top. Zartman notes that, despite failing to punish the terrorists for their crime, such a solution is balanced. It uses a concession only to restore the original situation which the government found acceptable, but the terrorists did not.[19] This assertion seems to be supported by the fact that following the Bangkok incident, Black September strongly criticized their operatives for backing down and losing face for the organization. At the same time, it should be pointed out that, despite the factual return of the situation to the pre-incident status, the terrorists managed to gain publicity and therefore did succeed in fulfilling one of their main objectives.

Even more important, it is imperative to recognize that, in the era of the so-called 'new terrorism', characterized by increasing lethality and the prevalence of religious justifications for violence, dealing with the barricade/ hostage scenario will probably be much more complicated than in the past. First, the terrorists' overt pronouncement of a 'desire for martyrdom' will make the question of free passage a highly delicate matter, as such a proposal could be interpreted as an offensive second-guessing of the fighters' commitment to God, and thereby possibly escalating the situation. Secondly, the terrorists' prior knowledge of the processes that typically make it difficult for hostage takers to kill in cold blood will possibly lead the terrorist to the conscious obstruction of these dynamics, which, in combination with the advanced level of enemy dehumanization associated with religious sanction of their actions, will almost certainly make the moral appeals on the terrorists' conscience unsuccessful. And, thirdly, the alleged absence of a politically mindful constituency on behalf of the 'new terrorists' will make the negotiation emphasis on the success associated with a high level of publicity already achieved a less persuasive argument.

Ominously, more recent attacks such as the Air France Flight 8969 hijacking (1994), Budyonnovsk Hospital (1995), Moscow Theatre siege (2002) or the Beslan school siege (2004), have demonstrated the existence of terrorist hostage takers of the 'new' breed, who possess much greater willingness to execute hostages, employ large teams of willing-to-die hostage takers who have the capability to effectively repel a rescue operation, and who have a detailed knowledge of the hostage negotiation and rescue teams' 'playbook'. Responding to these types of terrorist sieges will require a number of different adjustments in expectations, analytical tools, and negotiation approaches. We have dealt with this issue in detail elsewhere,[20] but the key additional recommendations are summarized in Figure 3.

Figure 3: Additional Guidelines for Negotiations with 'Terrorists'

1. Always keep in mind that negotiation is not just about reaching 'deals' and making quid pro quo exchanges; it is also about *exercising influence over the thinking, behaviour, and decision making* of others. Any information gained in conversation—and the very act of *having* the conversation itself—may present such opportunities at any time.

2. Be (and remain) self-diagnostic: understand your own biases and constantly question your assumptions about the hostage takers, their motives, and their willingness to negotiate (keeping in mind that there is a big difference between self-*diagnosis* and self-*doubt*). Do not cling to conclusions out of frustration or disgust, or you will miss important clues and opportunities.

3. Do not negotiate with the 'terrorist', negotiate with the *rational human being who, for some set of reasons, has chosen— or felt forced into—an extreme, violent course of action.*

4. Use an active listening approach to the negotiations, not just a bargaining approach; focus at least as much on asking good questions, learning, and understanding grievances and motives as on making quid pro quo substantive deals.

5. Ask for as many details as possible about the reasons/justification the perpetrators use to explain their actions. The answers will provide criteria that may be useful in other ways later.

6. Look for empathetic ways to acknowledge or validate legitimate grievances behind the terrorists' actions while differing with the actions themselves. This will make it harder for them to label you as unreasonable, it will create chances to de-escalate the situation emotionally, and it may help you to create a wedge between their grievances and their actions, which in turn may help them to question the connection.

7. Brainstorm with them. Rather than simply trying to stall with the 'good cop, bad cop routine', genuinely look for ways to address the more legitimate grievances in ways that do not require unwise, unreasonable, or impossible concessions.

8. Make sure someone is looking at the bigger picture, beyond this incident.

Source: Dolnik, Adam, and Fitzgerald, Keith M., *Negotiating Hostage Crises with the New Terrorists* (Westport, CT: Praeger Security International, 2008)

THE LAL MASJID NEGOTIATIONS

Let us now return to the Lal Masjid case. Following the breakout of violence on 3 July, General Musharraf laid the blame on the clerics, describing the mosque as a 'fort ready for battle',[21] adding that the government was 'open to negotiations and dialogue, but not at the cost of a compromise in the fight against terrorism and extremism'.[22] This statement basically outlined the general approach to negotiations, which were viewed as simply synonymous with 'compromise'—an unfortunate term, tainted with perceptions of 'weakness', 'giving in', and 'rewarding extortion'. The value of tactical negotiations as a law enforcement influence tool was clearly not appreciated and the political need to publically appear 'tough' prevailed over a more nuanced negotiation approach. What is important to realize, is that tactical tools and influence tools are not mutually exclusive, but are two parts of the same toolkit. Throwing half the toolkit away for political reasons when hundreds of lives are at stake is simply not prudent.

'SURRENDER OR DIE'

Given the general lack of appreciation of law enforcement negotiation strategies, it is not surprising that the principal 'negotiation tactic' initially used by the authorities in the Lal Masjid siege relied precisely on the pre-1972 practice, which had historically been found to *increase*, as opposed to *decrease*, the likelihood of a violent confrontation. Right after imposing a curfew in the Lal Masjid area, a government spokesperson announced that the plan was to first ask the militants to surrender via loudspeakers, and those that would heed the call would be 'spared'. Those who did not surrender and tried to fight back would 'face what people who break law face'.[23] This archaic zero-sum game approach established a pattern of mutual threats and an escalatory rhetoric on both sides that was a sign of bad things to come.

To be fair, it is easy to see how the authorities would feel impatient, having bent over backwards for months in trying to appease the brothers in the futile hope that by satisfying most of their demands the government could make the problem go away. But, as was discussed in the previous chapter, this approach had achieved just the opposite effect. It raised the clerics' expectations that they could achieve anything; it undermined the credibility of the government's tough rhetoric; and it created a situation in which the authorities felt that the only way left to gain influence over the outcome was through intimidation and threats to use force. In many ways, the negotiation pattern established during the months before the barricade crisis had already paved the way for a tragic outcome later on.

It is also important to recognize that the Pakistani authorities did not just use a one-dimensional tactic, relying on an ultimatum and a deadline alone. In an effort to minimize the number of potential casualties, the security forces also attempted to add a proverbial 'carrot' to the 'stick', and announced the government's promise to provide an amnesty, Rs. 5,000 in cash, and a 'better institution' to study in to all those who would surrender and come out of the mosque without a weapon.[24] This offer was set to expire at 11:30 a.m.

Several students started surrendering at around 11:15 a.m. and the deadline was regularly extended through loudspeakers in the hope that more may surrender. By dusk, 1,100 students had left the mosque and the adjacent madaris,[25] among them 200 burqa-clad girls. Despite the fact that many of those who had surrendered had been debriefed, the number of remaining militants in the mosque and the women's madrasa remained uncertain, as most of the surrendered students failed to provide accurate testimonies (claims ranged from 600–1,500 left inside) and there was no other source of intelligence to confirm or disprove their claims.[26] Either way, some progress with respect to reducing the potential number of victims of a violent resolution through the surrender of a high quantity of students had been achieved.

Clearly intent not to let up on the pressure, as well as to avoid the perception of government weakness, armoured personnel carriers kept a tight vigil at Lal Masjid and helicopter gunships also circled overhead in an overt display of force.[27] In addition, the authorities also resorted to the manipulation of anxiety levels among the students inside by cutting off electrical supplies throughout the night, again accompanied by a 'carrot' in the form of repeated pleas through every possible means, including megaphones, land lines, and media, to those inside the complex to surrender. Having made preparations beforehand, the mosque's administration restored the electricity through the use of power generators, negating the effects of government action. Frustrated with the slow rate of progress, the Pakistani forces decided to escalate the pressure and started tear gas shelling of the complex to drive out those still inside. In what would become a pattern throughout the standoff, the militants inside responded by a show of force of their own, and resorted to retaliatory firing, leading to heavy exchange of fire between the two sides. Quite predictably, the quid pro quo process of one side's threats being met with the other side's threats, and likewise any violent show of force being reciprocated in kind by the other side, pushed the standoff in an increasingly escalatory direction.

On Day 2 of the siege, negotiations were underway between a delegation of the country's top religious symbols and Abdul Rashid Ghazi. The former insisted on unconditional surrender by the Ghazi brothers and other militants holed up in the mosque and seminaries. In accordance with his previous statements, Rashid Ghazi accused the ulema of 'compromising their Islamic obligations in favour of a heretic, authoritarian ruler'. The situation was further complicated by the emotionally charged atmosphere within the mosque, in which the brothers tried to strengthen the students' cohesion by staging a collective oath to 'embrace martyrdom to lay the foundation of a powerful country-wide movement to protect mosques and implement Sharia'. This public oath would further complicate future surrenders of students, as the act of having made an explicit and public commitment to martyrdom, in combination with the in-group dynamics and collective siege mentality augmented by an existential outside threat, made it psychologically more difficult for individual students to renege on their public promise and surrender peacefully. Another complication in the students' possible decision to surrender was presented by the fact that snipers positioned in nearby buildings were rather trigger-happy, picking off anyone escaping and walking out from the wrong direction.[28] And even some of those who surrendered peacefully were detained for seven days, which was known to the students inside through media coverage, and ran contrary to the overt promise of amnesty given by the authorities over loudspeakers.[29]

WILLINGNESS TO SURRENDER

Despite the confrontational tactics that characterized the first part of the siege, the containment dynamic, in combination with passage of time and a regression toward more basic needs, did begin to deliver some signs of progress.

As the evening fell on the second day, the Ghazi brothers' demands hinted at traces of flexibility and reconciliation. At this point, Rashid Ghazi offered a negotiated settlement; this included surrender to a delegation of religious leaders, as opposed to the military. According to Maulana Hyderi, the head of the Sunni sectarian outfit Sipah-e-Sahaba Pakistan (SSP), who was part of the ulema negotiation team, Ghazi was willing to give up, provided that the security forces were withdrawn from the area.

Rashid Ghazi also demanded safe passage for his family and companions to return to their hometown in the Rajanpur district. However, senior officials at the scene said they were not prepared to discuss any such condition. The government insisted that the Ghazi brothers had to face the legal consequences of challenging the authority of the state in the capital itself. The government declared that the two brothers would receive no amnesty and would face trial for terrorism, murder of Rangers personnel, and for the abduction of Chinese nationals in Islamabad on 27 June.[30] Abdul Rashid Ghazi remained defiant and refused to surrender unconditionally. In television interviews conducted from inside the mosque over a mobile phone, he offered to lay down arms, return the mosque and the madrasa to the institution that runs and manages mosques and seminaries, and denied having any suicide bombers inside. All he wanted now was safe passage for himself and his men.[31]

The desire of the Ghazi brothers to survive in spite of their overt commitment to martyrdom was confirmed later in the day, when Maulana Abdul Aziz was detained when trying to escape the Lal Masjid disguised in a burqa. This development provided the opportunity of using the imam's authority to persuade more of his students to surrender peacefully. Unfortunately, this opportunity became a double-edged sword when Maulana Aziz was openly ridiculed in a television interview aired on the following day. On Day 3, Abdul Rashid Ghazi contacted Maulana Taqi Usmani, a respected figure among the Deobandi school, with a request for the latter to mediate his safe passage. In a discussion with Maulana Zahoor Alvi, who went inside the mosque on the second day of the crisis following the arrest of Aziz, Rashid Ghazi repeated his agreement to surrender only 'after the forces withdraw'.[32]

After the Interior Ministry once again refused this offer of conditional surrender, and proclaimed that the 'time for negotiations had passed',[33] Rashid Ghazi dug in his heels and now stated, in a media interview, that he and his companions had decided to be 'martyred' but would not surrender: 'We are sacrificing our lives for our religion and for the enforcement of Islamic laws. We have no regrets and we will embrace martyrdom. We are writing our wills, and we want to be buried in the mosque,' he said. At the same time, despite stating this intent to be martyred, he continued bargaining for conditional surrender throughout the rest of the crisis. In an effort to alleviate Ghazi's fear of public humiliation, Information Minister Mohammad Ali Durrani pledged at a press conference that he would not be humiliated if he surrendered.[34]

Security forces kept announcing safe passage for surrendering students throughout the day, and by Friday night the number of students who abandoned the mosque premises had reached 1,221 (795 male and 426 female).[35] The authorities simultaneously continued their 'stick and carrot policy', suspending gas supply to the area, and conducting the longest spell of firing and shelling on the mosque in order to increase pressure on the militants. Some 19 people had been killed and 98 injured up to this point. Rashid Ghazi once again repeated his determination to become a martyr: 'We have decided that we can be martyred but we will not surrender. We are ready for our heads to be cut off but we will not bow them. We are more determined now.'[36]

On the same day, Chaudhry Shujaat Hussain made another contact with Abdul Rashid Ghazi via telephone. He offered to have him sent to a 'rest house' along with his mother, and not to jail. Ghazi refused the offer.[37] Shujaat spoke to him once on Friday and reported that Ghazi had declined to surrender, because 'those with him in the Lal Masjid were not ready to surrender'.[38] The imam was allegedly seeking time to consult with his companions which, according to Shujaat, showed that he was not acting independently.[39] What is more likely, however, is that he simply used the same deferment of authority approach crisis negotiators routinely rely on.

The extent to which Shujaat had the authority to make his offer to Ghazi is uncertain. What must be pointed out, though, is that such a step itself is rather unorthodox, in the sense that negotiators typically avoid making any offers themselves, for the simple reason that this gives the subject too much power. Not only is a direct offer from negotiators not consistent with the deferment of authority strategy, it also runs a high risk of locking the negotiator in a position that would be very difficult to later move away from without fatally damaging trust between the two parties. For this reason, negotiators typically focus on dealing with demands coming from the stronghold, while refraining from making any proactive offers or counter-offers of their own.

By Day 5 of the crisis, rations and ammunition inside the mosque had started to become scarce, and the students had to rely on rainwater collected in the pool for ablution as their main source of drinking water.[40] To increase pressure further, the security forces carried out several controlled explosions in the early morning hours to create holes in the outer wall of the compound. In a pattern established earlier, the Lal Masjid students reciprocated force with force, and the subsequent cross-fire injured the son of Maulana Abdul Aziz and also resulted in the death of Colonel Haroon, a senior commander of SSG, who had been leading the operation. The killing of a senior army officer by the Lal Masjid militants infuriated President Musharraf, who issued an ultimatum: 'The people inside the mosque should come out and surrender, otherwise I am saying it here, they risk being killed.'[41]

LAST-DITCH NEGOTIATIONS

In the meantime, a team of ulema attempted a last-ditch negotiation effort in order to prevent all-out bloodshed. This effort lasted 11 hours and featured many ups and downs, in which Rashid Ghazi kept rapidly changing his position. He also frequently failed to answer the phone because he was talking to the media. He continually expressed concern about the possibility of mistreatment upon surrender, which the negotiators tried to alleviate by pointing out that the presence of the world press on the scene would prevent this from happening.[42] What is important to point out here is that Rashid Ghazi seemed to be very close to giving up at this stage. As discussed earlier, the psychological de-escalation process has many peaks and valleys, especially at the end, when the hostage taker or the barricaded subject is about to surrender. While, to an unqualified eye, the continual changes of positions could appear as a sign of inability to commit due to a lack of genuine intent, experienced negotiators would recognize this pre-surrender stage fairly quickly and see it as a sign of the need to take charge in leading the subject through the surrender process.

According to one member of the delegation, Maulana Rafi Usmani, the team reached Islamabad in the morning and immediately went to see Chaudhry Shujaat who agreed to forward the 'solutions' proposed by the ulema team to President Musharraf, 'because he seemed convinced that these were fair offers to end the crisis'.[43] According to Usmani, the formula proposed by the team was 'quite effective because it could be face-saving for both the government and Red Mosque people as it allowed the law to be abided and yet avoid further bloodshed'.[44] The proposed solutions were also presented to Ijaz ul-Haq, the Minister for Religious Affairs, who after 'some reluctance' agreed to put the proposals up for the Prime Minister's consideration. Usmani then asked Ijaz ul-Haq whether the Prime Minister was in a position to decide about this issue, to which he is believed to have answered affirmatively.[45] It should be pointed out here that Ijaz ul-Haq, in a later interview, argued that, although he had been close to the Lal Masjid administration, he had distanced himself when the Wafaq-ul-Madaris decided to de-register the Lal Masjid madaris due to their hardline stands. He added that he only decided to be part of these last minute negotiations on the insistence of Prime Minister Shaukat Aziz.[46] In a further attempt to resolve the standoff, the Prime Minister extended the mandate of the ulema and Shujaat to continue their efforts on the negotiations front, and a ray of hope emerged for a peaceful resolution to the crisis.[47]

The next day, a 12-member delegation, including Chaudhry Shujaat, Ijaz ul-Haq, Information Minister Durrani, Maulana Abdus Sattar Edhi, Bilqees Edhi, and religious leaders Mufti Rafi Usmani and Dr Abdur Razzaq reached the 'Red Zone' at 6:30 p.m. and conveyed to Rashid Ghazi an invitation for talks through a megaphone.[48] Ghazi refused to come out for talks, stating that he feared being arrested or killed by security forces the moment he stepped out the door.[49] He asked Usmani to bring the delegation inside Lal Masjid,[50] but the security agencies opposed the idea, fearing they might be taken hostage. The agencies also alleged that Ghazi himself was hostage to some of the other militants inside.[51] Taking benefit of the mobile phone provided by the delegation, Ghazi contacted a private TV channel and conveyed to reporters that he was offering to guarantee the security of the delegation. He also said that the ulema wanted to come inside the mosque but they were prevented by the authorities.[52] In the end, the meeting never took place, but the delegation managed to talk with Ghazi for almost eleven hours from outside the premises through mobile phone and walkie-talkie. According to Shujaat, around 2:00 a.m., an agreement was reached with the following clauses:

1. All the women and children captured inside the building will be released to the civil authorities. Armed men will lay down their arms and hand over the Children's Library after vacating the madrasa established there.
2. Maulana Rashid Ghazi, together with his family, will be allowed safe passage to his ancestral town. He will not be formally arrested but will remain under the protection of the police.[53]

The government members of the delegation returned to brief the President about the situation, after spending five hours in unsuccessful attempts to remove the lack of trust shown equally by the government and the Lal Masjid administration.[54] Meanwhile, Sessions Judge Rafi-uz-Zaman arrived at the scene on the order of the Supreme Court to supervise the process of surrender by the Lal

Masjid occupants. In the presence of the Sessions Judge, the security forces once again repeated their offer of amnesty for those militants who were surrendering and leaving the complex.[55]

Maulana Usmani provides an insightful account of the events that unfolded on 9 July 2007.

> The next day (9th July morning) when we met the Prime Minister the entire formula was placed before him and after some talks, he agreed to the proposal that Ghazi will not be arrested. Ghazi was insistent that he would rather die with dignity than surrender to face the humiliation that those who were arrested faced including his elder brother, Maulana Aziz. Ghazi had agreed to leave the mosque premises if he was allowed a 'safe passage' with his family to his hometown and had agreed to give up on both the seminaries, the mosque, the occupied state-owned Children's Library, surrender all the weapons inside the mosque premises.[56]
>
> Once the agreement was reached, the Prime Minister ordered that the proposal be implemented. This was afternoon time [sic]. In order to implement this formula, the team of ulema flanked by Chaudhry Shujaat, Minister of Religious Affairs Ijaz ul-Haq, Information Minister Mohammad Ali Durrani and Telecommunication Minister Mr Tariq Azeem all proceeded to the mosque.

Mufti Usmani went on to describe the journey and how and why one of the Rangers' official stopped them from entering the mosque as he believed there was a risk of their being taken hostage. He apparently did not know that an agreement had been reached for resolution of this matter.[57]

Mufti Usmani also stated that some of his colleagues were also not in favour of entering the mosque which was surrounded by the Rangers who could attack them and shift the blame onto Rashid Ghazi. Hence they all agreed and proceeded to a house under paramilitary supervision, where they put down in writing the 'formula' agreed upon with the Prime Minister.[58]

The ministers in the team prepared the draft that was then discussed and amended. Meanwhile one of Ghazi's representatives arrived and the team began a discussion with Ghazi on his mobile phone which was replaced when its battery died down. In Mufti Usmani's words:

> Ghazi agreed on all the points but insisted that all the Ministers shall come inside so that he could show them the amount and quantity of weapons that we have inside the mosque (this was perhaps to dispel the government's allegations that there was a huge quantity of sophisticated weaponry inside the premises which was being used in resistance). But all avenues into the mosque were closed by the government for us, the ministers and the media. Finally, the agreement was written and we were all very happy and excited.[59]

Mufti Usmani continued that the ministers then left to discuss the agreement and on their return said that they needed to go to the President's House to seek permission to implement the terms agreed.[60] This was surprising because the terms had been approved by the Prime Minister in the presence of the ministers and Chaudhry Shujaat: they questioned the need for the President's approval, particularly when they had mentioned during their meeting with the Prime Minister that the matter had also been discussed with the President. Despite this the ministers left, saying they would return shortly.

The remaining members, exhausted by the day's proceedings, did not expect that the decisions taken would be overturned by this last minute development. However, the ministers returned, visibly upset, after two and a half hours. They had a sort of official paper with three points noted: the bottom line was that all the terms of the agreement had been rejected. For example, the point about where Ghazi and his companions would be shifted was changed from 'his hometown' to something akin to 'house arrest', which Ghazi had emphatically refused to accept. When the ulema asked for reversal to the original terms, Tariq Azeem said that there could be no change to the final terms laid down by the President, and that the ulema had just half an hour to accept this proposal. The latter's response was that these were not the terms agreed by the team as well as Rashid Ghazi hence they could not take the responsibility of having the terms accepted by him, but these points could be conveyed to him by his representative (who was present there). Ghazi refused outright.[61]

As the team continued their efforts to negotiate, someone from the Rangers or army entered the room, and pointedly indicated that their time was running out. Mufti Rafi Usmani said that there was no purpose in their staying on any longer as it was obvious that the government was 'not sincere in its commitments and agreement'. Hence they left, very disappointed.[62] Yet there a faint hope as Ghazi's representative was still there with the government's people and was trying to contact Ghazi over the phone. The ulema had turned off their mobiles as they did not want the media to know and circulate that the talks had failed as this could 'sabotage' any possibility of rescuing the situation peacefully. Thereafter, they returned to their hotel rooms, agreeing to decide later what statement should be issued; but soon they came to know that the Lal Masjid operation had begun. Mufti Usmani said that when asked by a media person as to who was responsible for the operation, he said it was the President.[63]

The last conversation the negotiators had with Rashid Ghazi took place at 3:25 a.m.[64] Even after this time, he still continued to talk to the media, keen to share his version of how the talks collapsed on that fateful night. Speaking to Aaj TV, he claimed that the government was 'behaving arrogantly and did not wish to resolve this crisis amicably'. He said that he had wanted to have the issue resolved with full transparency, alluding to his demand for all the ministers to come into the mosque and see the quantity and type of weapons they had inside the mosque, which, according to his claim, were not more than 14 Kalashnikovs. The government wanted to make a deal quietly and he was not ready to accept that because he worried that this could give the government the opportunity to twist the reality and vindicate its own 'baseless propaganda', which of course also included the presence of foreign militants inside the mosque.[65] Rashid Ghazi also insisted on his leadership of the people inside the mosque, and dismissed the claim that someone else was leading the resistance as mere government propaganda.[66] This statement was intended to rebut rumours that Ghazi had taken a backseat or was not in control or had been taken hostage by more militant elements inside. Ghazi also reiterated that he would rather 'die with dignity' than submit and surrender to the use of 'brutal force'. He stated that there were only 25 people inside who were fighting against the government forces. Most significantly, he accused some of the ulema, who had come for the negotiations, of themselves being politically motivated and, instead of having the crisis resolved, actually wanted to have him and his fellows killed.[67] Ghazi wanted to make the same point in another of his last interviews with Geo TV, when he was interrupted with a different question. He called them *Siyasi* ulema' i.e. political scholars. In the same interview he again, insisted that he wanted the truce to be 'transparent' and wanted the ulema and the media to be part of it to 'see the reality so that it cannot be twisted or planted later on by the government in order to prove its claims right'.[68]

Rashid Ghazi's public relations effort throughout the crisis seemed to pay immediate dividends, as a number of protests and demonstrations in support of the Lal Masjid were held across the country. More than 20,000 armed tribesmen and members of Pakistani Taliban held a demonstration in Bajaur agency of the Federally Administered Tribal Areas (FATA). The crowd condemned the government and vowed to launch revenge attacks and country-wide jihad if the military moved inside the mosque.[69] Similarly, more than 700 armed men calling themselves 'mujahideen' blocked the historic Silk Route and demanded an end to the siege of the Red Mosque.[70] Nevertheless, the decision to proceed with the operation had already been taken.

On Tuesday morning, Rashid Ghazi bid his farewell: 'This is my last chance to say anything, and I would like to say that we fought with courage. We were asked to bow before power, but we refused to do so,' Ghazi told a private news channel. 'We will fight until martyrdom, but the people will take revenge from the rulers ... I offered surrender in the presence of media so that the entire world could see what sort of weapons we had and those were my last words with them [negotiators],' he said. 'We did not commit any crime, for which we are being punished so tremendously; the government is using naked aggression with reckless blind force against us ... This is gross injustice; the people conducting the operation are American agents and carrying out this operation on USA's bidding.' Ghazi further added: 'The prevalent system is creating problems, where some families are in possession of power and afflicting everybody with misery ... these problems will stay unresolved until the Islamic system is established.' Later on, he telephoned a TV channel and said: 'Commandos have reached my room.' Telephone contact was lost immediately afterwards.[71]

NOTES

1. Michael J. McMains and Wayman C. Mullins, *Crisis Negotiations: Managing Critical Incidents and Hostage Situations in Law Enforcement and Corrections*, 4th edn. (New Providence, NJ: Mathew Bender & Company Inc. Publishing, 2010), 3.

2. Thomas M. Davidson, *To Preserve Life: Hostage-Crisis Management* (San Rafael, CA: Cimacom, 2002); James L. Greenstone, *The Elements of Police Hostage and Crisis Negotiations: Critical Incidents and How to Respond to Them* (Binghamton, NY: Haworth Press, 2005); Frederick Lanceley, *On-Scene Guide for Crisis Negotiators*, 2nd ed. (Boca Raton, FL: CRC Press, 2003); McMains, et al., *Crisis Negotiations*; Gary Noesner, *Stalling for Time: My Life as an FBI Hostage Negotiator* (Random House, 2010); James Poland and Michael McCrystle, *Practical, Tactical and Legal Perspectives of Terrorism and Hostage Taking* (Lewiston, NY: Edwin Mellen Press, 2000); Randal Rogan, Mitchell Hammer and Clinton Van Zandt, *Dynamic Processes of Crisis Negotiation* (Westport, CT: Praeger, 1997); Adam Dolnik and Keith M. Fitzgerald, *Negotiating Hostage Crises with the New Terrorists* (Westport, CT: Praeger Security International, 2008); Arthur A. Slatkin, *Communications in Crisis and Hostage Negotiations* (Springfield, IL: Charles C. Thomas Publishers, 2005); Thomas Strentz, *Psychological Aspects of Crisis Negotiation* (New York: CRC Press, 2006); William Zartman ed., *Negotiating with Terrorists* (Leiden: Martinus Nijhoff Publishers, 2006).

3. Adam Dolnik, 'Contrasting Dynamics of Crisis Negotiations: Barricade versus Kidnapping Incidents', *International Negotiation*, 8/3 (2003), 53–84.

4. This does not always have to be the case. In some situations, such as the 2004 Beslan school siege, the hostage takers have negated this advantage of the passage of time by executing hostages, or by denying their captives water.

5. Thomas Strentz, 'The Cyclic Crisis Negotiations Time Line', *Law and Order* (1995).

6. Ibid.

7. Arthur A. Slatkin, *Communications in Crisis and Hostage Negotiations* (Springfield, IL: Charles C. Thomas Publishers, 2005), 19.
8. Ibid. 20.
9. Psychotherapists make a living precisely on this natural desire of people to share their problems and their need to feel heard and understood.
10. Dolnik and Fitzgerald, *Negotiating Hostage Crises*, 162.
11. McMains & Mullins, 142.
12. Mitchell R. Hammer and Randall G. Rogan, 'Negotiation Models in Crisis Situations: The Value of a Communication-Based Approach', in Rogan et. al., *Dynamic Processes of Crisis Negotiation* (Westport, CT: Praeger, 1997), 9.
13. Dwayne Fuselier, 'What Every Negotiator Would Like His Chief to Know,' *FBI Law Enforcement Bulletin* (March 1986).
14. McMains & Mullins, *Crisis Negotiations*, 117.
15. McMains and Mullins describe how the negotiator can suggest taking a lunch break and continuing the discussion later. The mentioning of food has the potential of reminding the hostage taker of his primary needs.
16. McMains & Mullins, *Crisis Negotiations*, 107.
17. In the United States for instance the basic legal grounding relies on United States vs. Crosby, 1983; State vs. Sands, 1985.
18. Richard Hayes, 'Negotiations with Terrorists,' in Victor Kremenyuk, ed., *International Negotiation* (San Francisco: Jossey-Bass, 2001).
19. William Zartman, 'Negotiating Effectively With Terrorists', in Barry Rubin, ed., *The Politics of Counterterrorism* (Washington, D.C.: The Johns Hopkins Foreign Policy Institute, 1990), 164.
20. Dolnik and Fitzgerald, *Negotiating Hostage Crises*, 162.
21. Khalid Qayum, 'Pakistan Red Mosque Was 'Fort Ready for Battle', Musharraf Says', *Bloomberg* (US) (13 July 2007) <http://www.bloomberg.com/apps/news?pid=20601091&sid=aWFb.nCpxO.o&refer=india> accessed 3 May 2010.
22. 'Pak forces set to storm Lal Masjid; state on alert', *IBN Live* (4 July 2007) <http://ibnlive.in.com/news/pak-forces-set-to-storm-lal-masjid-state-on-alert/44008-2.html> accessed 12 April 2010.

23. Ibid.
24. 'Chief cleric held in burqa escape bid: 1100 students surrender, G-6 residents brave siege', *Dawn* (5 July 2007) accessed 2 April 2010.
25. Syed Irfan Raza, '1100 students surrender', *Dawn* (5 July 2007).
26. Interview with an FIA official, Islamabad, 27 September 2009.
27. K. Varma, 'Lal Masjid: 800 Students Surrender', *Rediff* (4 July 2007) <http://www.rediff.com/news/2007/jul/04pak3.htm> accessed 4 April 2010.
28. Interview with an FIA official, Islamabad, 27 September 2009.
29. Interview with Lal Masjid student who surrendered on the second day (27 September 2009).
30. Varma, 'Lal Masjid'.
31. Syed Irfan Raza, 'Besieged cleric seeks safe passage', *Dawn* (6 July 2007).
32. 'Chief cleric held in burqa'.
33. Ibid.
34. Syed Irfan Raza, 'Ghazi, militants vow to fight till bitter end', *Dawn* (7 July 2007).
35. Zulfiqar Ghuman, Irfan Ghauri and Azaz Syed, 'Lal Masjid militants stand defiant', *Daily Times* (Lahore) (7 July 2007).
36. Ahmed Hassan, 'Musharraf blamed for talks failure', *Dawn* (11 July 2007).
37. Raza, 'Besieged cleric'.
38. 'Ghazi snubs Shujaat over house arrest', *Daily Times* (Lahore) (7 July 2007).
39. Hassan, 'Musharraf blamed'.
40. Interview with an FIA official, Islamabad, 27 September 2009.
41. Saleem Shahid, 'Musharraf tells Hafsa brigade to surrender or die', *Dawn* (8 July 2007).
42. Interview with Tariq Azeem, Islamabad, 16 January 2009.
43. Maulana Mufti Muhammad Rafi Usmani, '*Lal Masjid aur hukumat kay darmian muzakrat kiun naakaam hue* [Why the negotiations failed between Lal Masjid and the government]', *Binaat* <http://www.banuri.edu.pk/ur/node/230> accessed 6 March 2010.
44. Ibid.
45. Ibid.

46. 'Interview with Ijaz ul-Haq on Morning Show (Urdu)', *ATV* (Pakistan); <http://www.youtube.com/watch?v=oL6ECAQpbiA& feature=related> accessed 14 May 2010.

47. Maulana Zahid Al-Rashdi, '*Lal Masjid tanaza'e par muzakarat kaise sabotazh kiye gaye* [How the Lal Masjid talks were sabotaged]', *Islam* (Urdu) (12 July 2007).

48. Shakeel Anjum, 'Solution to Lal Masjid crisis in sight', *The News* (Pakistan) (10 July 2007); <http://server.kbri-islamabad.go.id/ index.php?option=com_content&task=view&id=1101&Itemid=5 3> accessed 14 March 2010.

49. Interview with Mufti Rafi Usmani, Karachi, 24 January 2009.

50. Anjum, 'Solution'.

51. '*Sadr Musharaf ke tayyare ko nishana bananeki koshish aur khudkush hamla, Lal Masjid Operation ka radd-e amal?*' [Attack on President Musharraf's plane and suicide attack reaction to Lal Masjid Operation?] *Ausaf* (Urdu) (Pakistan) (7 July 2007).

52. Anjum, 'Solution'.

53. Interview with Chaudhry Shujaat Hussain, Islamabad, 16 January 2009.

54. Anjum, 'Solution'; Interview with Mufti Rafi Usmani, Karachi, 24 January 2009.

55. Anjum, 'Solution'.

56. Usmani, '*Lal Masjid aur hukumat*'.

57. Ibid.

58. Ibid.

59. Ibid.

60. In another narrative by the ulema as covered by *Pak Tribune*, it was Chaudhry Shujaat who insisted that the agreement must be approved by President Musharraf. See Abid Ullah Jan, 'Lal Masjid Massacre: What really happened?' *Haqeeqat.Org* (15 July 2007) <www.haqeeqat.org/.../lal-masjid-massacre-what-really-happened-abid-ullah-jan/> accessed 3 May 2010.

61. Usmani, '*Lal Masjid aur hukumat*'.

62. Ibid.

63. Ibid.

64. Interview with Tariq Azeem, Islamabad, 16 January 2009.

65. 'An Interview with Ghazi Abdul Rashid (purportedly his last interview) (Urdu)', *Aaj Television Channel* (Pakistan) <http://www.youtube.com/watch?v=8BIQcPHwNkU> accessed 10 April 2010.

66. '*Sadr Musharaf ke taiyyare ko*'.

67. 'An Interview with Ghazi Abdul Rashid'.

68. Ibid.

69. 'Bajaur tribals announce support for Lal Masjid *mullah*', *Daily Times* (Lahore) (10 January 2007).

70. Urdu *Daily Express* (Lahore) (10 July 2007).

71. 'Nation would take revenge from dictatorial [*sic*] rulers after my martyrdom: Ghazi', *Online International News Network* (11 July 2007); <http://www.onlinenews.com.pk/details.php?newsid=114879> accessed 19 December 2014.

6

Negotiation Analysis

Having covered the basic principles and processes of crisis negotiations as well as the chronology of the negotiation efforts at the Lal Masjid, the following chapter will apply these tools to offer an analytical negotiability assessment, along with highlighting the indicators of volatility and de-escalation, as well as identifying successes, failures, missed opportunities, and the lessons learned during the Lal Masjid siege.

INCIDENT TYPE

The Lal Masjid incident bore a number of interesting characteristics of a hybrid situation. On the one hand, the Lal Masjid militants were not voluntary barricade subjects, in the sense that the final siege appears to have been a product of the spontaneous unfolding of events, as opposed to prior planning. The militants did not simply deliberately occupy the stronghold with the intention of taking hostages and expecting a siege. In situations where the barricaded subjects find themselves in their respective situations as a result of unexpected developments or spur of the moment decisions, facilitation of the passage of time and a gradual regression toward more basic human needs are typically very successful strategies, as an unprepared counterpart is more likely to question his or her decisions with passing time.

At the same time, it is important to highlight that, while not exactly a pre-planned incident, the barricade crisis did not catch the Lal Masjid militants off guard completely. The possibility of an armed assault on the mosque and its madaris had publically been debated for many months, and the militants inside had made specific preparations for such a possibility, such as stockpiling of food, weapons, ammunition, and perhaps most importantly, developing a mental expectation of the possibility of a dangerous, prolonged siege. In this sense, much of the element of surprise from the perspective of the authorities was lost, and the time needed for the barricade subjects to regress to their basic needs would inevitably be longer due to the availability of food as well as the possibility to stand guard in shifts, allowing periods of rest. Similarly, given the fact that the militants operated on their own turf, this resulted in a situation where many essential items were already available to them, decreasing the number of opportunities to introduce items for trade. So for instance, when the Pakistani military engaged in an effort to pressure the students by cutting off electricity supply to the mosque, this effort was easily countered by the use of generators.

A point of specific concern in the 'incident type' analysis stage is to distinguish between hostage and non-hostage incidents. In hostage incidents, the barricaded subjects are in possession of considerable leverage, as possession of hostages creates a 'good' that hostage-takers can use to trade for specific measures the group seeks to achieve, and also gives them the opportunity to severely punish the authorities for non-compliance with their demands by executing hostages. In addition, the possession of hostages also provides a deterrent to a possible assault by the security forces, via the use of hostages as human shields. In non-hostage incidents, the barricaded subjects tend to have much less leverage precisely due to the absence of hostages. From this perspective, the Lal Masjid was once again a hybrid situation. On the one hand the presence of 'hostages' was a widely debated issue, with the government claiming on a number of occasions that some of the students were held inside against their will. A ten-year-old boy, introduced as Jawad Ahmad, who claimed to have escaped through a window and a hole in the wall, was paraded in front of the media stating: 'inside they had guns and everything ... and said that whoever would leave would be shot'.[1] There were other additional claims of the presence of hostages inside, including an assertion that some of the Jamia Hafsa female students who were still inside on 7 July, had started a hunger strike in protest of the stiff attitude of militants around Rashid Ghazi, and that the militants had pointed guns at them in order to enforce discipline.[2]

In our interviews with some of the Lal Masjid students who were inside the mosque during the siege, we were told that they were never held inside by force. In addition, we should not forget that hundreds of students had safely surrendered throughout the crisis and were not prevented from doing so.[3] This of course did not necessarily translate into complete freedom to leave, as psychological factors such as peer pressure, ideological references to the importance of martyrdom as the highest form of religious conviction, brainwashing, emotional extortion based on abandoning comrades in a moment of crisis, scare rhetoric about what awaited outside, as well as presence of high authority figures whom the students were used to unquestionably obeying—all combined to create a situation in which leaving the mosque was certainly not an easy decision to make.[4] Similarly, even if we accept that the students inside were not 'hostages' in the true sense of the word, the presence of so many civilians inside the mosque provided an analogous human shield element common to barricade hostage crises, as the government could ill afford to be seen as causing the deaths of large numbers of civilians in the process of an armed assault. Perhaps even more important was the symbolic value of the mosque itself, both at the level of popular following of the Lal Masjid imams throughout the country, as well as at the more general level of feeding potentially devastating propaganda images of Pakistani military attacking and killing 'true Muslims at a sacred place of worship at the behest of their Western masters', which would fit perfectly into the al-Qaeda narrative.

Finally, a third layer of protection against government action was provided by the credible threats of using suicide bombers against the government in retaliation for a possible use of force, which provided an external threat dynamic that almost no barricade siege in history has ever witnessed.

This was augmented by statements from influential militant figures such as Maulana Fazlullah, alias Maulana Radio, the head of the Pakistani Taliban in Swat, who demanded the government to stop military action against the mosque or face suicide attacks. He also threatened to breach a peace deal with the government signed earlier that year.[5] In this sense, the management of the crisis had to incorporate significant factors beyond the incident itself, which were arguably even more important for the future of Pakistan than the tactical scene at the Lal Masjid itself. In essence, the siege would become an important contest for the 'hearts and minds' of the Pakistani population.

ASSESSMENT OF VOLATILITY

From the crisis negotiation standpoint, Lal Masjid carried several signs of high volatility from the beginning. The first was the clear presence of a considerable quantity of automatic weapons, as well as apparent experience of the people inside in how to use them. Preparations for armed resistance to any police action had clearly been made in advance, with sandbags erected on walls, multiple automatic weapons with plenty of ammunition having been stockpiled, the presence of gas masks, and organized water buckets and wet rags to help counter the use of tear gas. Conventional wisdom suggests that such a premeditated incident is naturally quite challenging to negotiate due to the perpetrators' preparedness to adapt to any development, and the process is likely to be significantly longer in duration than in the case of spontaneous incidents.

Further, the presence of multiple subjects available to handle the negotiations made the situation even more unpredictable: building rapport with barricade subjects is much more challenging if they are under direct pressure from their peers and if they can effectively negate the formation of a personal relationship with the government negotiator by simply switching representatives. Moreover, the psychological process known as 'groupthink' affects the situation, as group hostage-takers in general have the ability to be more radical, and the collective standpoint they assume on any given issue is likely to be more extreme than the sum of the individual positions held by specific people within the group.

Secondly, the fact that at least nine people had been killed in the initial shootout that marked the beginning of the barricade crisis also was a terribly negative development, not just because of the lives lost, but also due to the fact that a threshold of lethal violence had already been crossed. In situations where barricade standoffs take place without the killing of anyone, negotiators have the option of calming the subjects down over time, later explaining that nothing 'that bad' had happened *yet*, that not everything had yet been lost. In situations where deaths have already occurred, it becomes much more difficult for negotiators to make this argument, since sometimes creating a sense of fait accompli in which the barricaded subjects are aware of the unavoidable consequences, makes them more averse to the option of peaceful surrender. In addition, the killings tarnish the hostage takers' 'clean bill of health' and, since the law has at this point been clearly severely violated, calm communication with the subjects becomes politically difficult and highly unpopular among decision-makers, who come under tremendous pressure from the public to 'do something'. Moreover, in incidents like the Lal Masjid, where some of the people killed in the initial shootout were part of the tactical team in charge of resolving the incident (Army-Rangers), tensions and emotions rise at the perimeter, frequently triggering aggressive determination to avenge the death of lost comrades. This was an especially significant risk at the Lal Masjid siege, where the tactical teams spent eight days at the perimeter sleeping no more than one hour a day while sitting up in chairs and receiving no psychological support whatsoever in the process.[6] In such a high-pressure situation, negotiations sometimes become dismissed as too 'soft' an approach, thereby creating the unfortunate situation in which violence becomes increasingly likely.

Finally, the declared desire on the part of the militants to die and become martyrs suggested a high level of volatility. The contemporary crisis negotiation paradigm suggests that the desire to live is a basic pre-condition of a negotiated settlement in barricade situations—if the hostage-takers are indifferent to staying alive, it is difficult to make them focus on personal safety and thus draw their attention away from their original demands. Also, the threat of force posed by the tactical units becomes much less powerful as a bargaining tool when survival plays no part in the hostage-takers' calculation of the outcome. Under circumstances in which the captors see it as their primary—or at least secondary—objective to kill themselves and take as many of their victims with them as possible, negotiation logically has very little chance of success. This argument is based on Maslow's hierarchy of needs, and assumes that since the desire to live is stronger than any other need, in its absence there is nothing for the negotiators to offer.[7]

However, such situations are extremely infrequent, especially in the realm of barricade crises involving ideologically inspired perpetrators. After all, one major reason for creating a barricade situation is to protect one's own safety during the ensuing standoff. In sum, there is little doubt that at last some of the militants who remained inside the stronghold until the bitter end, were *prepared* to die, as the likelihood of such a result was very high. At the same time, it seems almost certain that death did not constitute their *preferred outcome*. There are many shades of grey between a bluff and true, unswerving suicidal intent. It seems more likely that the repeated declaration of readiness to 'be martyred' was a rational course of action aimed at nullifying the government's threat level: the credible proclamation of the desire to die weakened the deterrent value of threats by the government to resolve the situation forcefully, strengthening the militants' own bargaining position.[8] Even the suicidal rhetoric itself adds to the incident's fear factor—a useful tool for the militants. For these reasons, the declared preparedness to die on part of the perpetrators might have made negotiations challenging, but certainly did not exclude the possibility of nonviolent resolution altogether—or at least the chance that continued negotiations would result in the surrender of more students or in the public perception that the authorities were handling the situation wisely and with appropriate caution. As previously argued by Slatkin, even though the militants may have a desire to become martyrs, 'it should not be assumed that they are ready or willing to die on *that day* [emphasis in original]'.[9] This is especially the case given the fact that Abdul Aziz clearly tried to survive by escaping the location in a burqa, while Rashid Ghazi's proclamations about wanting to become a martyr had also been simultaneously accompanied by demands for free passage to his hometown.

INDICATORS OF DE-ESCALATION

Besides the above-stated indicators of high volatility, positive signs hinting at the encouragingly strong possibility of a peaceful resolution were also present as the incident progressed. First, and most importantly, the incident witnessed a gradual progression over time in which the barricade subjects continually reduced their demands—from high level, abstract, open-ended, highly ambitious demands such as implementation of Sharia in the country, towards much more basic demands for survival and safety. In barricade incidents, it is quite common for subjects to start the bidding high and make completely unrealistic demands, but this is typically followed by a reduction of demands as the incident progresses, and as their exhaustion triggers a regression to a hierarchically low (more basic) set of needs, such as hunger, thirst, and sleep.[10] At the same time, the presence of multiple barricade subjects prolongs this process significantly, as the militants not only have the option of resting some of their crew by working in shifts but also are able to feed off the energy and determination of their comrades. Particularly when the hostage-takers widely publicize their original demands and thus publicly lock themselves into their position, it becomes more difficult to negotiate a peaceful solution, as the one thing the image-conscious and fear-dependent religious militants worry about most is widespread perception of their weakness and failure. It becomes the negotiator's key role to diminish and soften the perception of surrender as weakness and failure, in order to facilitate a non-violent conclusion to the incident.

As mentioned earlier, in 'negotiable situations', hostage-takers' demands are initially highly ambitious but, with the help of negotiators, should become more realistic over time. Similarly, the hostage-takers' behaviour is likely to undergo rapid changes as the incident progresses, starting with rage and excitement, followed by increasing frustration, stress, and then fatigue.[11] The key implication of this is that the frequent changes in mood are a natural and an uncontrollable occurrence, and can be overcome only with passing time. This development of rapidly changing demands and positions, while leading many uninformed observers to conclude that negotiators have no chance of success, actually represent an *encouraging* sign. In other words, not only are these rapid changes in positions normal and do not typically suggest the lack of sanity or sincerity on behalf of the subject, the variability in specific portions of their demands also provides many opportunities for negotiators to introduce further nuanced options in order to dissect the demands and make them more manageable—a process known as 'fractionization'. In the Lal Masjid case, the militants' vagueness opened up opportunities for the introduction of new options that they might not have considered before, but ones that would satisfy some of their core interests in alternate, yet still acceptable, ways. This is especially true given the fact that over time, the militants' demands regressed from unrealistic toward hypothetically more achievable ones.

This brings us to the second and closely associated positive sign in the crisis, and that was the absence of any clear hostages or threats to kill people inside the stronghold as a pressure tool designed to extort the government into granting specific concessions. In the absence of this dynamic, the position of the militants inside was quite weak as, despite their considerable rations of food and gasoline (for the power generators), they were clearly going to run out eventually. In the absence of any hostages inside, the militants had little 'currency' in forcing the government to accept their demands through threats to kill hostages at deadlines. In such a situation, the cost of doing nothing is relatively low, as no lives are in immediate danger and time is clearly on the side of the negotiation team. Further, prolongation of the incident also provides the tactical unit with more time to study the behavioural patterns of the perpetrators and to prepare for a possible assault should it at some point become the preferred course of action.

The final encouraging element in the ordeal was the periodic safe surrender of hundreds of students, without any demands or concessions attached. These surrenders clearly indicated the willingness of the militants to deal with the authorities, as well as a desire to demonstrate their 'good will' to their desired audience (or, at least, their sensitivity to how they were perceived). Even more importantly, peaceful surrender of students sets a precedent for future deals, and establishes an opportunity for the government to clearly demonstrate its commitment to fulfilling its promises. This would not only serve to increase the government's credibility in offers and guarantees made to the militants still holed up inside the Lal Masjid, but also would satisfy one of the government's key concerns for a favourable impression in the eyes of the public.

THE NEGOTIATIONS: MISSED OPPORTUNITIES

The negotiability or non-negotiability of the Lal Masjid crisis will always be an issue of much political contention, and one that can never be answered with absolute certainty. Nevertheless, the lack of a negotiation strategy—or the successful implementation of a strategy *not to negotiate*— clearly translated into missed opportunities and probably a higher body count. This section will analyse some of the missed opportunities of the negotiations in Lal Masjid in order to draw lessons for the future.

COMMUNICATIONS

The first obvious limitation of the Lal Masjid negotiations was the failure to establish clear and reliable communication links. Effective means of communication are the precondition of any successful negotiation. In barricade incidents, establishment of a communication line is the first action that takes place after the perpetrator's location has been secured. The more reliable the contact links between the parties, the lesser the chances of miscommunication and potentially catastrophic consequences. Similarly, the more direct the means of communication that exist, the greater the opportunities for the negotiator to establish a level of familiarity and rapport with the militants, increasing his or her ability to exercise influence over the subjects' conduct and to gather useful intelligence. In cases where the perpetrator refuses to communicate, prompt answering of the telephone is going to be the first concession the negotiator will seek in exchange for minor favours, such as food, drink, or turning the electricity back on.[12]

Much of the communication in the Lal Masjid siege was conducted through loudspeakers, which is an acceptable but far from ideal form of communication, given the fact that it is essentially a unidirectional conveying of messages and not a reciprocal dialogue in which the rapport building techniques that make crisis negotiations effective could be satisfactorily employed. In addition, loudspeakers are a very public means of communication and participants can lock themselves more firmly into initial positions, creating the need for more robust face-saving mechanisms later on. That being said, loudspeakers are frequently used in police negotiations as the initial means of establishing first contact, in order to persuade the barricaded subjects to accept a field phone, or to agree to establish another, more direct means of communication.

In addition to being the primary means of communication throughout some parts of the crisis, loudspeakers also played an important supplementary role in the Lal Masjid siege, providing a direct avenue for conveying messages to the students inside about the offer of risk-free surrender, circumventing the possibility of those messages being censored by the Lal Masjid leadership. In other words, direct access to the decision makers inside the stronghold was essential in providing an opportunity for the negotiation process to work, while at the same time relying solely on this means of communication might have resulted in the messages intended for everyone at the mosque not reaching their audience. In this sense, this public nature of the communication could have played a vital and positive role.

Another means of communication were cellphones, which, in recent times have become very common, but provide several distinct disadvantages against the standard telephone option. First, one of the key elements negotiators strive to achieve in a barricade crisis is the monopolization of the communication process in order to increase the dependence of the subject on the negotiator, who tries to position himself or herself as an intermediary between the subject and the authorities. In cases where communication is effectively monopolized, the subject's dependence helps strengthen the rapport building process in which the subject's reliance on the negotiator, along with the negotiator's empathetic, caring, and nonjudgmental approach combine for a powerful dynamic of influence. In cases where the perpetrators are communicating to various parties throughout the crisis, building this dynamic will prove to be a more challenging and a longer term process.

Moreover, the global reach of the Internet presents the terrorists with an independent communication channel to the media and the outside world, which will allow them to present their own version of events, along with documentary evidence, making censorship and media manipulation a much less effective or even a counterproductive incident management tool than was the case in the past. Moreover, in such a situation, providing access to the media, as a minor concession used to initiate trades, will also become a decreasingly important instrument in the negotiators' toolbox.

In addition, the immediate ability of the subjects to consult with their leadership outside of the siege location via cellphone can deprive the negotiators of much of the influence they typically strive to gain by disrupting the hostage takers' chain of authority, thus forcing the perpetrators to make their own decisions in isolation from their leadership. And, while terrorist hostage takers of the past had often gone on operations with minimal instructions from their leaders, and thus frequently found themselves in a position of having to make decisions on their own, today's technological reality that gives the militants immediate access to their superiors has radically altered the situation. Since the leaders—unlike the hostage takers—will not be confined to the location under a constant threat of immediate forceful resolution, the processes that form the baseline foundation of the contemporary practice of crisis negotiation will not take place, making the task of lowering the terrorists' expectations much more difficult. This element was fortunately not present in the Lal Masjid case, as all the key decision makers were personally located inside the stronghold.

Another disadvantage of the lack of a monopolized line with the stronghold is the possibility of the barricade subjects frequently communicating with outside channels such as the media. In the Lal Masjid, this element played a very important role in the negotiation process. According to the authorities, over 80 SIM cards and 12 Lal Masjid telephone lines that were used for Abdul Rashid Ghazi's conversations with the media and other outside parties had been blocked in the course of the crisis.[13] According to other sources, Ghazi allegedly had some 200 pre-paid SIM cards at his disposal and someone on the outside was charging up the balances on his behalf.[14]

Abdul Rashid Ghazi was fond of technology and was good with computers. He reportedly had up to date communication equipment installed at the mosque, including computers, faxes, printers, and a scanner. He broadcast his speeches on the Web and maintained his own website (which was founded in March 2007, and received over 6,000 hits within the first month). In addition, he allegedly monitored all incoming and outgoing calls through a computerized exchange, and also operated an illegal FM radio station (supposedly blocked by the government on 10 April) out of the mosque.[15] Throughout the siege, this shrewd media communicator made frequent phone calls to different media outlets, conducting a PR campaign designed to draw in popular support from among the Pakistani population, in an effort to increase popular pressure on the government to refrain from using force to resolve the crisis. According to Minister Tariq Azeem, Rashid Ghazi 'was more media savvy than any government spokesman that you can think of. In fact, if he was still alive, we should send government media spokesmen to him for training.'[16]

Besides conducting media interviews and press conferences, Rashid Ghazi even held live on-the-air debates with various politicians, such as on the night of Day 4 when he confronted Federal Minister Aftab Sherpao in a televised phone interview on the Geo TV network. Needless to say, live media encounters between barricade subjects and government ministers are a risky strategy, for several reasons. First, allowing the barricade subject to gain direct access to a decision-maker disrupts the deferment of authority tactic, which helps the negotiators explore any issues without commitment, in order to buy time and to decrease the subject's expectations. Secondly, a televized debate is not a good setting for reaching a peaceful resolution on a barricade crisis, as both parties focus primarily on winning public perceptions through appearing 'tough' and inadvertently hardening their positions, as opposed to focusing on joint problem solving. By actively encouraging confrontation in order to trigger media-attractive sound bites, as opposed to facilitating a meaningful dialogue, the media interaction can trigger further escalation of the situation. This was particularly the case here, where the Geo TV interviewer confronted Rashid Ghazi by asking him to clarify how he justified his position on religious grounds, when some of his own religious teachers had condemned his approach and had asked him to surrender. In such a setting, a heated public confrontation that has a tendency to push parties further apart is the most likely outcome, especially when 'tough' statements made in front of millions of television viewers tend to create pressure to maintain consistency with those statements, complicating future negotiations. And, finally, discussions between political decision-makers and barricade subjects live on air can result in missed opportunities, given the negotiators' inability immediately to follow-up on a demand or a statement made by the subject. For instance, in the Geo TV interview, Ghazi said that he was flexible in his stand but would only surrender his weapons, and not himself or his fellows.[17] Had a trained negotiator been a part of this conversation, he or she would have quickly exploited the public indication of his in-principle agreement with the idea of surrendering weapons, while he still remembered his own words and would find it difficult to backtrack from this de facto promise. Setting Ghazi's refusal to accept unconditional surrender aside for the moment and focusing instead on achieving the surrender of weapons would have definitely been a prize worth pursuing. It had the potential to stabilize the situation and to de-escalate it emotionally, while at the same time also reducing the likelihood of further violence by diminishing the firepower of the militants inside. Unfortunately, these opportunities were left unexploited.

On a final point relating to the media, the great media interest surrounding the case turned Abdul Rashid Ghazi into a contemporary celebrity, which increased rather than diminished his sense of importance and invulnerability, complicating the negotiation efforts designed to achieve his peaceful capitulation. In addition, the sheer number of phone calls Ghazi engaged in made it difficult to follow progress in the negotiation effort. As mentioned earlier, the perpetrator's demands typically are initially highly ambitious but, with the help of effective negotiators, should become more realistic over time. Similarly, the barricade subjects' behaviour is likely to undergo rapid changes as the incident progresses. In order to observe and analyse whether these processes are taking place, the negotiation team needs to have meticulous knowledge of *all* communications with the outside, so it can monitor details such as the changes in the suspect's tone of voice, specific vocabulary used, speech and breathing patterns, etc. In a situation where the perpetrators speak to a different person each time, while also making live interviews with media outlets, such detailed monitoring is much more difficult. Similarly, in this indirect communications scenario, the negotiators' inability immediately to follow-up on a demand or a statement made by the hostage takers, is likely to result in missed opportunities.

ABSENCE OF TRAINED CRISIS NEGOTIATORS

Besides the indirect and chaotic means of communication, another critical problem was the apparent absence of any trained crisis negotiators throughout the siege to begin with. Only on Day 6 of the standoff did the Prime Minister announce that two Pakistani hostage negotiators trained by the FBI would be sought and that they would negotiate on behalf of the government.[18] However, whether these trained negotiators were actually involved in any way is uncertain, and, even then, their impact would have probably not made an immediate difference for two reasons.

First, negotiation is a skill that needs to be constantly practised in order to build experience and maintain currency. The FBI course that these two negotiators had taken a part in provides only basic training, which the negotiators needed to build on through exercises and real-life exposure to incidents, in order to reach a level of proficiency. In addition, negotiation is a highly culture-specific phenomenon and, while most of the basic principles of the psychology of influence are universal, the specific communication techniques taught in the FBI course need to be adjusted to other language, culture, and context specific modes in order to reach their full potential. In other words, while the FBI course provided a very good starting point, it did not turn a person into a skilled negotiator in the absence of follow-up exposure to negotiations.

Secondly, the fact that the new negotiators were brought in only on Day 6 of the crisis, meant that they required additional time for these negotiators to build rapport and trust and to engage in damage control, in order to roll back the mistakes that had already been made up to that point. For instance, in seeking to establish the deferment of authority tactic by positioning themselves as intermediaries between the subject and the authorities, the newly appointed negotiators would have had a very difficult time convincing Rashid Ghazi that he would now have to communicate only through them and would not be granted direct access to decision-makers any more. Since Rashid Ghazi had for months spoken directly to government ministers, backtracking from this established pattern would simply not be easily achieved, especially in the absence of a prior relationship with the new negotiators and the absence of rapport and trust. Similarly, the unfortunate practice in which the ulema and the ministers made proactive counter-offers to Ghazi without having any authority to do so (such as suggesting the possibility of the subject's free passage to his home town) created a situation in which these suggestions now constituted official offers in the subject's mind, but in reality any guarantee that the deal would be backed by the authorities was absent. If he had decided to accept the offer at any point, only to find out that it was actually not officially sanctioned, all trust would be lost and this would constitute a colossal setback in the negotiations. This is ultimately what happened following General Musharraf's rejection of the agreement that Rashid Ghazi had assumed to be a done deal.

Nevertheless, despite all these limitations, the FBI-trained negotiators still could have played a positive role in serving as strategic advisors and as coaches to the individuals who served as primary communicators, to help them avoid further errors and to guide the negotiations in the right direction. Unfortunately, even the limited crisis negotiation skills available to the authorities at the time of the crisis were not properly utilized.

THIRD PARTY INTERMEDIARIES

An issue closely related to the lack of engagement of trained negotiators was the practically exclusive reliance on outside parties in this role. In negotiator jargon, the term third party intermediary (TPI) describes a person, who is not affiliated with the security services but is allowed to speak to the subject in a barricade/hostage crisis. In most jurisdictions, using TPIs is not the preferred option by any means, under the rationale that intermediaries lack specialized training, are out of the negotiation team's direct control, and may have a past relationship with the subject that can be destabilizing.[19] Nevertheless, there are situations where TPIs can play a positive role, and it is thus important to consider the 'who, why, when, and how' an intermediary might be used, as opposed to whether or not they should be used at all.[20]

One of the main reasons is that the dynamic between ideologically or religiously driven militants and the authorities is almost always one of mutual animosity, in which neither side can back down or make concessions, to the other. Introducing a third party can change that confrontational dynamic into one in which a credible third party may make suggestions that both sides might consider without having to cede credit for it to an enemy. For this reason, the involvement of well-known figures, such as journalists, politicians, celebrities, academics, clerics, or private negotiation professionals, whose perspective on the issue at hand is seen as neutral or sympathetic by the militants, can be a good idea—when managed skilfully.

After all, in negotiation, one's currency is influence. Logic would suggest that in situations where the authorities' main source of influence over the hostage takers (the ability to coerce them with threats) is minimized through preparation, tactical counter-measures, independent channels of communication, and the ability to work in shifts, a useful next step would be securing new sources of influence—one of which is an intermediary that has a different relationship to the barricade subjects and a higher level of credibility with them.

Although the practice is generally discouraged, this category of intermediary sometimes makes it possible to hold face-to-face negotiations with the subjects,[21] provided that this opportunity is used to extract some concession, such as the release of some hostages, or even only a public guarantee of the intermediary's safety. While this latter may seem like a small concession, the mere fact of getting the hostage-taker into the habit of making promises not to hurt people is a useful starting point for establishing a better process than the mutual coercion that is likely to result in violence if left to fate (from this perspective, Rashid Ghazi's public promise guaranteeing safety to the ulema delegation on the seventh day of the siege is quite significant, but often overlooked). Alternatively, a condition could be attached allowing the militants to select only one person to act as mediator throughout the entire crisis, in order to allow for the development of rapport between this individual and the hostage-takers, to establish credibility and consistency in the process, and to make keeping track of events, demands, and changes in moods more feasible.

In the Lal Masjid negotiations, a wide range of TPIs were used, from PML-Q President Chaudhry Shujaat Hussain, to Ministers such as Ijaz ul-Haq, Tariq Azeem, Aftab Sherpao, and Mohammad Ali Durrani, to prominent religious personalities such as Muhammad Rafi Usmani, Maulana Zahoor Ahmed Alvi, Maulana Dr Sher Ali Shah, Maulana Zahid Al-Rashdi, humanitarian NGO representatives such as Abdul Sattar Edhi and his wife Begum Bilqees Edhi, and to leaders of militant groups such as Maulana Fazlur Rehman Khalil and Maulana Sher Ali Hyderi. Applying the conventional crisis negotiation wisdom, there were several problems with the engagement of these particular negotiators.

First, they lacked training and lacked even basic instructions from the authorities on how to behave, what to say, what to do in certain situations, and what to avoid. Also the scope of their authority was never fully clarified and some of the TPIs, either accidentally or deliberately, clearly overstepped the reasonable boundaries of their role as simple mediators between the two sides. Secondly, the different TPIs were sometimes in significant opposition to each other, and frequently pursued their own agenda. For instance, when the operation began, the Wafaq-ul-Madaris in their 10 July joint press conference held the government responsible for the failure of talks and said that the Federal Ministers were issuing misleading statements in the process.

The ulema accused the government of creating a deadlock on the issue at the last moment and foiling all efforts to resolve it in a peaceful manner.[22] They ulema claimed that Musharraf changed the draft agreement completely, thereby making it unacceptable to Rashid Ghazi. Chaudhry Shujaat, on the other hand [at the time],[23] maintained the official position and said that the draft was only given a 'legal shape' and was 'not changed drastically'.[24] He also said that Ghazi had been informed of the need to keep him under house arrest for security reasons. The ulema disagreed, stating that all three main points of the agreement had been changed—i.e. it was agreed with Ghazi that he and his family along with personal belongings could be shifted to his village, which was changed to 'legal action will be taken after his house arrest in his village'.[25] The section dealing with the associates of Rashid Ghazi—who were to be detained for inquiry and those found innocent were to be sent home—was also totally changed. And, finally, the ulema alleged that the section about the fate of Lal Masjid and its madaris was also changed. The Wafaq-ul-Madaris delegation claimed that, according to the original deal, it was agreed that 'control of Jamia Hafsa and Lal Masjid would be given to Wafaq-ul-Madaris but the new draft said the government would take over both places'.[26]

This entire disagreement points to several issues. Firstly, it demonstrates the risks of using TPIs with questionable allegiance to the government, which can backfire once all the parties involved start distancing themselves from the failure of the negotiations and focus on laying blame on the government. That is not to say that the involvement of the Wafaq-ul-Madaris clerics did not have the potential to be useful—after all they were perfectly positioned to send the right message to the Lal Masjid militants by validating their cause and goals, while differing on the utility of using radical methods as a useful tool for achieving those goals. They also had the option of credibly praising Rashid Ghazi for his successes and simultaneously appealing to him not to waste everything that had been achieved by driving the crisis into a violent showdown. As Maulana Salimullah Khan remarked, 'The ulema had supported the demands of the management of Lal Masjid and Jamia Syeda Hafsa, which included the withdrawal of un-Islamic amendments in the Hudood Ordinance, enforcement of Sharia and reconstruction of demolished mosques, but the path adopted by the management of Lal Masjid and Jamia Hafsa was wrong.'[27]

Unfortunately, despite the tremendous potential of this message to be persuasive, it backfired simply because Abdul Rashid Ghazi perceived the ulema as 'traitors' who had only exploited the Lal Masjid movement to pressure the government into implementing their own agenda, and then threw the Ghazi brothers overboard. In addition, the fact that the Wafaq-ul-Madaris ulema were apparently pursuing their own agenda in the talks, such as gaining control of the Lal Masjid and its seminaries following the end of crisis, also clearly had a negative impact on Rashid Ghazi's perception of them, and negated any influence their otherwise persuasive message might have had.

MEDIA STRATEGY

Media coverage of barricade and hostage crises has been the topic of many heated debates, with one side arguing for the right to free speech and the other drawing a link between media coverage and the contagion of hostage taking tactics. In barricade situations, the sensational nature of the incident always succeeds in attracting wide media attention, which can have both positive and negative effects.

On the negative side, an irresponsible approach by the media can directly affect the outcome of the incident. In several instances, the media have provided the hostage takers with critical intelligence, putting the hostages in grave risk. During the 1977 hijacking of a Lufthansa aircraft to Mogadishu, for example, a radio report revealed that one of the pilots on the airplane was secretly passing information to the authorities during routine transmissions to the ground. The hijackers heard the broadcast and reacted by executing the German Captain. In another incident in Cleveland, Ohio, the local television station transmitted footage showing police snipers moving into position just as the incident was about to conclude. Having seen the report, the perpetrator thought he was about to be attacked by the tactical team, resulting in prolongation of the incident. Another possible damaging effect of media inquiry is the establishment of direct contact with the hostage takers. During the 1977 coordinated barricade hostage crisis sprawling over three buildings in Washington DC, a reporter asked one of the terrorists whether a deadline had been set. The police, who saw the lack of a deadline as one of few positive aspects of the situation, were outraged.[28]

In the Lal Masjid siege, the importance of media coverage cannot be overemphasized. Given the fact that the centre of gravity in the siege was public opinion about the [il]legitimacy of the government's use of force in resolving the crisis, a well-planned and managed media strategy was absolutely crucial. This was not lost on the country's leadership and, as early as February 2007, President Musharraf stated that the government would take armed action against the Lal Masjid students, if the media agreed not to show any pictures of dead bodies. In the end, however, despite having more than six months to prepare for all eventualities, the media strategy was poorly coordinated, and too heavily reliant on deception and unpersuasively clumsy propaganda. In the age of the digital media, cellphones, and 'citizen reporting', censorship and media manipulation are much less effective, even counterproductive, incident management tools than they were in the past.

Throughout the crisis, the government insisted on various claims designed to overcome the public opposition to an armed operation, as well as to decrease the negative political impact associated with the probable high level of civilian casualties. One such claim made by the government was that those fighting inside the mosque were 'known hardcore militants', including foreign fighters. The government had mentioned the name of one Abu Zar as a high profile terrorist hiding inside the mosque and this was released as latest news on various national television channels as well as on the print media. Abu Zar was dubbed as the assistant to Amjad Farooqi, who had allegedly masterminded the attacks on General Pervez Musharraf.[29] However, until today, there is no clear evidence in this regard, which has caused various negative public reactions, ranging from to conspiracy theory claims to the public questioning of the legality of the operation.[30] In the end, the government version received a strong hit after Ijaz ul-Haq conceded in a television interview that he was misled on this issue by the intelligence agencies of Pakistan and that, subsequently, it was conceded by the Interior Ministry itself that no foreign militants were found inside the mosque.[31]

The government's case was not helped by the poorly communicated and widely resented restrictions on media coverage in the aftermath of the crisis. Major General Ashraf Qazi, ex-ISI Chief, argued that the government did not want the nation and the world to see the shocking scenes of carnage inside the mosque, with security troops walking in with their boots.[32] But, while this explanation makes logical sense, many media observers who were banned from the scene accuse the government of planting large caches of sophisticated weapons, ammunition, gas masks, explosive devices, and other equipment after the raid, before allowing the media to come in. This scepticism of the government's claims was further augmented by that fact that, during the crisis, Rashid Ghazi had repeatedly pointed out the likelihood of this very scenario in the event that he and his comrades were killed in the operation.[33] He revealed, in one of his interviews to the media, that the government had asked him to have a 'quiet safe passage' but that he had instead insisted on a 'transparent safe passage' in which he wanted the media, the ministers and the ulema to see the actual situation inside the mosque with regard to the state and quantity of the weapons and the presence of foreign militants before he left. After the media were finally allowed to enter the scene post-operation, they were presented with a huge quantity of weapons and ammunition which were freshly oiled and some even looking brand new, sparking widespread suspicions about how these weapons survived the fire in the mosque in such good shape when everything else had been turned to charcoal.

Overall, the unsubstantiated claims such as the alleged presence of foreign militants, underground trenches, the supposed huge quantity of sophisticated weapons inside the mosque, suspicions about the actual number of casualties, in combination with the government's rejection of Rashid Ghazi's demand for a 'transparent safe passage', and the ban on the media entering the mosque in the aftermath of the operation—all these factors combined to raise serious suspicions in the eyes of the public about the true course of events. In an effort to rally public opinion behind the armed assault on the mosque, the government made a case based on the above allegations, many of which turned out not to be true. In the end, this effort backfired, as it resulted in loss of support for the operation, which would have been crucial in managing the strategic fallout of the crisis. Even more damagingly, it played directly into the anti-government propaganda of militant groups in Pakistan and abroad.

THE ABDUL AZIZ INTERVIEW

A further strategic error in media management of the crisis was the television interview with Maulana Abdul Aziz following his apprehension while fleeing the mosque in a burqa. Aziz's surrender provided a huge opportunity to use the media to convince his followers inside the stronghold that they could surrender into the hands of government troops safely. However, despite that fact that the call for surrender directly from Abdul Aziz to his followers was the *content* of the media interview, the *form* through which this was presented was counterproductive. When the Maulana appeared in front of the television camera with his face covered in a burqa, only to be asked by the media host to remove it, it sent exactly the opposite message—a message of public humiliation. Who was responsible for one of the most important blows to the negotiation process? This was one of the questions posed by the one-man Judicial

Commission formed by the Supreme Court in 2012 to the Managing Director of Pakistan Television (PTV), who replied that he had instructions from senior Information Ministry officials to air the interview of Abdul Aziz in a burqa in order to humiliate the cleric.[34] The section of Information Ministry in Pakistan assigned to deal with media reportedly usually comprises officers from the Secret Services.

To an extent, the government's instinct to try to delegitimize Abdul Aziz is understandable, given the all-important value of public opinion in this case. The fact that Abdul Aziz called himself a mujahid and constantly enticed his followers to martyr themselves for the cause, only to try to escape dressed as a woman, had left him open to ridicule, and the government naturally tried to exploit this fact to their advantage. On the other hand, the fact that he was so publicly humiliated only resulted in greater defiance by his brother, Abdul Rashid Ghazi, who constantly repeated that he would 'rather be martyred than publicly humiliated like [his] brother'. Thus, in the end the strategy designed to delegitimize the cleric essentially backfired, and only contributed to a violent outcome of the crisis. Had the authorities allowed Abdul Aziz to save face and to send a message to his followers to surrender for the sake of preventing bloodshed and destruction of the mosque and the madrasa on his own terms, the end result would have likely been more productive or, at the very least, less destructive.

HANDLING DEMANDS

Another significant flaw in the operation was the manner in which the authorities handled the militants' demands. There seems to have been an unfortunate and excessive focus on the substantive nature of the demands, emphasizing the political unacceptability of 'giving in' to people who tried to directly challenge the legitimacy of the government. The situation was then basically framed as a zero-sum game, leading many to mistakenly conclude that there was no possibility of a negotiated settlement.

However, the militants' primary demand had many expressive components to which the negotiations could have been diverted: the desire for equal application of justice; acknowledgement of the failure of the state to enforce its own laws; and so on. In order to explore these expressive components, the negotiators simply could have kept asking good questions in an effort to understand the specific origins of the demands, and to listen for legitimate grievances that could be acknowledged with little political risk. The answers to such questions often seem obvious but, in crisis negotiations, such questions need to be asked, as they provide opportunities to find 'negotiable nuance', to relieve or influence the emotional state of the perpetrator, and/or to gain useful information about what might eventually be acceptable substitutes for giving into initial demands. This in turn gives the negotiator a chance to engage the spokesperson on the other side on a more personal level, by asking about his or her personal experience with the alleged injustices and abuse—in this case, for instance, Rashid Ghazi's frustration with the failure of the government to investigate and punish the murder of his father Maulana Abdullah. This then provides an opportunity for the negotiator to express empathy. In ideological barricade/hostage situations, it is usually very difficult to move the discussion away from ideology toward a more personal level and this approach provides one of the best possible ways for achieving this. Forming genuine personal rapport between the negotiators on both sides is one of the critical principles upon which the crisis negotiation practice is based. Importantly, Ghazi seemed very keen to talk about both his ideological and personal grievances. As with any conflict, those who use violence are partly motivated by the frustration of not being listened to by those in authority. The simple act of listening and demonstrating interest in the grievance (even without the intention of doing something to address it) is significant—and has the effect of reducing the level of frustration and bitterness that leads people to violent action in the first place.

Another pragmatic reason why asking good questions is important is the fact that answers provide an insight into the subjects' underlying interests and the motivations behind their core demands. If these interests are understood, new options that could address the militants' legitimate concerns, but would stop short of giving in to any of their original demands, can be introduced. And, the deeper and broader the understanding of their interests, the broader will be the scope to generate potential options. Through active listening and by introduction of new options, the subjects' expectations may be shaped. Also, shaping the militants' perception of having achieved some success gives them a stake in the outcome, and can prevent them from taking radical steps that would waste everything that had already been accomplished. This is why it is important in the beginning to focus on the demands that are easier to fulfill, in order to achieve some early success. And, since with time the militants in the Red Mosque began to transform their initial demands from the rebuilding of all razed mosques built illegally on government land and the implementation of Sharia throughout the country, to more specific and more realistic options, such opportunities were clearly present. Effective crisis negotiation is not just about trying to manipulate or outsmart the hostage takers. *Understanding* them is the key to exercising the kind of influence that might move all parties toward a better outcome.

WILLINGNESS TO SURRENDER

And, finally, this leads us to some observations relating to Abdul Rashid Ghazi's statements throughout the crisis about the prospect of surrender, which was eventually the main remaining obstacle to the peaceful end of the crisis. First, Ghazi's statements on the issue were an important indicator of progress, especially given the declining unreasonableness of his demands over time. He first demanded that the troops leave the scene, then sought to surrender into the hands of clerics as opposed to the military. He later insisted on safe passage to his home village and, finally, demanded a surrender in the presence of the media.

Notwithstanding that Rashid Ghazi's statements about surrender always had conditions attached to them, instead of rejecting these out of hand, negotiators should have focused on reinforcing and rewarding the in-principle decision to surrender, and should have assisted the cleric in developing a face-saving mechanism to help him mentally justify the gradual softening of his hard-line position. Facilitating a face-saving mechanism in barricade situations is especially important, since the standoff begins with the subject perceiving his position to be one of absolute power, but usually ends with an inglorious capitulation. This is particularly the case in situations where the subject has locked himself in his original position by making public statements. Because of the complications that such public statements can bring later on, it is typically recommended, to the extent that it is possible, to limit spectators of the standoff, especially during the concluding stages.[35] Rashid Ghazi's situation in this case was rather different, however, as one of the conditions he held on to until the end was to have a very public surrender, in order to avoid mistreatment and to document the fallacies of some of the government claims about the situation inside.

In order to facilitate the hostage-taker's decision to surrender, it is extremely important to prevent the feeling of humiliation by providing reasoning support and by stressing the hostage-taker's 'admirable display of courage' in peacefully surrendering to the authorities. Ghazi's stated conditions for surrender could have been explored and discussed right from the beginning, without committing to any sort of agreement. This is where a negotiator's position, of someone who can explore anything but lacks the authority to make any final decisions, is especially useful. So, in the case of the Lal Masjid, the negotiator might have discussed Ghazi's conditions for surrender, asking clarifying questions about those conditions and the logic and justification behind them, on the pretext of being able to accurately brief the authorities and to perhaps try to convince them about the reasonability of some of those conditions. Following a period of silence, the negotiator might point out to the suspect in a non-threatening manner that the issue of pulling back the troops from the scene had not been agreed to by the decision makers, as the troops are needed to maintain order in the area and to make sure no outside influences disrupt the scene or destabilize the situation. This could have been presented as being in Ghazi's interest as well.

The issue of the coming out plan was something that could have been discussed in great detail, and the negotiator could have focused the conversation specifically on this important point, leveraging Ghazi's commitment to the idea of eventual surrender by discussing a detailed plan for how this surrender should occur, in order to satisfy Ghazi's need for safety and for saving face in the process. Such detailed discussions also typically help reinforce the subject's commitment to the idea, by the negotiator treating the issue as not a question of 'if' the surrender will take place, but rather a question of 'when and how' this will happen (at this point the negotiator would use sentences such as 'WHEN you decide to come out ...').

And finally, the issue of granting Ghazi safe passage to his home village could have been another issue the negotiator could have explored without commitment, in order to buy more time. The final decision on this issue would have been a political one, out of the hands of law enforcement or military decision makers, who in most cases would not be in favour of such a concession. Nevertheless, even a denial of safe passage could have been communicated to the subject in a non-threatening and non-definitive way, with the negotiator expressing the need for more time in order to attempt to convince the authorities, also asking the subject for some concession or confidence building steps in order to help the negotiator 'make the case with the bosses'. This strategy then would have likely bought more time for fatigue and regression to basic needs to play their role in altering Ghazi's position over time.

CONCLUSIONS

We will never know with certainty the answer to the question of whether Ghazi would have eventually surrendered peacefully, as the only person who could conclusively clarify this is dead. What is clear, however, is that based on crisis negotiations experience collected in this specialized field for over forty years, the Lal Masjid siege appeared to feature all of the standard characteristics of a 'negotiable incident'.[36] It was in essence a classic barricade crisis in which the subjects were located in a contained and stabilized location, they had presented demands and showed a willingness to negotiate, there were ongoing communications between the parties, and time was clearly on the negotiator's side, providing ample opportunity to develop trust and to facilitate the subjects' regression to more basic needs. This crisis setup was further backed by a credible threat of force by the security agencies and, despite the proclaimed desire for martyrdom, survival was clearly the preferred option for the subjects holed up inside the stronghold. Admittedly, the crisis also carried some signs of volatility, such as evidence of pre-planning, presence of multiple suspects with access to considerable firepower, the militants' proclaimed desire for martyrdom, and the fact that the threshold of lethal violence had already been broken at the beginning of the crisis. On the other hand, as the absence of hostages made it difficult for the militants to pressurize the authorities in any way, a pattern for surrender of suspects had already been firmly established, and Ghazi's demands became more and more focused on basic needs with passing time. Under such circumstances, is seems reasonable to assume that, with the proper application of crisis negotiation fundamentals, such as active listening, empathy, and rapport building, in combination with the deferment of authority strategy and a passage of time, the prospects for Ghazi's eventual acceptance of unconditional surrender were good. Unfortunately, many of the opportunities that existed were never followed up on, and despite the many positive indicators even basic and straightforward gains of the negotiation approach were never achieved.

At this point, we should also remind ourselves that the main key to the crisis was the fate of the Jamia Hafsa, the largest girls' madrasa in the world, which had been the pride and legacy of the cleric brothers' family. The entire crisis began with the CDA-initiated demolition of mosques and madaris built illegally on government land and Jamia Hafsa was also on the list. The sole purpose claimed by Maulana Abdul Rashid Ghazi's and Maulana Abdul Aziz's campaign was to avert this outcome. In the final negotiation, Rashid Ghazi also made the fate of the Jamia Hafsa part of the agreement he reached with the ulema, to ensure its survival in the aftermath of the crisis. And, finally, when we asked Maulana Abdul Aziz about his biggest regret in the whole Lal Masjid saga, he did not choose to highlight the demise of his mother, his son, or his brother in the siege, but rather the 'loss of Jamia Hafsa' as the greatest tragedy of all. In our view, it was the securing of the fate of Jamia Hafsa through a negotiated agreement that held the main key to the peaceful end of the crisis and Rashid Ghazi's surrender.

In the end, despite all the errors of the unsystematic and largely unqualified negotiation effort to end the crisis, it was a political decision at the very top that spelled doom for the negotiation process. General Musharraf changed the conditions of the agreement to terms that were not going to be immediately acceptable to Rashid Ghazi, and issued a 30-minute deadline for the negotiation team to get these terms accepted, which was simply impossible, as much more time would have been needed to rebuild the damaged trust and to persuade him to accept the significantly amended agreement. While Musharraf's desperate need to appear 'tough' in this case is at some level politically understandable, the end result in the form of the death of over 100 people and the subsequent mobilization of militant organizations to unite in an all-out conflict against the Pakistani state, makes it hard to portray this decision as anything but a disaster. Following the siege, an undated last will of Rashid Ghazi had surfaced:

'When this letter reaches you those inside Lal Masjid might have been martyred. Around 15,000 security forces and paramilitary troops with all their sophisticated weaponry would have crushed unarmed and innocent students. They would have conquered the Lal Masjid and Jamiah Hafsah. Lal Masjid is looking like Karbala at this time. The scattered bodies of martyrs, the cries of wounded students, the destroyed minarets of mosque and its four walls are crying for we have been punished only for demanding Islamic Shariah for which 600,000 people were martyred when Pakistan came into being.

In this entire scenario the unexpected arrest and interview of the Head Cleric of Lal Masjid and the founder of the student's movement Maulana Abdul Aziz dressed in a Burqa caused a lot of disappointment among the Islamists. The Media deliberately tried to paint a wrong picture of it and most of the people were deceived. Ordinary people thought that Maulana Abdul Aziz was trying to escape from the fear of death and he was leaving behind his sincere companions and students. Those people who don't have any abilities to analyse the situation should think that if Maulana Abdul Aziz was really trying to escape from death then why would his son, daughter, mother, wife, and myself (his brother), his sincerest companions and students not follow the same strategy?

I believe that instead of refuting allegations of our opponents it is more relevant to tell our broken hearted supporters that Maulana Abdul Aziz became a victim of enemy's conspiracy. Even though there is a certain mystery is drawn over his arrest, with the passage of time the truth will be revealed. We know how much Maulana Abdul Aziz loves martyrdom in the way of Allah and what an enthusiastic Mujahid he is in the caravan of jihad. The only mistake he made was trusting some people at a very critical time and he will have to suffer the consequences of this mistake. The truth is that Maulana Abdul Aziz was not afraid of death; neither was he fleeing from it. He had written his will, taken Ghusl and was waiting for martyrdom but then a ray of hope that the lives of the rest of the people could be saved created the resulting trouble. Rest assured, that in the near future the truth will be revealed, I must say that Maulana Abdul Aziz and his companions started the movement only for the pleasure of Allah and implementation of Shariah. The amendments in Hududullah [limits set by Allah], destruction of mosques, the spreading of vulgarity and nudity, self made explanations of Islamic creed, military assaults on the jihadists, handing over Muslims to Kuffar's prisons like sheep and goats, and the wide-spread secularism were not bearable for us and these are the reasons why we decided to launch the movement. I also want to clarify that none of the students inside Lal Masjid or Jamiah Hafsah were forced to stay with us. All the students remained with us at their own will. Their hearts have been changed by hearing the speeches of Maulana Abdul Aziz.

I also want to mention that we want the just system of Islam in our country. We are looking forward to seeing the implementation of Sharia laws in the courts of justice. We want the poor to have justice and bread. We want to end bribery, illegal methods, favoritism, injustice, and vulgarity. The solution to all these problems is the implementation of Islam and that is the only solution. This is the order of Allah and also a demand of the constitution of Pakistan. We have denied the comforts of this life and instead have chosen the difficulties of this path. We are fully aware of what we are doing and we have chosen the life of the hereafter over the life of this world.

The courage of students with me is sky high and I would not be wrong in saying that their courage is a source of motivation for me. I ask what crime have these students committed? Is the punishment of standing in the way of Allah with the intention of correction of some wrong people a reason to destroy innocent people with explosives? There are people who claim that we challenged the writ of the state but why did they deny the laws of Allah and challenged His writ? These people who have fired bullets on the bodies of students of Quran and Hadeeth are oppressors indeed.

On this occasion the media has also shown its biased behavior. But we leave this matter with Allah. In the end, as a part of my will, I would repeat my words to the Islamists, the members of our movement, the students, their relatives and the media that our movement was started with sincere purposes. We remain firm on our demands of implementation of Sharia. We are satisfied that we chose the way of sacrifice. Sacrificing life for the implementation of Islam is an honor to us. We are not disappointed in the mercy of Allah and we believe that our blood will become the message of revolution. This world sometimes labelled us as the agents of taghut and sometimes they labelled us as mad fanatics. But today the rain of bullets is proof that we are fighting in the way of Allah. Indeed the people of truth faced different trials. If our Amir Sayyidina Hussein R.A. was martyred in helplessness then we are proud to be part of the same caravan. InshaAllah, the Islamic revolution will come to this country.

The Gardens will perceive spring but we will not be there to see it'.

Ghazi Abdul Rashid[37]

NOTES

1. 'Inside the Red Mosque', *Al Jazeera Special Witness* (aired on 27 July 2007).
2. Abdul Sattar Khan, 'Hafsa girls revolt in the making', *The News* (8 July 2007).
3. Assessment of Lal Masjid operation by Pakistani think tank Brasstack.
4. Interviews with Lal Masjid Taliban, Islamabad, 2009.
5. Urdu *Daily Express* (Lahore) (4 July 2007).
6. Interview with FIA official, Islamabad, 27 September 2009.
7. Michael McMains and Wayman Mullins, *Crisis Negotiations: Managing Critical Incidents and Hostage Situations in Law Enforcementand Corrections*, 2nd edn. (Dayton, OH: Anderson Publishing, 2001), 50.

8. William Zartman, 'Negotiating Effectively With Terrorists', in Barry Rubin ed., *The Politics of Counterterrorism* (Washington, D.C.: The Johns Hopkins Foreign Policy Institute, 1990).

9. Arthur A. Slatkin, *Communications in Crisis and Hostage Negotiations* (Springfield, IL: Charles C. Thomas Publishers, 2005), 87.

10. Thomas Strentz, '13 indicators of Volatile Negotiations', *Law and Order* (September 1991).

11. Thomas Strentz, 'The Cyclic Crisis Negotiations Time Line', *Law and Order* (March 1995), 73–75.

12. McMains & Mullins, 108.

13. Syed Irfan Raza, 'Commander's killing raises spectre of all-out assault', *Dawn* (9 July 2007).

14. Interview with FIA official, Islamabad, 27 September 2009.

15. Zahid Hussain, *The Scorpion's Tail: The Relentless Rise of Islamic Militants in Pakistan and How it Threatens America* (New York: Free Press, 2012), 115.

16. Interview with Tariq Azeem, Islamabad, 16 January 2009.

17. Kamran Khan, 'Live Interview with Rasheed Ghazi by Kamran Khan', *Geo Television Channel* (Pakistan) (2007); <http://www.youtube.com/watch?v=2J6ijPP8uyg&feature=related> accessed 10 March 2010.

18. Syed Irfan Raza and Munawer Azeem, 'Breakthrough in sight', *Dawn* (10 July 2007).

19. Thomas Strentz, *Psychological Aspects of Crisis Negotiation* (New York: CRC Press, 2006), 34–36.

20. Slatkin, *Communications*, 11.

21. Dwayne Fuselier, 'What Every Negotiator Would Like his Chief to Know', *FBI Law Enforcement Bulletin* (March 1986); Strentz, *'Psychological Aspects'*.

22. Muhammad Anis, 'ulema blame govt for talks failure', *The News* (11 July 2007); <http://www.thenews.com.pk/top_story_detail.asp?Id=8946> accessed 13 March 2010.

23. When interviewed by the authors several years later, Shujaat backed the Imam's version.

24. Ahmed Hassan, 'Musharraf blamed for talks failure', *Dawn* (11 July 2007).

25. Ibid.

26. Anis, 'ulema'.

27. Ibid.

28. Grant Wardlaw, *Political Terrorism: Theory, Tactics, and Counter-Measures* (Cambridge: Cambridge University Press, 1982), 79.

29. Talat Hussain, 'Lal Masjid: Many unanswered questions [Urdu]', *Aaj Television Channel* (Pakistan) <http://www.youtube.com/watch?v=2kRwZfaEF8Y> accessed 4 May 2010; *'Lal Masjid ke askariat pasandon ke barey main sansanikhaiz inkishafat* [Sensational revelations about the Lal Masjid militants]', Aaj (Urdu) (9 July 2007).

30. Hussain, 'Lal Masjid: Many unanswered questions'.

31. 'Interview with Ijaz ul-Haq on Morning Show [Urdu]', *ATV* (Pakistan) <http://www.youtube.com/watch?v=oL6ECAQpbiA&feature=related> accessed 14 May 2010; *'Lal Masjid ke askariat pasandon'*.

32. Hamid Mir, 'Lal Masjid Incident on Capital Talk with Hamid Mir [Urdu]', *Geo Television Network* (Pakistan) <http://www.youtube.com/watch?v=zP62BoWQcCs> accessed 5 March 2010.

33. Abid Ullah Jan, 'Lal Masjid Massacre: What really happened?' *Haqeeqat.Org* (15 July 2007) <www.haqeeqat.org/.../lal-masjid-massacre-what-really-happened-abid-ullah-jan/> accessed 3 May 2010.

34. 'Lal Masjid probe: Commission seeks copy of former PM Shaukat Aziz's written orders', *The Express Tribune* (10 February 2013); <http://tribune.com.pk/story/505215/lal-masjid-probe-commission-seeks-copy-of-former-pm-shaukat-azizs-written-orders/> accessed 20 April 2013.

35. McMains & Mullins, 77.

36. McMains & Mullins.

37. The last will of Abdul Rashid Ghazi: 'The Last Will and Testament of Ghazi Abdul Rashid', *PureIslam* (10 July 2008); <http://www.pureislam.co.za/index.php?option=com_k2&view=item&id=895:the-last-will-and-testament-of-ghazi-abdul-rashid> accessed 1 December 12.

Epilogue

THE STRATEGIC FALLOUT OF OPERATION SUNRISE

> The nation should be ready for jihad because only jihad can bring a revolution ... The students of schools, colleges, and universities should spread in the nook and corner of Pakistan and work for bringing Islamic revolution.[1]

—Maulana Abdul Aziz

By the second week of July 2007, Pakistan Army's elite units had concluded the operation and civil authorities had buried the corpses in mass graves in H-8 graveyard of the capital Islamabad, while the general public was left confused and outraged over the conduct and outcome of 'Operation Sunrise'. According to serving military officers interviewed for this book, the public anger against army and other agents of the state showed up in unprecedented ways. For instance, in the immediate aftermath of the operation, a group of military personnel in uniform was on the way to the General Headquarter (GHQ) of Pakistan Army in Rawalpindi when their vehicle broke down and they decided to use a public van. Uncomfortable in the presence of military personnel, the passengers aboard reportedly stared at the newcomers and left the vehicle in protest. It was an expression of increasing hatred towards an institution that has been admired and respected for generations. Such incidents in the heart of Rawalpindi, the centre of Pakistan's breeding lands for martial races, reflected the communication breakdown between the state and the people and also signalled the radical transformation of the militant landscape in the country.

The storming of the Lal Masjid in Islamabad marked the start of an all out confrontation between the state and its erstwhile allies—the militant outfits and radical madaris. Although there was widespread understanding of the need for a security operation at Lal Masjid, its actual conduct was deemed as having been excessively heavy-handed. Mishandling of this particular operation and the high number of casualties[2] resulted in an unprecedented public dismay over President Musharraf's coercive approach. He failed to anticipate how the operation would touch people's sentiments in the religiously sensitive society of Pakistan. Musharraf believed that a show of strength followed by a powerful assault would force the new breed of anti-state Islamists into submission. However, the opposite turned out to be true, and the consequences would prove to be catastrophic, not only for Pakistan, but the security of the region as well.

Loss of popular support for the regime and the Pakistan Army came as the major strategic fallout of 'Operation Sunrise', the outcomes of which drew frequent comparisons with the 1984 'Operation Blue Star', in which the Indian Armed Forces assaulted Sikh militants in the Golden Temple in Amritsar, the holiest shrine in the Sikh religion.

The Indian government had been battling Sikh rebels who were struggling for regional autonomy in the Indian Punjab, the province with Sikh majority, and whose demands for more political, economic, and religious rights were met with strong resistance from the Indian state. A systematic clampdown was launched against Sikh dissidents alienating them from political mainstream, and consequently a radical leadership among the Sikhs of the Indian Punjab replaced the moderates and vowed to fight till death to gain an independent Khalistan, a separate country for the Sikhs. Sikh militant outfits launched attacks targeting the Indian state and the majority Hindu population. The Indian government believed that Sant Jarnail Singh Bhindranwale, the leader of Sikh separatists, was using the Golden Temple as his operational headquarters, and 'Operation Blue Star' was initiated on 31 May 1984 to clear the temple of militants in a seven-day long siege. The desecration of the holiest shrine for the Sikhs further radicalized the wider Sikh community and its global diaspora, and also led to the assassination of then Prime Minister Indira Gandhi, who was killed by her own Sikh bodyguards. Over 4,000 Sikh soldiers deserted their regiments, slew their officers, and tried to get to Amritsar. Several Sikh members of the Lok Sabha (Lower House) and the Punjab legislature resigned; a Sikh diplomat in Norway asked for political asylum; and several distinguished men of letters returned 'honours' that the government had bestowed on them. Additionally, many young Sikhs took up arms to fight for a separate Sikh state.[3]

The 1979 siege of Mecca[4] is another case in point to compare with the Lal Masjid assault. It started when an armed contingent of religious zealots numbering over 300, led by Juhaiman al-Utaibi, stormed and took over the Grand Mosque, one of the most sacred of Islam's holy places. According to Juhaiman, the Saudi royal family had become a 'spineless servant of American infidels', and by seizing the Grand Mosque and eventually taking control of the Saudi state itself, they sought a return to the glory days of what they saw as pure Islam.[5] The takeover was violent and it left 50,000 worshippers trapped inside the compound. The siege lasted for two weeks and caused hundreds of deaths and massive damage to the Grand Mosque. Though the Saudi government was finally able to free the Mosque with the help of French advisors and Pakistani commandos, the ideology and grievances championed by al-Utaibi prospered and later played a significant role in the birth of a movement that became known as al-Qaeda.

'Operation Sunrise' evoked negative reactions. The ideology of the Lal Masjid imams transformed the militant landscape of Pakistan and gave birth to a new generation of religious zealots. The tribal areas of Pakistan and Khyber Pakhtunkhwa (KPK) province, which were already suffering from the threat of radicalization due to the spill-over effects of the Afghan war, emerged as hotbed of a new and more devastating wave of militancy targeting officials, security forces, and anyone deemed as 'pro-government' by the militant outfits.

THE BIRTH OF THE NEO-TALIBAN IN PAKISTAN

As discussed in Chapter 1, the history of violent extremism in Pakistan dates back to 1979, when the idea of holy war was invoked under state patronage to obstruct the Soviet expansion into Afghanistan. However, it is worth noting that, during the ten years of the Afghan jihad, the threat remained localized as the mujahideen factions concentrated all their energies and resources on targeting Soviet interests within Afghanistan. But, following the Soviet withdrawal, various Afghan factions became involved in a prolonged and bloody civil war to capture power in Kabul. At the same time, a notable number of international fighters from the Middle East, South and South-East Asia relocated to other conflict zones stretching from Kashmir to the Horn of Africa. Militancy in Kashmir intensified as thousands of Pakistani fighters trained and armed for Afghanistan moved to fight against the Indian rule over Kashmir. Meanwhile, a sectarian conflict in Pakistan also escalated with the return of the 'Afghan-Trained Boys'[6] who were vital in forming sectarian terrorist outfits such as Lashkar-e-Jhangvi.

As stated above, the jihadi culture in Pakistan had been cultivated for decades prior to the Lal Masjid incident, but the difference was that, throughout this time, the Pakistani authorities exercised effective control over the leadership and cadres of these groups. 'Operation Sunrise' came as an important turning point in the history of violent extremism in Pakistan, as in its bloody aftermath the state's proxies turned against their former sponsors, and the 'heretic, pro-American and puppet Pakistani state'[7] replaced the 'occupying' forces in Afghanistan as their top target. The militant groups in Pakistan gave up their pro-Pakistan nationalist tendencies in favour of al-Qaeda's agenda of global jihad, with initial focus on establishing a Caliphate in Pakistan. They intensified attacks against the state institutions and resorted to more lethal tactics. Suicide attacks, a rare occurrence in the time period until July 2007, emerged as the preferred *modus operandi* of a new generation of religiously motivated fighters that can be aptly described as the neo-Taliban of Pakistan.

One of the effects of the siege of Lal Masjid was the spillover of violent activities in the tribal areas of Pakistan into the urban areas as well. The first ever missile attack on an army base in Khyber Pakhtunkhwa was reported in Landi Kotal on 5 July 2007, during the time of the siege of Lal Masjid. Four missiles were fired, two of which landed inside the base but caused no damage. As mentioned in Chapter 3, another attack that took place during the operation was an apparent assassination attempt against Musharraf, when his aircraft came under fire on 6 July in an attack carried out by militants tied to Lal Masjid. 'Operation Sunrise' also inspired the anti-state militia to abandon their basic strategy of selective violence against official targets, in favour of indiscriminate terrorist attacks for the sake of vengeance. Until this point, Islamist militants from the tribal areas, commonly known as the 'local Taliban', had reserved their violent activities for the security forces. Following the Lal Masjid stand-off, terrorist attacks were extended to the urban areas of Pakistan, targeting political personalities, rival sects, funerals, mosques, and other public places frequented by the Armed Forces, government officials, and anti-Taliban clerics. The terrorist groups operating in the country expanded their already broad definition of 'legitimate targets' for terror strikes to include anyone who was not actively continuing the unaccomplished mission of Lal Masjid, and actively taking part in the jihad to overthrow the 'un-Islamic regime of Musharraf'. The neo-Taliban also targeted those top religious clerics of Pakistan who did not endorse their violent activities. The assassinations of Maulana Hasan Jan and Maulana Sarfaraz Naeemi, the two top leaders of the Deobandi and Barelvi schools of thought, respectively, at the hands of Tehrik-e-Taliban Pakistan (TTP) came as a stark reminder of Islamist militants' expanding pool of potential targets.

Pakistan's Inter-Services Intelligence (ISI), the driving force behind nurturing the culture of militant jihad in Pakistan during the 1980s, lost the confidence of its erstwhile proxies. On 4 September 2007, a suicide bomber struck a 70-passenger bus carrying ISI officials in the cantonment area of Rawalpindi, in the first-ever suicide attack targeting this powerful agency. The attack killed 24, the biggest single loss suffered by the ISI since the creation of Pakistan. The Rawalpindi attack demonstrated that militants would not hesitate to target the nerve centre of the Pakistani military establishment, including its former sponsors.

Beyond the borders of Pakistan, the siege of Lal Masjid also became a rallying cry for global militants, including the top leadership of al-Qaeda, which repeatedly called for punishing Musharraf and his allies for killing Abdul Rashid Ghazi. In the immediate aftermath of the military operation, al-Qaeda's then second-in-command Ayman al-Zawahiri urged Pakistanis to avenge the storming of Lal Masjid and the sacrifice of the 'martyrs' for the cause of Islam.[8] Abu Yahya al-Libbi, another senior al-Qaeda leader, also joined al-Zawahiri in urging Pakistanis to revolt against President General Pervez Musharraf for killing Rashid Ghazi.[9] In a 21-minute video, with pictures of President Musharraf and slain Abdul Rashid Ghazi in the background, al-Libbi urged: 'Ghazi, the son of the martyr, who spoke of truth at the time of submission. In the midst of the siege and in the midst of enemies' heightening strikes, he said, 'I prefer death to give up my cause or to submit to surrender ... O people of jihad in Pakistan ... hurry up and get rid of this corrupt and tyrannical apostate and his secular infidel rule. Destroy the fortifications of his weak army and the nests of his filthy intelligence agency and the core of his infidel rule.'[10] Finally, in September 2007 Osama bin Laden also issued a statement, in which he vowed: 'We in al-Qaeda call on God to witness that we will retaliate for the blood of Ghazi and those with him against Musharraf and those who help him.'[11]

This was not for the first time in the history of al-Qaeda that the group publicly challenged the Pakistani government. In September 2003, al-Qaeda's Ayman al-Zawahiri had called upon the Pakistani Army to overthrow President Musharraf and, a few months later, successive assassination attempts were made against him, with junior officers of the armed forces reportedly involved in both attempts. In April 2006, Ayman al-Zawahiri repeated his appeal once again. But, while even these earlier calls had a significant mobilizing effect, in this case the timing of al-Qaeda's post-Lal Masjid propaganda ensured even greater impact, as the statements were issued at a time when Osama bin Laden enjoyed greater popularity in Pakistan than Pervez Musharraf. According to a September 2007 poll conducted by Terror Free Tomorrow, Musharraf's approval rating was only 38 per cent, 8 per cent less than the number of respondents who expressed their support for bin Laden (46 per cent). In the Islamist-ruled Khyber Pakhtunkhwa, bin Laden's ratings then soared to a staggering 70 per cent.[12] Given these numbers, it is not completely surprising that calls for Pakistanis to rise up against their US-allied military leader struck a chord among an angry, extremist segment of the society.

Al-Qaeda's local allies in Pakistan were quick to respond to the repeated calls to arms. Maulana Sufi Muhammed, the leader of pro-Taliban extremist organization Tehrik-e-Nifaz-e-Shariat-e-Muhammadi (TNSM), called for jihad against the Musharraf government. Sufi's son-in-law Maulana Fazlullah, who was leading TNSM during his imprisonment, had threatened the government with breaking the peace deal that was in place at the time, if it did not cease military action against Lal Masjid. As both sides headed towards confrontation, the 2006 truce between the government and the local tribal leaders and militants in the Malakand Agency of KP and FATA indeed came to an end. The wave of revenge attacks in different parts of Pakistan during the eight days of the Lal Masjid siege (from 3 to 11 July 2007) killed more than 100 people, mostly among the security forces. The involvement of Lashkar-e-Jhangvi (LeJ), the militant wing of Sipah-e-Sahaba (SSP), a Sunni sectarian outfit that fully supported the Lal Masjid imams, compounded the situation as the group had extensive presence and experience in urban warfare in Pakistan's non-tribal areas. LeJ cadres were instrumental in recruiting and training aspiring fighters from the mainland of Pakistan.

The combination of tribal and urban militants increased the number and sophistication of attacks. Prior to the Lal Masjid siege, 28 suicide attacks had been recorded since the emergence of *the idea of popular militancy in the name of religion* in Pakistan in 1979. Between 11 July and 31 August 2007 alone, 18 suicide bombings occurred in different parts of Pakistan, four of them right in the political and military capitals of Rawalpindi and Islamabad. In the year 2007, Pakistan became the world's third worst-hit country by suicide attacks after Iraq and Afghanistan.[13] Apart from ambushes, road-side bomb blasts, and targeted killings of political leaders, nearly 60 suicide attacks were reported throughout the year 2007, which killed at least 770 people and injured 1574 others.[14] Out of these, 37 suicide attacks specifically targeted security forces and installations. This rise was in stark contrast to the 'mere' seven suicide bombings, which were recorded in Pakistan in 2006. A dramatic increase was also witnessed in the number of suicide attacks in the Punjab in July–August 2007.[15] A senior Punjabi Taliban leader also signalled the shifting patterns of attacks from tribal areas to the mainland, stating that 'the mujahideen had planned to fight this war against the US in Washington, New York and Kabul. But Pakistani generals acting as American lackeys brought it to Islamabad for the sake of dollars'.[16] In the first quarter of 2008, Pakistan even surpassed war-torn Iraq and insurgency-hit Afghanistan in terms of the number of suicide bombings, with at least 18 such attacks rocking the country between 1 January and 1 March.[17] Initially, suicide attacks against the security forces were largely viewed as 'justified' by a large segment of the Pakistani society, because the army and other law enforcement agencies were perceived by the masses as 'mercenaries' fighting the unpopular US war on Pakistani soil. The spate of attacks also greatly demoralized the soldiers, eroded the traditional respect for the Army, and bolstered the prestige of the militants.

Threats to the state came not only from the militants— different religious-political groups and parties also announced their intention to have a 'final round' with the government following the Lal Masjid debacle. *Wafaq-ul-Madaris Al-Arabia*, a collective platform of 8199 registered Deobandi madaris in Pakistan called for a countrywide movement against the Musharraf government. Qazi Hussain Ahmad, the central leader of Muttahida Majlis-e-Amal (MMA), an alliance of religious parties, and the head of Jamaat-e-Islami Pakistan, announced his resignation from the National Assembly in protest against the storming of the mosque. Unfortunately for Pakistan, the mainstream political parties remained fragmented and without much influence on domestic public opinion. This vacuum left by the moderates gave a chance to the radical groupings to expand their public standing at the expense of moderate voices.

The Islamist forces manipulated the issues to gain public sympathy and support against the authoritarian rule of General Pervez Musharraf, who was accused of disregarding political solutions in favour of excessive force to resolve the Lal Masjid issue. The involvement of the army's elite units and the dubious roles played by the intelligence agencies and political forces in the 'Lal Masjid massacre' were projected by the jihadi groups as demonstrating the state's ruthlessness against the 'Islamic forces to appease American Crusaders and Israeli Zionists'.[18] Consequently, popular support tilted in favour of anti-government hardline Islamist forces. A poll conducted by World Public Opinion Poll in the aftermath of the Lal Masjid siege revealed that 64 per cent of the participants opposed the government's use of force to regain control of Lal Masjid.[19] The same survey also showed that 60 per cent of Pakistanis believed in the stated goal of the Lal Masjid clerics that 'Sharia should play a larger role in Pakistani law'. The poll found only 44 per cent support for the Pakistan Army pursuing al-Qaeda, while only 48 per cent of respondents answered that they support the Pakistan's Army actions against 'Taliban insurgents who have crossed over from

Afghanistan'.[20] Given the importance of popular support in the effort to counter violent extremism, the decision to initiate a country-wide campaign against extremists, at a time when the enemy enjoyed greater popular sympathy and support than the government, was inherently fraught with challenges.

IMPACT ON THE ARMED FORCES

The Red Mosque siege had deep socio-political impacts and caused further polarization in a society already confused over the discourse on jihad. The Armed Forces of Pakistan and law enforcement agencies were no exception. Pro-jihadi elements within these powerful institutions either deserted or continued to operate as 'sleeper cells' of anti-state militant organizations. The insiders' involvement appeared to be a prominent feature in the earlier wave of revenge attacks against the state's institutions. A case in point is the suicide attack on 13 September 2007 against the SSG elite commando unit of Pakistan's Army that took part in the Lal Masjid siege, which killed 22 military commandos and injured 35 more.[21] According to investigators, the suicide bomber who carried out the attack, was an insider who had lost his sister during 'Operation Sunrise'.[22] The targeted base also housed the Special Operations Task Force that rose to prominence after the 9/11 attacks in the United States, and participated in numerous operations against Islamist militants. Similarly, the November 2007 suicide attack on a Pakistan Air Force bus in Sargodha that killed eight people was allegedly masterminded by Ahsanul-Haq, a retired army major.[23] Authorities later arrested Haq and five of his associates from Sargodha, based on information provided by a former army official. Haq ran a militant training camp in Afghanistan during the Taliban rule and was said to have been close to the Afghan guerrilla commander Younis Khalis, who fought against the Soviet forces in the 1980s and later established links with the Taliban.[24]

Beyond becoming direct targets of terrorist attacks, the government personnel who took part in the siege also came under social pressure for 'violating the sanctity of the mosque'. A number of Rangers officials were obliged to publicly apologize and express regret over taking part in the operation and 'killing innocents'.[25] Prevalent confusion in the Armed Forces, resulting partly from the state's inability to communicate its decision to sever links from former allies, had a dramatic impact on the morale of the Pakistani troops fighting the Taliban on the Afghan-Pakistan border. Incidents of desertion in the armed forces became commonplace. Questions were raised about the willingness of the army's and law enforcement agencies' personnel to fight against this new generation of militants. Hundreds of Pakistani soldiers who were deployed in the Waziristan tribal region refused to fight against the militants in the area, saying they do not want to fight against their own people.[26]

In August 2007, not even a month after 'Operation Sunrise', militants led by Baitullah Mehsud in South Waziristan captured 300 military and paramilitary personnel[27] who had gone into the city of Wana and offered no resistance when challenged by Mehsud's men. Those mediating the release of the captured soldiers stated the belief that the latter had actually surrendered voluntarily, as they were not ready to fight against their fellow Muslim brothers.[28] Likewise, one of the 26 surrendered soldiers from the paramilitary Frontier Corps, who were released by the militants on 20 September 2007, was quoted as saying that he did not desert the force because he feared death, but actually did so 'because he was not sure whether the ongoing fighting in Waziristan was Islamic or not'. The man, who refused to serve in the tribal areas, claimed that the same query was haunting many other soldiers and the confusion was stopping them from putting up a tough fight against Islamist militants in the region.[29]

LAL MASJID AND INTERNAL SPLITS WITHIN THE JIHADI MOVEMENT

In the aftermath of the Lal Masjid siege, another very interesting development took place, as prominent jihadi leaders, such as Maulana Masood Azhar of Jaish-e-Muhammad (JeM), Hafiz Saeed of Lashkar-e-Taiba (LeT), and Fazlur Rehman Khalil of Harkat-ul-Mujahideen (HuM) had lost appeal to their cadres, who blamed the jihadi clerics for wrongly siding with the government in the Lal Masjid episode. Consequently, JeM, LeT, and HuM, which had been traditionally known as well-organized and controlled proxies of the state, suffered substantial fractionalization as numbers of foot soldiers deserted and formed their own cells, or relocated to the Federally Administered Tribal Areas (FATA) and its adjacent regions to join the Pakistani Taliban. In August 2007, a Pakistani intelligence source confirmed that the dissidents of three militant groups— JeM, LeJ, and SSP—had joined anti-Pakistan groups, including al-Qaeda, with the goal of engaging in attacks targeting the Pakistan Army, government personalities, and installations.[30] What held together these scattered elements, led by Abu Ali Tunisi, an al-Qaeda operative hailing from Tunisia, was a desire for vengeance against Pakistan Army and its intelligence services. They felt betrayed and called themselves '*Muntaqim*' (an Urdu word that translates as 'revenge seekers').[31] They denounced their past links with ISI-sponsored jihadi groups and threatened their former commanders and fellow ideologues, whom they called 'Army officers without the uniforms'.[32] In 2008, the rivalry between the two camps (pro- and anti-Pakistan Army groups) became so strong that Hafiz Saeed, the head of LeT and one of the top figures of the pro-Army militant camp, allegedly had to buy a bullet and bomb proof vehicle to prevent any backlash from the neo-jihadis.[33]

THE CASE OF ASMATULLAH MUAVIYA

The cases of Asmatullah Muaviya and Ilyas Kashmiri in particular present an interesting account of the massive disintegration of mainland militant outfits due to the state's action against Lal Masjid. Asmatullah Muaviya was once a key commander of JeM and the Pakistani establishment's blue-eyed boy for actions in the Indian-held Kashmir. He was born in Kabirwala, a town in district Khanewal, and never attended any religious seminary. Upon joining JeM, Muaviya sought jihadi training in camps located in Azad Kashmir, after which he took an active part in the violent struggle in Kashmir. He was not involved in militancy in Pakistan. However, Pakistan's decision to side with the international community irked many militant outfits, and Asmatullah Muaviya was also among those who considered the international campaign in Afghanistan to be a part of the West's 'crusades', in which Pakistan played a role only to appease her Western masters.[34] In a video statement, Muaviya accused Pakistan Army generals of forcing 'sons of the soil' to take up arms against their own country.[35]

Pakistan's military operation against the brothers aggravated his anger and, within JeM, Muaviya argued strongly in favour of a head-on collision with the state during the Lal Masjid crisis. The top leadership of the group, however, turned down his proposals and instead blamed Maulana Abdul Aziz for the outcome of the crisis.[36] Muaviya and many other members of JeM willing to rebel against their former masters over the Lal Masjid issue were allegedly told by Maulana Masood Azhar, head of the JeM, mockingly: 'You may quit JeM and fulfil your desire to confront the government, we are not keen to retain your allegiance.'[37] Muaviya claimed that he held a final meeting with Maulana Masood Azhar but 'Maulana crossed all moral limits and accused Maulana Abdul Aziz of harbouring ambitions to become the leader of Muslims without any credentials to assume such a status.'[38]

As both Ghazi brothers and Muaviya hailed from South Punjab, Muaviya's allegiance to the Lal Masjid clerics was intensified by their similar regional, and also linguistic (Seraiki) background. Disappointed with JeM's unwillingness to confront the government, Muaviya opted to split away, along with dozens of his followers, and to turn their guns against the 'pro-American' government and anyone supporting it. He left Jaish-e-Muhammad and went to South Waziristan where he became one of the founding members of the Punjabi Taliban. Muaviya also formed 'Ibna-e-Hafsa' (The Sons of Hafsa), a specialized cell consisting of former male students of Jamia Faridia, to avenge the killing of the Lal Masjid imams and students. In the tribal areas, Asmatullah Muaviya was tasked with recruitment and training of young men from Punjab and Azad Jammu and Kashmir for suicide attacks across the country.[39] During the military operation in South Waziristan in June 2009, he was in charge of mining the region on the orders of Baitullah Mehsud, in order to complicate any potential military offensives in South Waziristan.[40] 'Our jihad will continue until the US-led forces depart from Afghanistan and the Pakistani authorities enforce Sharia in our country!'[41] Muaviya stated in a message after the killing of Osama bin Laden in May 2011.

Muaviya's rebellion against the state and jihadi clerics infuriated the JeM commanders. A four-member committee was reportedly formed, consisting of top commanders Maulana Masood Azhar, Mufti Khalid, Mufti Abdul Rauf, and Maulana Asif Qasmi, to examine the matter. In one of the meetings, Mufti Khalid allegedly proposed the hunting down and killing of all the rebellious JeM ex-members, including Muaviya. Masood Azhar approved the plan and a country-wide manhunt was launched by the organization in which 18 rebels were tracked down, abducted, and taken to the group's Balakot training centre, where they were badly tortured. A number of JeM's religious scholars, including Maulana Karim Bakhsh, Qari Mansoor Shah, and Mufti Hammad Abbasi, who opposed their leaders' tacit approval of the Lal Masjid operation, were also apprehended and publically humiliated.[42] Such was the level of disintegration and internal frictions within the JeM caused by 'Operation Sunrise'.

THE CASE OF ILYAS KASHMIRI

Another important case demonstrating the impact of the Lal Masjid siege is the case of the notorious Ilyas Kashmiri,[43] a dangerous terrorist whose name was among those discussed in the context of potential successors to Osama bin Laden after the latter's death in May 2011. According to some sources, Kashmiri was a former SSG (Special Services Group) commando of the Pakistan Army,[44] but former SSG commandos, and journalists who had interviewed Kashmiri, passionately refute this claim.[45]

Trained by the Pakistani intelligence agencies to fight in Afghanistan against the Soviets and subsequently in Kashmir against India, Kashmiri was considered a 'strategic asset' for decades by Pakistan's security establishment until he reportedly 'turned rogue'.[46] Kashmiri passed the first year of a mass communication degree at Allama Iqbal Open University, Islamabad, but could not continue his education due to his heavy involvement in jihadi activities. In the Afghan jihad, in which he lost an eye fighting against the Soviets, he was known as an expert on mines, which were supplied to the Afghan mujahideen by the US.[47] During that period, Ilyas Kashmiri was based in the Miranshah area of North Waziristan, where he worked as an instructor at a training camp. Following the Soviet withdrawal from Afghanistan, Kashmiri shifted his focus to Indian-held Kashmir and also carried out attacks in the heartland of India.

In 1994, Kashmiri launched the 'al-Hadid' operation in New Delhi, to achieve the release of some of his comrades from Indian prisons. His group of 25 people also included Sheikh Omar Saeed, the abductor of US reporter Daniel Pearl in Karachi in 2002. In order to achieve its aims, the group kidnapped several foreigners, including American, Israeli, and British tourists, and took them to Ghaziabad near Delhi, where they demanded the release of their colleagues in exchange for the lives of the hostages. The Indian security forces were able to identify the kidnappers' stronghold and launched a rescue operation, from which Kashmiri escaped unhurt[48] but Sheikh Omar was injured and arrested, only to be later freed in another hostages-for-prisoners swap initiated by the infamous hijacking of Indian Airlines Flight 814.

On 25 February 2000, the Indian Army crossed the Line of Control (LoC) that separates the Indian and Pakistani sides of the disputed region, and killed 14 civilians in the Lonjot village in Pakistan-administered Kashmir. In this incident, the Indian commandos allegedly abducted several girls and took them back to the other side of the LoC, beheading them, and throwing their severed heads at Pakistani soldiers on the other side of the LoC. The very next day, Kashmiri conducted a guerrilla operation against the Indian Army in Nakyal sector after crossing the LoC with 25 fighters of the 313 Brigade. They kidnapped an Indian Army officer who was later beheaded and his head was paraded in the bazaars of Kotli in the Pakistan-controlled territory. The most significant operation conducted by Kashmiri then took place in the Aknor cantonment in Indian-administered Kashmir against the Indian Armed Forces, following the massacre of Muslims in the Indian city of Gujarat in 2002.[49]

Kashmiri's outfit was banned by Musharraf after 9/11 and Kashmiri himself was arrested after an attack on the life of Pervez Musharraf in December 2003. He was reportedly tortured during interrogation.[50] The United Jihad Council led by Syed Salahuddin, the central leader of Kashmir's largest militant outfit Hizb-ul-Mujahideen, strongly protested against the arrest of Kashmiri. Following the pressure of Kashmiri militants, he was released in February 2004. Allegedly, a shattered man after his release, Kashmiri disassociated himself from the militants, remaining silent for over three years until the Lal Masjid operation prompted him to again become actively involved in the fight against the state.[51] He moved to North Waziristan—an area that was full of his friends and sympathizers, where he had spent many years as a jihad instructor.[52] He reorganized his 313 Brigade and joined hands with the Tehrik-e-Taliban Pakistan (TTP). Most of his fighters were recruited from the Punjab, Sindh, and Azad Kashmir, and, according to some reports, Kashmiri was also able to recruit a number of former Pakistan Army officers to join his struggle. The strength of the 313 Brigade in North Waziristan eventually reached more than 3,000.[53] In the days to follow, Kashmiri organized many terrorist attacks in different areas of Pakistan, including the assassination of Major General (R) Faisal Alvi, an SSG Commander who had led the first-ever army operation in Waziristan in 2004. Media reports suggest that Kashmiri had planned attacks on Alvi on the demand of the Taliban in North Waziristan.[54]

In May 2009, Ilyas Kashmiri was accused of colluding with al-Qaeda in the plot to assassinate Army Chief General Ashfaq Parvez Kayani, largely because of the latter's lead role in the ongoing war against terrorism.[55] An al-Qaeda cell in Pakistan reportedly tracked General Kayani's daily visits to the gym, with the plan of targeting him through a suicide bomber as soon as he stepped out of his car. However, the plan was abandoned after being leaked to the intelligence agencies.[56] Ilyas Kashmiri continued to unleash attacks against state institutions across Pakistan. His deadliest strike was on the Pakistan naval base in Karachi in May 2011, in which six militants held off dozens of security personnel, including commandos, for 16 hours and destroyed two P3C Orion aircraft, inflicting financial damage of more than 75 million dollars in a single attack.[57] Ilyas Kashmiri was reportedly killed in a US drone strike in South Waziristan on 3 May 2011, although there are still some doubts about his demise.

TEHRIK-E-TALIBAN PAKISTAN (TTP)

Apart from motivating large numbers of fighters to desert their organizations and turn against the state, the schisms that occurred in the aftermath of the Red Mosque siege gave birth to more violent and sophisticated terrorist organizations. Manipulating widespread popular support and anti-establishment resentments within the state institutions and masses at large, different factions of the Pakistani Taliban organized their rank and file to launch a sustained movement for the violent enforcement of their version of Sharia in Pakistan. A variety of Pakistani Taliban groups, which emerged in the spillover effect of the international intervention in Afghanistan and had hitherto operated independently, had in December 2007 amalgamated under the umbrella of Tehrik-e-Taliban Pakistan (TTP) on the back of the Lal Masjid siege. With the enforcement of Sharia as its core objective, the organization vowed to continue the unfinished agenda of the Lal Masjid.[58] At the time of its formation, pervasive anti-government sentiments over the siege provided the TTP with a pool of potential recruits in the tribal and settled areas of Pakistan. At one point in early 2008, the strength of TTP had reportedly surpassed 10,000 fighters.[59] The ideology of TTP was largely influenced by the Lal

Masjid and differed from that of the pre-9/11 class of jihadi groups in the country. Whereas groups such as LeT, JeM, and HuM had projected a pro-Pakistan character and sought to maintain cordial relations with Pakistan Army and the intelligence services, the post-'Operation Sunrise' breed of militants left no stone unturned to demonize Pakistani state institutions, political elite, religious clergy, and the media as anti-Islamic and pro-infidel forces. The leaders of LeT, JeM, and HuM had traditionally shown respect towards the symbols of Pakistani nationalism; this was not the case with groups like Tehrik-e-Taliban Pakistan, whose ideology challenged the traditional narratives upheld by the pro-ISI groups. For instance, Hafiz Muhammad Saeed, the founder of LeT, and Maulana Masood Azhar, the head of JeM, would always show great respect for the Quaid-e-Azam ('the Great Leader'—the title of Muhammad Ali Jinnah, the founder of Pakistan). On the contrary, Abu Zar, the chief ideologue of the TTP, did not hesitate to call the Quaid-e-Azam the 'Kafir-e-Azam' (The Great Infidel) for his Shia background and for dividing the Muslims of the subcontinent.[60]

The inception of the TTP broadened the rift between jihadi factions with purely anti-Indian and anti-American tendencies, and those aligned with Lal Masjid's mission to enforce Sharia in Pakistan as its main aim. While the pro-ISI groups termed the TTP and its allies as Indian/Israeli agents working on an anti-Pakistan agenda, LeT, JeM, HuJI, and al-Badar were in turn demonized by the other camp as front organizations of Pakistan Army, misguiding the Muslims in the name of jihad. Another distinct feature of the jihadi groups inspired by the Lal Masjid ideology was their global agenda, as they categorically condemned the idea of nation-states and advocated a global struggle for the establishment of a global Caliphate.[61]

The core of this militant force consisted of revenge-seeking fighters from mainland Pakistan, who once operated in Kashmir as state proxies and had previously regarded the military and its affiliated institutions as the defenders of Islam. Our interview with a disgruntled former Afghan Mujahid, who opted to fight against the state institutions after 'Operation Sunrise', provides insight into the strategic fallout of the operation. In reply to the question of why the Pakistan Army was now a target of the jihadi forces, the TTP-affiliated fighter simply asserted that the army had lost its 'Islamic identity' since the operation against Lal Masjid.[62] The army was alleged to have killed 'hundreds of children', many of whom came from earthquake the affected areas, and the Pakistani Taliban thus saw themselves as agents of revenge. Himself a member of the Punjabi Taliban, an allied group of the TTP, the interviewee argued that the army disregarded the potential for a peaceful solution between the Ghazi brothers and the Deobandi ulema, widening the rift between the ulema and the army.[63] He further disclosed that the footage of the Lal Masjid operation and of other military operations in FATA had been compiled into a series of recruitment videos, and young boys were now being instructed in the main training centre in Kari Kot, South Waziristan, on how the Pakistan Army and the government had become mere puppets controlled by the American government.[64] This again shows the facilitating effect that the government's approach to the Lal Masjid crisis had on the recruitment process of militant groups in Pakistan.

This influx of battle-hardened militants, largely from the Punjab, Sindh, and Azad Kashmir, strengthened the TTP, and by displaying the characteristics of an insurgent fighting force, this highly motivated, well-funded and well-fortified group began to operate against the Pakistani military. The aforementioned August 2007 abduction of more than 300 Pakistani troops at the hands of Baitullah Mehsud came as a particularly mortifying incident. The tribal belt of Pakistan became a safe haven for al-Qaeda's fugitives and served as a launching pad for attacks against the US and other foreign forces stationed in Afghanistan.

Within a few months of its inception, the TTP was able to consolidate its foothold in South Waziristan and its adjacent regions. The tribal areas of FATA steadily fell to the Taliban groups and the 'Waziristan Shura' came into existence. Army operations to regain control of the lost terrirories proved to be ineffective due to the lack of military success and the TTP's rejection of any offers of a cease-fire. Having captured FATA, the TTP began to extend its influence to the adjacent settled areas of KP. The Swat district of Malakand was the first to fall. Although Tehrik-e-Nifaz-e-Shariat-e-Muhammadi (TNSM) had spearheaded the movement to enforce Sharia in Swat since 1992,[65] the Red Mosque operation proved to be the trigger for an intensification of this campaign, as a more ruthless and uncompromising breed of militants assumed leadership, sidelining aging Sufi Muhammed, the founder of TNSM.

The majority of the students involved in the Lal Masjid stand-off belonged to the Malakand Agency and its adjacent areas,[66] making a strong reaction from these areas to 'Operation Sunrise' practically inevitable. Fazlullah, the self-proclaimed leader of TNSM, vowed to avenge the killing of the 'innocent students and teachers' in Lal Masjid, and established links with the Taliban factions of FATA to fight against their common enemy—the state and the security forces of Pakistan. In December 2007, TTP was formed to unite all the scattered Taliban groups and the TNSM leaders were given key designations in the newly formed organization. Fazlullah was appointed as the General Secretary and Maulvi Faqir Muhammed (TNSM's representative in Bajaur) was selected as the Deputy of TTP. By merging the TNSM with the TTP, Fazlullah was obliged to allow the Taliban of Waziristan, Bajaur, and other agencies to establish footholds in the Malakand Agency. The increasing strength of the Pakistani Taliban in Swat also attracted hundreds of militants from mainland Pakistan to settle their scores with the security forces. Locals claimed that, soon after July 2007, huge explosions started to rock the area at night but no one could identify where exactly these explosions were taking place. Later it was revealed that those were test explosions set off by the Punjabi militants in the process of training their counterparts from Swat in the manufacture and use of improvised explosive devices.[67] Within a few months, the Pakistani Taliban took control of Swat and the government of Pakistan signed a peace deal surrendering the valley to the militants.[68]

The fourteen points of the agreement reached between the TNSM and the government were in line with the unfinished agenda of Abdul Rashid Ghazi: implementation of Sharia law in Swat, including the whole Malakand Division; withdrawal of the armed forces from the region; and a prisoner swap with the Taliban.

The other points of agreement included:

- The government and the Taliban will exchange prisoners
- The Taliban will recognize the writ of the government and they will cooperate with the local police
- The Taliban will halt attacks on barbers and music shops
- The Taliban will not display weapons in public
- The Taliban will turn in heavy weapons like rocket launchers and mortars to the government
- The Taliban will not operate any training camps
- The Taliban will denounce suicide attacks
- A ban will be placed on raising private militias
- The Taliban will cooperate with the government to vaccinate children against diseases like polio
- The madrasa of Maulana Fazlullah in Imam Dherai will be turned into an Islamic University

- Only licensed FM radio stations would be allowed to operate in the region
- The Taliban will allow women to work without fear[69]

Through increasing public sympathy for the Islamists and persistent pressure on the government in the form of escalated suicide attack across the country, TNSM achieved the goals set forth by the Ghazi brothers in 2007. Having established their control in Swat, al-Qaeda and its local allies, including TNSM, TTP, and Lashkar-e-Jhangvi, intended to expand their 'Islamic rule' beyond Malakand, thus fulfilling the 'divine prophecies' of Maulana Abdul Aziz. In accordance with the May 2008 peace agreement, Sufi Muhammed was bound to persuade the Swati Taliban to lay down their arms, which would in return allow the government to announce the enforcement of Sharia in Malakand. However, Sufi Muhammed failed to disarm the Taliban,[70] and instead the TTP, while taking advantage of the peace deal, covertly reorganized itself and started a three-pronged assault on the state.[71] First, the Swat chapter of the TTP started large-scale recruitment and the construction of bunkers in different parts of Swat in preparation for further fighting. Secondly, the Swat chapter of the TTP, in line with their comrades in FATA, started readjusting and relocating therein, and started expanding their assaults from the north to the south of the KPK province. The onslaught by the Taliban on Buner and Dir was part of this strategy. Thirdly, the Taliban started consolidating their positions vis-à-vis the security establishment by taking over the strategic passes and side valleys of Swat, Buner, Shangla, and Dir.[72] In fact, Sufi Muhammed attempted to persuade the militants to adhere to the deal, but the TTP defied him. The TTP also threatened to assassinate Sufi Muhammed if he insisted that the Taliban lay down their arms,[73] and the differences between the two outfits ensued in violent clashes.

For its part, the government not only ignored the violations of the agreement by the militants, but also went ahead with fulfilling its own part by imposing the Nizam-e-Adl Regulation in Malakand Division, which introduced Sharia to this region. On 13 April 2009, Asif Ali Zardari, then President of Pakistan signed Nizam-e-Adl after the National Assembly accepted the militants' terms.[74] In the meantime, attacks on the security forces continued, and there were indications that Sufi Muhammed was under immense pressure from more hard-line militants led by his son-in-law to make further demands on the government. The peace agreement did not last for more than three months and the government finally opted for an all out military action against the Taliban to stop their advance towards the urban areas of Pakistan.

Shortly thereafter, the Pakistan Army successfully dislodged the Tehrik-e-Taliban Pakistan, the terrorist group spearheading the anti-state militancy in the area, as well as largely dismantling their operational infrastructure. The majority of the militants who were involved in the 'Talibanization' of Swat fled to the adjacent areas of Khyber Pakhtunkhwa and neighbouring Afghanistan. Reportedly, a handful of very dangerous militants from the ranks of the Swati Taliban also fled to Saudi Arabia, Muscat, the United Arab Emirates, Thailand, Malaysia, and Indonesia.[75] Although the physical infrastructure of the TTP and its allies was significantly damaged during the military operations in Bajaur, Swat, and South Waziristan, a total victory is yet to be achieved. While the militants eventually were driven out, they will continue to pose a threat until the systemic causes of violent radicalization in Pakistan are dealt with in a more systematic way.

CONCLUSION

In sum, the operation against Lal Masjid and its adjacent madaris impacted the militant landscape of Pakistan in three ways: it widened the rifts between the state and its erstwhile militant allies; caused fractionalization within militant outfits; and most importantly, deprived the state of much needed popular support to counter the alarming level of militancy in Pakistan. In addition, it provided an opportunity for al-Qaeda to make inroads into different segments of the Pakistani society by manipulating the post-Operation Sunrise sentiments. The Islamist forces, instead of submitting to the more assertive policies of the government, became stronger, more organized and more sophisticated. The 'Talibanization' along Pakistan's border regions escalated rapidly in the aftermath of the Lal Masjid siege.

The continuing effects of the Lal Masjid operation are still haunting Pakistan. Despite successive military operations and continued US drone strikes, the tribal areas of Pakistan continue to serve as the epicentre of national, regional, and global terrorism. In fact, there is a gulf of political polarization and mistrust between the Pakistani Taliban and the state caused by ill-conceived and poorly-coordinated actions such as 'Operation Sunrise'. Therefore, the military initiatives of Pakistan and its allies are highly unlikely to yield long lasting peace in the region, until there are conscious efforts to resolve the legacy of the Lal Masjid incident, one of the major rallying cries for violent radicalization in Pakistan. A big part of this effort, of course, is learning the lessons of the Lal Masjid siege in order to avert such outcomes in the future. It is our hope that this book can contribute in some small way toward that end.

Notes

1. Maulana Abdul Aziz addressed a huge gathering at the mosque after he was released by the court. He also vowed retaliatory Jihad against Pakistani authorities. See video of: Maulana Abdul Aziz, *Jamia Hafsa* (17 January 2008); <http://jamiahafsa.multiply.com/video/item/52/Latest_video_speech_of_Molana_Abdul_Aziz_sbDAMAT_BARAKATUHUM> accessed 5 March 2011.

2. The government sources put the casualties figure at 98. However, independent sources claim that more than 300 students of Jamia Hafsa and Jamia Faridia lost their lives during the operation.

3. Ijaz Hussain, 'Lal Masjid and Golden Temple', *Daily Times* (1 August 2007); <http://archives.dailytimes.com.pk/editorial/01-Aug-2007/comment-lal-masjid-and-golden-temple-ijaz-hussain> accessed 25 November 2014.

4. For a detailed account, see: Yarsolav Trofimov, *The Siege of Mecca* (Doubleday, 2007).

5. Ibid. 15.

6. This particular term is used by Pakistani Law Enforcement Agencies to describe fighters who were recruited, trained, and armed to fight against the Soviets in Afghanistan.

7. Frequent reference to Pakistani state in Pakistani Taliban's propaganda material such as audio/video CDs, pamphlets, and magazines.

8. Arabinda Acharya and Khuram Iqbal, 'Extremism in Pakistan: Time for Decisive Action', *RSIS Commentaries* (18 July 2007); <http://www.rsis.edu.sg/publications/Perspective/RSIS0762007. pdf> accessed 23 April 2012.

9. 'Libi urges Pakistanis to topple govt', *The Post* (Lahore) (2 August 2007).

10. Ibid.

11. 'Osama declares war on Musharraf', *Daily Times* (Lahore) (21 September 2007).

12. 'Osama more popular than Gen Musharraf in Pakistan', *Daily Times* (Lahore) (13 September 2007).

13. Khuram Iqbal, 'Drivers of Suicide Terrorism in Pakistan', *RSIS Commentaries* (27 February 2008); <http://www.pvtr.org/pdf/ commentaries/RSIS0212008.pdf> accessed 24 December 2008.

14. *Pak Institute for Peace Studies* (Islamabad: Pakistan Security Report, 2008).

15. Ibid.

16. 'Molana Asmatullah Muaviya New Bayan', (19 May 2012); <http://www.youtube.com/watch?v=5cAeJWTQ9Hg> accessed 11 September 2012.

17. Raza Hamdani, '*Khudkush hamle: Pakistan sar-e fihrist* [Suicide attacks: Pakistan on top of the list]', *BBC Urdu.com* (23 March 2008); <www.bbc.co.uk/urdu/pakistan/story/2008/03/080323_ suicide_attacks_sen.shtml> accessed 25 March 2008.

18. The Red Mosque administration established a publication unit called *Tareekh-e-Lal Masjid* (The History of Red Mosque) Publishers, which to this date produces books and audio/video CDs to project the 'un-Islamic' features of the Pakistani state. The material published and released by Lal Masjid is widely

disseminated among the targeted population in tribal and mainland Pakistan.

19. 'Poll of Pakistan', *WorldPublicOpinion.org* (dates of survey 12–28 September 2007); <http://www.worldpublicopinion.org/pipa/pdf/oct07/PakAlQaeda_Oct07_quaire.pdf> accessed 16 May 2011.

20. Ibid.

21. Investigations were carried out by two major agencies ISI (Inter-Services Intelligence) and MI (Military Intelligence)—'Tarbela attack likely an insider's job', *The Post* (Lahore) (15 September 2007).

22. Amir Mir, 'The costs of keeping Musharraf', *The Post* (Lahore) (28 September 2007).

23. 'Mastermind of Sargodha attack arrested', *Pakistan Post* (Lahore) (10 January 2008).

24. Ibid.

25. *'Bay-gunahon ko mara, khud ko gunahgar samajhtay hain: Ranger Ahalkar'* [Having killed innocents, we consider ourselves sinners: Ranger officials]'Urdu Daily *Ausaf* (Rawalpindi) (11 July 2007).

26. Mir, 'The costs'.

27. The commander of Mehsud Taliban threatened to behead five of the captives every day if the government did not release his 80 Taliban warriors captured by the Army. The government had no option other than surrendering to Baitullah Mehsud's demands. 80 hard core militants including a number of trainers and would-be suicide bombers were set free by the government to secure the release of 300 troops and senior officers.

28. Mir, 'The costs'.

29. Ibid.

30. Shakeel Anjum, 'Three militant outfits join hands with al-Qaeda', *The News* (Lahore) (27 August 2007).

31. Interview with Qari Aleemullah Sabir (a pseudonym), a former member of Sipah-e-Sahaba Pakistan (SSP) and Harkatul-Jihad-e-Islami, Dera Ghazi Khan, South Punjab, 18 July 2009.

32. 'Jamia Hafsa presents Q&A session with Mufti Abu Zar', the document originally in Urdu, dated 5 July 2012, was retrieved from <www.jhuf.net> on 16 August 2012.

33. Umar Cheema, 'Jihadi leader now scared of Jihadis', *The News* (18 September 2008).

34. Asmatullah Muaviya, *'Aatish-o-Aahan'*, (2004); <http://www.muslimtents.com/turepath/> accessed 11 January 2012.

35. See note 16.

36. *'Jaish-e-Mohammed Lashkar-e-Taiba ki Haqeeqat'*, (posted 8 March 2012); <www.youtube.com/watch?v=f7IMwdmKZxc> accessed 14 September 2012.

37. Ibid.

38. Ibid.

39. 'TTP Punjab commander killed in Shaktoi drone strike', *Daily Times* (17 January 2010); <http://www.dailytimes.com.pk/default.asp?page=2010%5C01%5C17%5Cstory_17-1-2010_pg7_24> accessed 23 July 2010.

40. 'Waziristan militants start mining region: report', *Dawn* (Karachi) (28 May 2009).

41. See note 16.

42. Ibid.

43. He was reported dead in a US drone strike in South Waziristan on 3 May 2011. However, this could not be confirmed by independent sources.

44. Hamid Mir, 'How an ex-army commando became a terrorist', *The News* (20 September 2009).

45. Colonel (R) Imam, an ex-SSG officer rejected the claim made by Hamid Mir and termed it 'total disinformation'. Similarly, Syed Saleem Shahzad, a journalist associated with *Asia Times Online* wrote 'Ilyas was never a part of Pakistan's special forces, nor even of the army'. See Syed Saleem Shahzad, 'al-Qaeda's guerrilla chief lays out strategy', *Asia Times Online* (15 October 2009); <http://www.atimes.com/atimes/South_Asia/KJ15Df03.html> accessed 26 May 2011.

46. 'Ilyas Kashmiri: end of a terrorist', *Daily Times* (Lahore) (6 June 2011).

47. Hamid Mir, 'Who was Ilyas Kashmiri?' *The News* (Lahore) (20 September 2009).

48. Ibid.

49. Ibid.
50. Ibid.
51. A Profile of Ilyas Kashmiri published in a Jihadi magazine: *Nawa-e-Afghan Jihad* 4/7 (August 2011), 49.
52. Ibid.
53. Ibid.
54. Mudassir Raja, 'Lashkar-e-Taiba killed Gen. Alvi, court told', *Dawn* (13 May 2009).
55. Amir Mir, 'Ilyas Kashmiri had planned to attack COAS', *The News* (18 September 2009).
56. Ibid.
57. Azeem Samar, 'Security of PNS Mehran was PAF's responsibility: Navy', *The News* (31 May 2011).
58. The three core objectives of the TTP are 'to enforce Sharia and to unite against the NATO forces in Afghanistan and to wage defensive jihad against the Pakistan Army'.
59. Although the TTP's former spokesman Maulvi Omar claimed to have 100,000 fighting soldiers in tribal areas, such numbers are usually exaggerated for propaganda purposes.
60. See note 32.
61. Ibid.
62. See note 31.
63. Ibid.
64. Ibid.
65. Tehrik-e-Nifaz-e-Shariat-e-Muhammadi (TNSM) is the first Taliban-style organization of Pakistan. TNSM is a pre-9/11 Islamist group. Initially referred to as the '*tor patki*' (Black Turban Movement), the TNSM was founded in 1992 by Sufi Muhammed, a former member of Jamaat-e-Islami, a mainstream religious political party.
66. Malakand Agency and its adjacent areas were affected the most by the massive earthquake in October 2005, which killed more than 80,000 people. The Asmatullah Muaviya administration provided free shelter and education to more than 300 females who had lost their families in the earthquake. The madrasa administration claimed that these female students of Jamia Hafsa had no place to

which to go; it is for this reason that they decided to stay inside the building during the operation.

67. Interview with Fayyaz Zafar, Bureau Chief Aaj TV, Mingora, Swat, 12 November 2010.

68. Bill Roggio, 'Pakistani government inks peace deal with Swat Taliban', *The Long War Journal* (21 May 2008); <http://www.longwarjournal.org/archives/2008/05/pakistani_government.php> accessed 1 June 2011.

69. Hamid Mir, 'Secret details of Swat peace accord', *The News* (11 April 2009).

70. Ghulam Farooq, 'Sufi says disarm, TTP says enforce Sharia first', *Daily Times* (Lahore) (15 April 2009).

71. *'Swat: Aarzi bandobast, Taliban ki tanzeem-e nau'* [temporary arrangements, the reconfiguration of the Taliban], *BBCUrdu.com* (9 April 2009); <www.bbc.co.uk/urdu/lg/pakistan/2009/05/090505_taliban_swat_rh.shtml?s> accessed 14 April 2009.

72. Ibid.

73. Haji Muhammed Adeel, the central vice president of the Awami National Party (ANP) and a witness to the Swat Peace Agreement, made this disclosure in a speech he delivered at the Express Forum. Extracts of his speech were reported in Urdu Daily *Express* (Lahore, 12 May 2009).

74. Zulfiqar Ghuman and Irfan Ghauri, 'President signs Nizam-e-Adl after NA nod', *Daily Times* (Lahore) (14 April 2009).

75. See note 67.

References

'A Chronology of the Lal Masjid Standoff', *Dawn* (Pakistan) (4 July 2007); <http://www.dawn.com/2007/07/04/nat6.htm> accessed 26 March 2010.

Abbas, Hassan, 'The Road to Lal Masjid and its Aftermath', *Terrorism Monitor* (19 July 2007); <http://www.jamestown. org/single/?no_cache=1&tx_ttnews%5Btt_news%5D=4322> accessed 15 March 2010.

Acharya, Arabinda, and Khuram Iqbal, 'Extremism in Pakistan: Time for Decisive Action', *RSIS Commentaries* (18 July 2007); <http://www.rsis.edu.sg/publications/Perspective/ RSIS0762007.pdf> accessed 23 April 2012.

Al Rashdi, Maulana Zahid, *'Lal Masjid tanaza'e par muzakarat kaise sabotazh kiye gaye'* [How the Lal Masjid talks were sabotaged], *Islam* (Urdu) (12 July 2007).

'An Interview with Molana Abdul Aziz after his arrest [Urdu]', *Pakistan Television* (2007); <http://www.youtube.com/ watch?v=3Z4Ss7OdgdM> accessed 15 March 2010.

'An Interview with Ghazi Abdul Rashid (purportedly his last interview) (Urdu)', Aaj Television Channel (Pakistan); <http:// www.youtube.com/watch?v=8BIQcPHwNkU> accessed 10 April 2010.

Anis, Muhammad, 'Ulema blame govt for talks failure', *The News* (11 July 2007); <http://www.thenews.com.pk/top_story_ detail.asp?Id=8946> accessed 13 March 2010.

Anjum, Shakeel, 'Army shows huge cache of "recovered" arms', *The News* (Pakistan) (13 July 2007); <http://www.thenews.

com.pk/top_story_detail.asp?Id=8988> accessed 10 March 2010.

———, 'Big plan to evict seminary students', *The News* (Lahore) (6 February 2007).

———, 'Govt gives in to Lal Masjid clerics', *The News* (Online Edition) (20 May 2007); <http://thenews.jang.com.pk/top_story_detail.asp?Id=7963> accessed 4 March 2010.

———, 'Lal Masjid declared a no-go area for cops', *The News* (18 April 2007).

———, 'Solution to Lal Masjid crisis in sight', *The News* (Pakistan) (10 July 2007); <http://server.kbri-islamabad.go.id/index.php?option=com_content&task=view&id=1101&Itemid=53> accessed 14 March 2010.

———, 'Three militant outfits join hands with al-Qaeda', *The News* (Lahore) (27 August 2007).

———, and Mobarik A. Virk, 'Lal Masjid standoff continues', *The News* (Lahore) (24 May 2007).

Asad, Tariq, *Lal Masjid ka muqaddimah qanoon ki nazar mein* (Azmat-e-Quran Foundation, 2008).

Aziz, Maulana Abdul, *Jamia Hafsa* (17 January 2008); <http://jamiahafsa.multiply.com/video/item/52/Latest_video_speech_of_Molana_Abdul_Aziz_sbDAMAT_BARAKATUHUM> accessed 5 March 2011.

Baabar, Mariana, 'Who wears the pants?', *Outlook India* (26 February 2007); <http://www.outlookindia.com/article.aspx?233987> accessed 5 March 2010.

'Bajaur tribals announce support for Lal Masjid *mullah*', *Daily Times* (Lahore) (10 January 2007).

'Banned terror group to help defend mosque', *Gulf Times* (23 April 2007); <http://www.gulf-times.com/site/topics/article.asp?cu_no=2&item_no=145195&version=1&template_id=41&parent_id=23> accessed 5 March 2010.

'*Bay-gunahon ko mara, khud ko gunahgar samajhtay hain*: Ranger Ahalkar' [Having killed innocents, we consider ourselves sinners: Ranger officials], Urdu Daily *Ausaf* (Rawalpindi) (11 July 2007).

Bukhari, Akram, '*Lal Masjid ke andar ki kahani—lamha ba lamha*' [The inside story of Lal Masjid—moment by moment], *Islam* (Urdu) (8 July 2007).

Cheema, Umar, 'Jihadi leader now scared of jihadis', *The News* (18 September 2008).

'Chief cleric held in burqa escape bid: 1,100 students surrender, G-6 residents brave siege', *Dawn* (Pakistan) (5 July 2007) accessed 2 April 2010.

'Cleric gives govt a week to impose Sharia', *Daily Times* (Lahore) (31 March 2007).

'Clerics suspend talks after 'surveillance'', *Dawn* (Karachi) (17 April 2007).

Davidson, Thomas M., *To Preserve Life: Hostage-Crisis Management* (San Rafael, CA: Cimacom, 2002).

Dolnik, Adam, 'Contrasting Dynamics of Crisis Negotiations: Barricade versus Kidnapping Incidents', *International Negotiation*, 8/3 (2003), 53–84.

———, and Keith M. Fitzgerald, *Negotiating Hostage Crises with the New Terrorists* (Westport, CT: Praeger Security International, 2008).

Farooq, Ghulam, 'Sufi says disarm, TTP says enforce Sharia first', *Daily Times* (Lahore) (15 April 2009).

'Fatwa makes minister fear for her life', *Indian Express* (India) (16 April 2007); <http://www.indianexpress.com/news/fatwa-makes-minister-fear-for-her-life/28473/> accessed 10 March 2010.

'Fierce gun battles rock capital: •Army troops deployed around Lal Masjid •Curfew imposed in area •Rangers man, journalist among 10 killed •Govt buildings torched', *Dawn* (Pakistan) (4 July 2007); <http://www.dawn.com/2007/07/04/top1.htm> accessed 18 April 2010.

Fuselier, Dwayne, 'What Every Negotiator Would Like His Chief to Know,' *FBI Law Enforcement Bulletin* (March 1986).

'Ghazi snubs Shujaat over house arrest', *Daily Times* (Lahore) (7 July 2007).

Ghumman, Khawar, 'Protests in Islamabad against 'moral police'', *Dawn* (Pakistan) (6 April 2007); <http://www.dawn.com/2007/04/06/top7.htm> accessed 5 March 2010.

Ghuman, Zulfiqar, and Irfan Ghauri, 'President signs Nizam-e-Adl after NA nod', *Daily Times* (Lahore) (14 April 2009).

_____, and Azaz Syed, 'Lal Masjid militants stand defiant', *Daily Times* (Lahore) (7 July 2007).

Gilgati, Maulana Mufti Riaz Mansoor, *Hayat-e-Shaheed* (Lahore: Iqra Quran Company, 2010).

'Grabbing Attention', *The News* (Lahore) (8 April 2007).

Greenstone, James L., *The Elements of Police Hostage and Crisis Negotiations: Critical Incidents and How to Respond to Them* (Binghamton, NY: Haworth Press, 2005).

Haider, Masood, 'Nilofar Urges SC action against Lal Masjid', *Dawn* (Online Edition) (4 July 2007); <http://www.dawn.com/2007/07/04/nat1.htm> accessed 2 November 2012.

Haider, Noreen, 'Stand-off grabbing attention', *The News On Sunday* (Pakistan) (8 April 2007); <http://jang.com.pk/thenews/apr2007-weekly/nos-08-04-2007/enc.htm#1> accessed 15 March 2010.

_____, 'Time for a showdown?', *The News* (Lahore) (18 February 2007).

Hamdani, Raza, '*Khudkush hamle: Pakistan sar-e fihrist*' [Suicide attacks: Pakistan on top of the list], *BBC Urdu.com* (23 March

2008); <www.bbc.co.uk/urdu/pakistan/story/2008/03/080323_
suicide_attacks_sen.shtml> accessed 25 March 2008.

Hammer, Mitchell R., and Randall G. Rogan, 'Negotiation
Models in Crisis Situations: The Value of a Communication-
Based Approach', in Rogan et. al., *Dynamic Processes of Crisis
Negotiation* (Westport, CT: Praeger, 1997).

Hasaan, Umme, *Saniha Lal Masjid: Ham par kya guzri'* [The
tragedy of the Red Mosque: What befell us], (Islamabad: Lal
Masjid Publications, 2007).

Hassan, Ahmed, 'Government decides to negotiate more with
clerics', *Dawn* (Karachi) (4 April 2007).

_____, 'Ijaz hits hard at Islamabad clerics', *Dawn* (Karachi)
(4 April 2007).

_____, 'Musharraf blamed for talks failure', *Dawn* (11 July
2007).

_____, 'Suicide bombers holed up in Lal Masjid: President',
Dawn (Pakistan) (30 June 2007); <http://www.dawn.
com/2007/06/30/top1.htm> accessed 26 March 2010.

Hayes, Richard, 'Negotiations with Terrorists,' in Victor
Kremenyuk, ed., *International Negotiation* (San Francisco:
Jossey-Bass, 2001).

Hussain, Zahid, 'The leap of faith that cost tourism minister
her job', *Times Online* (UK) (21 May 2007); <http://www.
timesonline.co.uk/tol/news/world/asia/article1820247.ece>
accessed 4 March 2010.

_____, *The Scorpion's Tail: The Relentless Rise of Islamic Militants
in Pakistan and How it Threatens America* (New York: Free
Press, 2012).

Hussain, Ijaz, 'Lal Masjid and Golden Temple', *Daily Times*
(1 August 2007); <http://archives.dailytimes.com.pk/
editorial/01-Aug-2007/comment-lal-masjid-and-golden-
temple-ijaz-hussain> accessed 25 November 2014.

Hussain, Talat, 'Lal Masjid: Many unanswered questions [Urdu]', *Aaj Television Channel* (Pakistan); <http://www.youtube.com/watch?v=2kRwZfaEF8Y> accessed 4 May 2010.

'Ilyas Kashmiri: end of a terrorist', *Daily Times* (Lahore) (6 June 2011).

Imran, Mohammad, 'Government will rebuild Hamza mosque', *Daily Times* (Lahore) (4 February 2007).

———, 'Seminar students reject govt-clerics agreement', *Daily Times* (Lahore) (5 February 2007).

'Interview with Ijaz ul-Haq on Morning Show (Urdu)', ATV (Pakistan); <http://www.youtube.com/watch?v=oL6ECAQpbiA&feature=related> accessed 14 May 2010.

Iqbal, Khuram, 'Children's Library to Enforce Sharia?', *South Asia Net* (2011); <http://san-pips.com/print.php?id=25> accessed 5 March 2011.

———, 'Drivers of Suicide Terrorism in Pakistan', *RSIS Commentaries* (27 February 2008); <http://www.pvtr.org/pdf/commentaries/RSIS0212008.pdf> accessed 24 December 2008.

'Islamists Free 3 Chinese Women, 6 Others After Massage Parlor Kidnapping in Pakistan', *Fox News* (US) (23 June 2007); <http://www.foxnews.com/story/0,2933,286390,00.html> accessed 21 March 2010.

'*Jaish-e-Mohammed Lashkar-e-Taiba ki Haqeeqat*', (posted 8 March 2012); <www.youtube.com/watch?v=f7IMwdmKZxc> accessed 14 September 2012.

'*Jamia hafsa aur Tank jaese waqeat ki Islam mein ijazat nahin hai—hukumat apni* writ *qaim kare*' [There is no permission for acts such as Jamia Hafsa and Tank in Islam—Government must establish its writ], *Jang* (Urdu) (30 March 2007).

'Jamia Hafsa presents Q&A session with Mufti Abu Zar', the document originally in Urdu, dated 5 July 2012, was retrieved from <www.jhuf.net> on 16 August 2012.

'Jamia Hafsa students start drive against video centres', *Daily Times* (Lahore) (27 March 2007).

'Jamia Hafsa to end library's occupation conditionally', *The News* (8 February 2007).

Jan, Abid Ullah, 'Lal Masjid Massacre: What really happened?' *Haqeeqat.Org* (15 July 2007); <www.haqeeqat.org/.../lal-masjid-massacre-what-really-happened-abid-ullah-jan/> accessed 3 May 2010.

Khaikaew, Thaksina, 'Female Pakistani students protest Govt', *Fox News* (US) (10 February 2007); <http://www.foxnews.com/printer_friendly_wires/2007Feb10/0,4675,PakistanMadrassaProtest,00.html> accessed 10 March 2010.

Khan, Abdul Sattar, 'Hafsa girls revolt in the making', *The News* (8 July 2007).

Khan, Iftikhar A., 'Lal Masjid cleric urges ulema to enforce Sharia', *Dawn* (Karachi) (4 April 2007).

Khan, Kamran, 'Live Interview with Rashid Ghazi by Kamran Khan', *Geo Television Channel* (Pakistan) (2007); <http://www.youtube.com/watch?v=2J6ijPP8uyg&feature=related> accessed 10 March 2010.

Khan, Sohail, 'Environment Ministry building, vehicles set on fire', *The News International* (4 July 2007) accessed 24 May 2008.

Khattak, Daud, 'Reviewing Pakistan's Peace Deals with the Taliban', *CTC Sentinel* (26 September 2012); <http://www.ctc.usma.edu/posts/reviewing-pakistans-peace-deals-with-the-taliban> accessed 2 November 2012.

Khattak, Inamullah, 'Seminaries plan Islamic Revolution', *Dawn* (Karachi) (4 April 2007).

Khattak, Iqbal, 'Musharraf ready to raid mosque but ...', *Daily Times* (Pakistan) (30 June 2007); <http://www.dailytimes.com.pk/default.asp?page=2007%5C06%5C30%5Cstory_30-6-2007_pg1_3> accessed 5 March 2010.

Keller, Bill, 'Last Soviet Soldiers Leave Afghanistan', *The New York Times* (16 February 1989); <http://partners.nytimes.com/library/world/africa/021689afghan-laden.html> accessed 23 November 2012.

'Lal Masjid "brigade" kidnaps 4 policemen', *Dawn* (Pakistan) (19 May 2007); <http://www.dawn.com/2007/05/19/top1.htm> accessed 3 March 2010.

'Lal Masjid clerics had contacts with terrorists, commission told' *Pakistan Today* (26 March 2013); <www.pakistantoday.com.pk/2013/03/26/news/national/lal-masjid-clerics-had-contacts-with-terrorists-commission-told/> accessed 26 November 2014.

'Lal Masjid gears up for attack on CD, video shops: Taliban jihad in NWFP backed', *Dawn (Pakistan)* (May 26 2007); <http://archives.dawn.com/2007/05/26/top7.htm> accessed 31 October 2011.

'Lal Masjid ignores Bilqees Edhi's offer', *Daily Times* (Lahore) (7 July 2007).

'*Lal Masjid ke askariat pasandon ke barey main sansanikhaiz inkishafat*' [Sensational revelations about the Lal Masjid militants], *Aaj* (Urdu) (9 July 2007).

'Lal Masjid operation called off', *Ibnlive.com* (India) (22 May 2007); <http://ibnlive.in.com/news/lal-masjid-operation-called-off/41078-2.html> accessed 1 March 2010.

'Lal Masjid probe: Commission seeks copy of former PM Shaukat Aziz's written orders', *The Express Tribune* (10 February 2013); <http://tribune.com.pk/story/505215/

lal-masjid-probe-commission-seeks-copy-of-former-pm-shaukat-azizs-written-orders/> accessed 20 April 2013.

'Lal Masjid set up *Shariat* Court today', *The News* (Pakistan) (6 April 2007); <http://www.thenews.com.pk/top_story_detail.asp?Id=6945> accessed 5 March 2010.

Lanceley, Frederick, *On-Scene Guide for Crisis Negotiators*, 2nd edn. (Boca Raton, FL: CRC Press, 2003).

'Libbi urges Pakistanis to topple govt', *The Post* (Lahore) (2 August 2007).

Linder, Evelin, *Making Enemies: Humiliation and International Conflict* (Westport, CT, London: Greenwood/Praeger Security International).

'*Madrasa Jamia Faridia par hamla hua to talibat apni jaanein de dain gi—Molana Abdul Aziz*', *Nawae Waqt* (Urdu) (27 January 2007).

'*Madrassa* students in Pak release Chinese nationals', *The Hindu* (India) (23 June 2007); <http://www.hinduonnet.com/thehindu/holnus/001200706232169.htm> accessed 24 March 2010.

Malik, Akram, 'Woman minister killed by fanatic', *Dawn* (Pakistan) (21 February 2007); <http://www.dawn.com/2007/02/21/top2.htm> accessed 4 March 2010.

'*Masajid-o-madaris ke tahaffuz ke liye kashtian jala di hain, qaum saath de—Molana Abdul Aziz*' [We have burnt our boats for the sake of the mosques and the seminaries: the nation should support us—Molana Abdul Aziz], *Daily Islam* (Urdu) (27 January 2007).

'Mastermind of Sargodha attack arrested', *Pakistan Post* (Lahore) (10 January 2008).

McMains, Michael, and Wayman Mullins, *Crisis Negotiations: Managing Critical Incidents and Hostage Situations in Law*

Enforcement and Corrections, 2nd edn. (Dayton, OH: Anderson Publishing, 2001).

———, *Crisis Negotiations: Managing Critical Incidents and Hostage Situations in Law Enforcement and Corrections*, 4th edn. (New Providence, NJ: Mathew Bender & Company Inc. Publishing, 2010).

Mir, Amir, 'Ilyas Kashmiri had planned to attack COAS', *The News* (18 September 2009).

———, 'The costs of keeping Musharraf', *The Post* (Lahore) (28 September 2007).

Mir, Hamid, 'How an ex-army commando became a terrorist', *The News* (20 September 2009).

———, 'Lal Masjid Incident on Capital Talk with Hamid Mir [Urdu]', *Geo Television Network* (Pakistan); <http://www.youtube.com/watch?v=zP62BoWQcCs> accessed 5 March 2010.

———, 'Secret details of Swat peace accord', *The News* (11 April 2009).

———, 'Who was Ilyas Kashmiri?' *The News* (Lahore) (20 September 2009).

Mirza, Abdul Quddus, '*Pervez Musharraf ki hatdharmi ki wajh se* surrender *nahi kiya tha*' [We did not surrender because of Pervez Musharraf's arrogance], *Ummat* (Urdu) (4 January 2013).

'MMA raps capital clerics', *Daily Times* (Lahore) (5 April 2007).

'Molana Asmatullah Muaviya New Bayan', (19 May 2012); <http://www.youtube.com/watch?v=5cAeJWTQ9Hg> accessed 11 September 2012.

Muaviya, Asmatullah, '*Aatish-o-Aahan*', (2004); <http://www.muslimtents.com/turepath/> accessed 11 January 2012.

'Musharraf changed success into failure, ordered Lal Masjid operation: Shujaat', *The News* (Pakistan) (21 March 2013).

'Musharraf escapes yet another assassination bid', *Daily Times* (Lahore) (7 July 2007).

'Nation would take revenge from doctorial [*sic*] rulers after my martyrdom: Ghazi', *Online International News Network* (11 July 2007); <http://www.onlinenews.com.pk/details.php?newsid=114879> accessed 19 December 2014.

Nawa-e-Afghan Jihad 4/7 (August 2011).

'No one injured in Pak suicide attack', *One India News* (30 December 2007); <http://news.oneindia.in/2007/12/30/no-one-injured-in-pak-suicide-attack.html> accessed 1 November 2012.

Noesner, Gary, *Stalling for Time: My Life as an FBI Hostage Negotiator* (Random House, 2010).

'Obituary: Abdul Rashid Ghazi', *BBC News* (10 July 2007); <http://news.bbc.co.uk/2/hi/south_asia/6281228.stm> accessed 7 May 2010.

Omar, Rageh, 'Inside the Red Mosque (Video Documentary)', *Witness on Al Jazeera Television Network (English)* (2007); <http://www.youtube.com/watch?v=RrKEaOeZs2o> accessed 12 February 2010.

'*Operation Khamosh: 102 jan bahaq, 198 zakhmi, 608 ke khilaf muqaddimat, 403 talibat, 152 bache riha*' [Operation Silence: 102 killed, 198 injured, Cases filed against 608, 403 students, and 152 children released], *Jinnah* (Urdu) (17 July 2007).

'Operation plan ready, but government hesitant', *Dawn* (Karachi) (24 May 2007).

'Osama declares war on Musharraf', *Daily Times* (Lahore) (21 September 2007).

'Osama more popular than Gen Musharraf in Pakistan', *Daily Times* (Lahore) (13 September 2007).

'Pak forces set to storm Lal Masjid; state on alert', *IBN Live* (4 July 2007); <http://ibnlive.in.com/news/pak-forces-set-to-

storm-lal-masjid-state-on-alert/44008-2.html> accessed 12 April 2010.

Pak Institute for Peace Studies (Islamabad: Pakistan Security Report, 2008).

'Pakistan foils plan for weeklong series of al-Qaeda attacks', *Taipei Times* (23 August 2004); <http://www.taipeitimes.com/News/world/archives/2004/08/23/2003199891> accessed 29 October 2011.

'*Pakistan mein nifaz-e-shari'at kay liye jihad ki shar'i haysiyyat* [The Islamic Justification of Waging jihad in Pakistan for the Enforcement of Sharia].

'Pakistan militant cleric killed', *BBC News* (10 July 2010); <http://news.bbc.co.uk/2/hi/south_asia/6288704.stm> accessed 12 March 2010.

'Pakistan's Red Mosque leader killed', *Al Jazeera* (English) (10 July 2007); <http://english.aljazeera.net/news/asia/2007/07/2008525124430212996.html> accessed 4 March 2010.

'Pakistani soldiers storm mosque', *BBC News* (10 July 2007); <http://news.bbc.co.uk/1/hi/world/south_asia/6286500.stm> accessed 10 May 2008.

Pennington, Matthew, 'Pakistani Students Abduct Brothel Owner', *Washington Post* (USA) (28 March 2007); <http://www.washingtonpost.com/wp-dyn/content/article/2007/03/28/AR2007032800290.html> accessed 2 March 2010.

Poland, James, and McCrystle, Michael *Practical, Tactical and Legal Perspectives of Terrorism and Hostage Taking* (Lewiston, NY: Edwin Mellen Press, 2000).

'Poll of Pakistan', *WorldPublicOpinion.org* (dates of survey 12–28 September 2007); <http://www.worldpublicopinion.org/pipa/pdf/oct07/PakAlQaeda_Oct07_quaire.pdf> accessed 16 May 2011.

Qayum, Khalid, 'Pakistan Red Mosque Was 'Fort Ready for Battle', Musharraf Says', *Bloomberg* (US) (13 July 2007); <http://www.bloomberg.com/apps/news?pid=20601091&sid=aWFb.nCpxO.o&refer=india> accessed 3 May 2010.

Raja, Mudassir, 'Lashkar-e-Taiba killed Gen. Alvi, court told', *Dawn* (13 May 2009).

Rana, Muhammad Amir, 'Conflict: Lal Mosque's Terror Link', *Pakistan Institute for Peace Studies Network*; <http://san-pips.com/print.php?id=28> accessed 15 March 2010.

Raza, Syed Irfan, '1,100 students surrender', *Dawn* (Pakistan) (5 July 2007).

———, *'Badkari ka ilzam: Jamia Hafsa ki talibat ne 3 khawateen to aghva kar liya'* [Allegations of Corruption: Students of Jamia Hafsa kidnap 3 women], *Jang* (Urdu) (29 March 2007).

———, 'Besieged cleric seeks safe passage: •Nerves as standoff continues •Govt sticks to its guns', *Dawn* (Pakistan) (6 July 2007); <http://www.dawn.com/2007/07/06/top1.htm> accessed 4 March 2010.

———, 'Commander's killing raises spectre of all-out assault', *Dawn* (9 July 2007).

———, 'Fatwa against Nilofar issued', *Dawn* (Pakistan) (9 April 2007); <http://www.dawn.com/2007/04/09/top2.htm> accessed 5 March 2010.

———, 'Ghazi, militants vow to fight till bitter end', *Dawn* (Pakistan) (7 July 2007); <http://www.dawn.com/2007/07/07/top1.htm> accessed 3 March 2010.

———, 'Government accepts Lal Masjid demands', *Dawn* (Karachi) (25 April 2007).

———, 'Lal Masjid clerics break off talks with government', *Dawn* (Karachi) (17 May 2007).

———, 'Lal Masjid threatens suicide attacks' *Dawn* (Pakistan) (7 April 2007); <http://www.dawn.com/news/241168/lal-masjid-threatens-suicide-attacks> accessed 19 November 2014.

———, *'Madressah* force on the offensive in Islamabad: Move to impose Talibanisation; three women kidnapped', *Dawn* (Pakistan) (29 March 2007); <http://www.dawn.com/2007/03/29/top4.htm> accessed 5 March 2010.

———, 'Major demand of Lal Masjid clerics accepted', *Dawn* (Karachi) (18 April 2007).

———, 'Two policemen freed in Lal Masjid swap: GHQ meeting looks for final solution', *Dawn* (Pakistan) (20 May 2007); <http://www.dawn.com/2007/05/20/top1.htm> accessed 2 March 2010.

———, 'Women freed after forced confession', *Dawn* (Pakistan) (30 March 2007); <http://www.dawn.com/2007/03/30/top2.htm> accessed 3 March 2010.

———, and Munawer Azeem, 'Breakthrough in sight', *Dawn* (10 July 2007).

Rogan, Randal; Hammer Mitchell; and Van Zandt, Clinton, *Dynamic Processes of Crisis Negotiation* (Westport, CT: Praeger, 1997).

Roggio, Bill, 'Pakistani government inks peace deal with Swat Taliban', *The Long War Journal* (21 May 2008); <http://www.longwarjournal.org/archives/2008/05/pakistani_government.php> accessed 1 June 2011.

'*Sadr Musharraf ke tayyare ko nishana bananeki koshish aur khudkush hamla Lal Masjid Operation ka radd-e amal?*' [Attack on President Musharraf's plane and suicide attack reaction to Lal Masjid Operation? *Ausaf* (Urdu) (Pakistan) (7 July 2007).

Sahni, Ajai, 'Pakistan: A Progression of Crises', *South Asia Terrorism Portal*; <http://www.satp.org/satporgtp/sair/Archives/5_52.htm> accessed 27 November 2014.

Samar, Azeem, 'Security of PNS Mehran was PAF's responsibility: Navy', *The News* (31 May 2011).

'Security personnel deployed around Lal Masjid', *Daily Times* (Lahore) (10 February 2007).

'Seminary students warn of protests', *Daily Times* (Lahore) (28 February 2007).

Shahid, Saleem, 'Musharraf tells Hafsa brigade to surrender or die', *Dawn* (8 July 2007).

Shahzad, Syed Saleem, 'Al-Qaeda's guerrilla chief lays out strategy', *Asia Times Online* (15 October 2009); <http://www.atimes.com/atimes/South_Asia/KJ15Df03.html> accessed 26 May 2011.

_____, *Inside Al-Qaeda and the Taliban: Beyond Bin Laden and 9/11*, 1st edn. (Pluto Press, 2011).

'Shujaat fears failure of Lal Masjid deal', *Dawn*, Karachi, 12 May 2007.

Siddiqui, Naveed, 'President allows use of force', *Daily Times* (Lahore) (7 February 2007).

Siddiqui, Wajiha Ahmed, '*Lal Masjid mein qazi ki adalat—hukumat ka iqdam kya hoga?*' [Establishment of Court in Lal Masjid—What will the government do?], *Ummat* (Urdu) (7 April 2007).

_____, '*Tahriri mu'ahida karne se sarkari idaron ka gureiz*' [Reluctance of the government departments to sign a written agreement], *Ummat* (Urdu) (10 February 2007).

_____, '*Shikayat ke bawajood police ne karavai nahin ki; makeenon ki shikayat par hamein iqdam karna para—Jamia Hafsa ke naib Maulana Abdul Rashid Ghazi se guftugu*' [Despite complaints Police did not take action: We had to take action on the request of the residents—Talking to Maulana Rashid Ghazi, the deputy of Jamia Hafsa], *Ummat* (Urdu) (31 March 2007).

Slatkin, Arthur A., *Communications in Crisis and Hostage Negotiations* (Springfield, IL: Charles C. Thomas Publishers, 2005).

Strentz, Thomas, '13 indicators of Volatile Negotiations', *Law and Order* (September 1991).

———, 'The Cyclic Crisis Negotiations Time Line', *Law and Order* (March 1995), 73–75.

———, *Psychological Aspects of Crisis Negotiation* (New York: CRC Press, 2006).

'Students being trained for suicide attacks: report', *The News* (Lahore) (23 April 2007).

'Students raid Islamabad 'brothel', *BBC* (28 March 2007); <http://news.bbc.co.uk/2/hi/south_asia/6502305.stm> accessed 12 March 2010.

Subramanian, Nirupama, 'Bid to hold talks with Lal Masjid cleric', *The Hindu* (India) (10 July 2007); <http://www.hindu.com/2007/07/10/stories/2007071057990100.htm> accessed 21 March 2010.

———, 'Pakistan policemen released', *The Hindu* (India) (25 May 2007); <http://www.hindu.com/2007/05/25/stories/2007052506751500.htm> accessed 3 March 2010.

———, 'Pakistan policemen released', *The Hindu* (Online Edition) (India) (25 May, 2007); <http://www.hindu.com/2007/05/25/stories/2007052506751500.htm> accessed 3 March 2010.

'Suicide bombers are present in Red Mosque: Umme Hasaan', *Urdu Daily Express* (Lahore) (4 July 2007).

'*Swat: Aarzi bandobast, Taliban ki tanzeem-e nau*' [temporary arrangements, the reconfiguration of the Taliban] *BBCUrdu.com* (9 April 2009); <www.bbc.co.uk/urdu/lg/pakistan/2009/05/090505_taliban_swat_rh.shtml?s> accessed 14 April 2009.

Syed, Baqir Sajjad, 'Changing colours of Lal Masjid', *Dawn* (Pakistan) (6 July 2007); <http://www.dawn.com/2007/07/06/nat13.htm> accessed 20 April 2010.

'TTP Punjab commander killed in Shaktoi drone strike', *Daily Times* (17 January 2010); <http://www.dailytimes.com.pk/default.asp?page=2010%5C01%5C17%5Cstory_17-1-2010_pg7_24> accessed 23 July 2010.

'Tarbela attack likely an insider's job', *The Post* (Lahore) (15 September 2007).

'The chronology of Lal Masjid clashes', *Times of India,* (10 July 2007); <http://timesofindia.indiatimes.com/world/pakistan/Chronology-of-Lal-Masjid-clashes/articleshow/2190609.cms> accessed 13 May 2010.

'The Last Will and Testament of Ghazi Abdul Rashid', *PureIslam* (10 July 2008); <http://www.pureislam.co.za/index.php?option=com_k2&view=item&id=895:the-last-will-and-testament-of-ghazi-abdul-rashid> accessed 1 December 12.

Trofimov, Yarsolav, *The Siege of Mecca* (Doubleday, 2007).

'Ulema reject claim of Lal Masjid mullah', *Daily Times* (Lahore) (5 July 2007).

Urdu *Daily Express* (Lahore) (6 July 2007).

_____ (4 July 2007).

_____ (10 July 2007).

_____ (12 May 2009).

Usmani, Maulana Mufti Muhammad Rafi, '*Lal Masjid aur hukumat kay darmian muzakrat kiun naakaam hue*' [Why the negotiations failed between Lal Masjid and the government], *Binaat*; <http://www.banuri.edu.pk/ur/node/230> accessed 6 March 2010.

Varma, K., 'Lal Masjid: 800 Students Surrender', *Rediff* (4 July 2007); <http://www.rediff.com/news/2007/jul/04pak3.htm> accessed 4 April 2010.

'Veiled women leave Jamia Hafsa, dazed and confused', *Dawn* (5 July 2007); <http://www.dawn.com/2007/07/05/nat2.htm> accessed 3 March 2010.

Walsh, Declan, 'The Business is jihad', *The Guardian* (UK) (20 March 2007); <http://www.guardian.co.uk/world/2007/mar/20/pakistan.declanwalsh> accessed 5 March 2010.

Waqar, Ali, 'Lahori clerics distance themselves from Ghazi brothers', *Daily Times* (7 July 2007).

Wardlaw, Grant, *Political Terrorism: Theory, Tactics, and Counter-Measures* (Cambridge: Cambridge University Press, 1982).

'Waziristan militants start mining region: report', *Dawn* (Karachi) (28 May 2009).

Wilkinson, Isambard, 'Bloody Pakistan mosque siege ends', *Telegraph* (UK) (11 July 2007); <http://www.telegraph.co.uk/news/worldnews/1557151/Bloody-Pakistan-mosque-siege-ends.html> accessed 5 March 2010.

———, 'Chief siege cleric killed as rebel mosque falls', *Telegraph* (UK) (10 July 2007); <http://www.telegraph.co.uk/news/worldnews/1557036/Chief-siege-cleric-killed-as-rebel-mosque-falls.html> accessed 11 March 2010.

———, 'Radical cleric sets up vigilante *Sharia* law court in Pakistan's capital', *Telegraph* (UK) (7 April 2007); <http://www.telegraph.co.uk/news/worldnews/1547930/Radical-cleric-sets-up-vigilante-sharia-law-court-in-Pakistans-capital.html> accessed 2 March 2010.

Witte, Griff, 'Mosque Siege Exposes Rift In 'Mullah-Military' Alliance', *Washington Post* (13 July 2007); <http://www.washingtonpost.com/wp-dyn/content/article/2007/07/12/AR2007071202083.html> accessed 12 April 2010.

———, 'Pakistani Forces Kill Last Holdouts in Red Mosque', *Washington Post* (12 July 2007); <http://www.washingtonpost.

com/wp-dyn/content/article/2007/07/11/AR2007071100367. html> accessed 2 November 2014.

Yasin, Asim, 'Government, Lal Masjid talks end on positive note', *The News* (8 May 2007).

———, 'Lal Masjid not involved Ghazi tells Shujaat', *The News* (Lahore) (4 April 2007).

Zartman, William, 'Negotiating Effectively With Terrorists', in Barry Rubin ed., *The Politics of Counterterrorism* (Washington, D.C.: The Johns Hopkins Foreign Policy Institute, 1990).

———, ed., *Negotiating with Terrorists* (Leiden: Martinus Nijhoff Publishers, 2006).

Index